CCEA

GCSE
BUSINESS STUDIES
THIRD EDITION

Hope Kerr

DYNAMIC LEARNING

HODDER EDUCATION
AN HACHETTE UK COMPANY

Orders: please contact Bookpoint Ltd, 130 Park Drive, Milton Park, Abingdon, Oxon OX14 4SE. Telephone: (44) 01235 827720. Fax: (44) 01235 400454. Email education@bookpoint.co.uk Lines are open from 9 a.m. to 5 p.m., Monday to Saturday, with a 24-hour message answering service. You can also order through our website: www.hoddereducation.co.uk

ISBN: 9781471899379

© Hope Kerr 2017

First published in 2017 by

Hodder Education,

An Hachette UK Company

Carmelite House

50 Victoria Embankment

London EC4Y 0DZ

www.hoddereducation.co.uk

Impression number   10 9 8 7 6 5 4 3

Year   2021 2020 2019

Cover photo © &#169 travel-imagery/iStock/Getty Images

Illustrations by Integra Software Serv. Ltd.

Typeset in India by Integra Software Serv. Ltd.

Printed in Dubai

A catalogue record for this title is available from the British Library.

CONTENTS

Acknowledgements   v

Introduction   vi

UNIT 1: STARTING A BUSINESS

1 Creating a business   2
  1.1 Entrepreneurs   2
  1.2 Business resources   6
  1.3 Business ownership   9
  1.4 Public sector ownership   25
  1.5 Business location   31
  1.6 Business aims and objectives   37
  1.7 Stakeholders   44

2 Marketing   49
  2.1 Marketing and market research   49
  2.2 Marketing mix – price   58
  2.3 Marketing mix – product   66
  2.4 Marketing mix – promotion   73
  2.5 Marketing mix – place   83
  2.6 Competition and customer service 88
  2.7 International trade   92
  2.8 E-Business   101
  2.9 M-Business   105

3 Business operations   109
  3.1 Types of production   109
  3.2 Methods of manufacturing   113
  3.3 Quality Assurance   123
  3.4 Health and safety in manufacturing 127

UNIT 2: DEVELOPING A BUSINESS

4 Human resources — 131

  4.1 Recruitment — 131

  4.2 Selection — 143

  4.3 Appraisal — 149

  4.4 Training — 152

  4.5 Motivation — 156

5 Business growth — 161

  5.1 Business success or failure — 161

  5.2 Business growth — 163

6 Finance — 171

  6.1 Sources of finance — 171

  6.2 Cash flow forecasts — 177

  6.3 Financial Statements — 182

  6.4 Ratios — 188

  6.5 Breakeven — 192

UNIT 3: PLANNING A BUSINESS

7 Business plan — 200

Assessment objectives and command words used in the GCSE (CCEA) Business Studies examination — 208

Glossary — 210

Index — 214

ACKNOWLEDGEMENTS

The author wishes to acknowledge the advice given by Dr David McAree, Mrs Jane Hanna and Mr John McLaughlin on various sections of the text.

The Publishers would like to thank the following for permission to reproduce copyright material.

Every effort has been made to trace all copyright holders, but if any have been inadvertently overlooked, the Publishers will be pleased to make the necessary arrangements at the first opportunity.

Photo credits

p.2 l Courtesy of Sinead Murphy/Shnuggle; r © Shnuggle.com; **p.5** © Audtakorn Sutarmjam - 123RF; **p.6** l © Ivan Baranov - 123RF; t r © Andreas Karelias - 123RF; b r © A. Singkham - 123RF; **p.9** © Ian Allenden - 123RF; **p.11** © Hope Kerr; **p.12** © gemenacom - 123RF; **p.13** © Blend Images/Alamy Stock Photo; **p.14** © Hope Kerr; **p.15** © Hope Kerr; **p.17** © Moy Park via Morrow Communications Ltd; **p.21** t © McDonald's Restaurants Limited; b © www.thezipyard.com; **p.22** t © Subway; b © 360b/Shutterstock; **p.25** © Robert Mayne/Alamy Stock Photo; **p.28** © Dmitry Kalinovsky - 123RF; **p.29** © City Living/Alamy Stock Photo; **p.30** © Kim Nayler/Divine Chocolate; **p.31** © Peter Samuels/Getty Images; **p.32** © Hope Kerr; **p.33** l © Jim Wileman/Alamy Stock Photo; r © Steffan Hill/Alamy Stock Photo; **p.34** l © Ana Blazic Pavlovic - 123RF; r © Hope Kerr; **p.35** © Steve Morgan/Alamy Stock Photo; **p.36** © AA World Travel Library/Alamy Stock Photo; **p.40** © Colin Hawkins/Getty Images; **p.45** © ALANDAWSONPHOTOGRAPHY/Alamy Stock Photo; **p.50** © Richard G. Bingham II/Alamy Stock Photo; **p.51** © RosaIreneBetancourt 3/ Alamy Stock Photo; **p.61** © Kurhan - 123RF; **p.66** © Nigel Cattlin/Alamy Stock Photo; **p.68** © Mary Evans Picture Library/Alamy Stock Photo; **p.71** © Nik Taylor/Alamy Stock Photo; **p.72** © Hope Kerr; **p.75** © Stephen Barnes/Alamy Stock Photo; **p.78** © urbanbuzz/Alamy Stock Photo; **p.80** © culture-images GmbH/Alamy Stock Photo; **p.86** © Wavebreak Media Ltd - 123RF; **p.89** © racorn - 123RF; **p.92** © javarman/Shutterstock; **p.95** © robertharding/Alamy Stock Photo; **p.101** © Alex Segre/Alamy Stock Photo; **p.106** © Translink (http://www.translink.co.uk/mLink/); **p.109** © Hope Kerr; **p.110** t © Brian Jackson - 123RF; b © Globuss Images/Alamy Stock Photo; **p.111** © Pat Eyre/Alamy Stock Photo; **p.114** t © Ted Horowitz/Getty Images; b © Hope Kerr; **p.116** t © macor - 123RF; b © tony french/Alamy Stock Photo; **p.121** © cheskyw - 123RF; **p.125** © Investors in People; **p.141** © Equality Commission for Northern Ireland; **p.168** © Robert Convery/Alamy Stock Photo; **p.182** © wirojsid - 123RF.

Text Permissions

p.37 © McDonald's Restaurants Limited; **p.38** © Culloden Estate and Spa; **p.141** © Equality Commission for Northern Ireland; **p.208–9** © CCEA.

INTRODUCTION

This third edition of GCSE Business Studies for CCEA revises, amends and updates the original textbook in line with the new CCEA GCSE Business Studies specification which is due to be taught for the first time in September 2017 and examined in 2018.

This revised textbook accurately and closely follows the order of the new specification. Like the specification, the book is divided into two main units with a short third unit. Each of the main units is divided into sections which are further divided into shorter units to provide coverage of the necessary material. This in no way aims to dictate the order in which the specification should be approached, however it is recommended that the material within each section should be studied together. The two main units will be examined separately.

Any examination questions which are included have been taken from previous GCSE (CCEA) papers. From experience, the author understands that many candidates do not answer questions appropriately because they fail to recognise the requirements of the command words used in questions. For this reason, a section on command words, related to the assessment objectives, is included at the end of the book. A section is included to explain the requirements of the GCSE examination and a further explanation of the new-style Controlled Assessment Task (replacing Coursework) is also included.

In addition, each unit includes activities which have been designed to reinforce learning and to make the student think further about the knowledge-based material provided as well as to give opportunities to develop the skills of application, analysis and evaluation. The author is aware of the wide range of ability in the candidature for this particular examination, so activities have been designed to cater for these varying abilities.

Each unit ends with a checklist of the material which should be understood at that stage and the glossary provides an easy reference for revision.

Hope Kerr

Examination papers

In the GCSE examination for Business Studies (CCEA) you will sit two examinations and undertake a Controlled Assessment Task (which now replaces coursework).

The first examination will last 1 hour 30 minutes and will examine the first three areas of the specification – Creating a Business, Marketing and Business Operations. Your answers will be written on the question paper in the spaces provided after each question. Paper 1 carries 40% of the total marks for the GCSE award.

The second examination also will last 1 hour 30 minutes and will examine the next three areas of the specification – Human Resources, Business Growth and Finance. As in Paper 1, your answers will be written on the question paper in the spaces provided after each question. Paper 2 carries 40% of the total marks for the GCSE award.

You will be assessed on the quality of your written communication. It is important that your work is legible, that your spelling, punctuation and grammar are accurate and that you organise information clearly.

Controlled Assessment Task (CAT)

The remaining 20% is awarded to the Controlled Assessment Task. The task is based on Unit 3 – Planning a Business and is synoptic which means that work could be included from any of the other six areas of the specification named on page vii.

The Controlled Assessment Task will be sent to your school in September of your Year 12. This will give you a question or situation which you have to research under the supervision of your teacher. You will be allowed a total of 12 hours to complete your research which you will record in Booklet A. You will be awarded up to 15 marks for your research in Booklet A. It is important that you acknowledge and reference any sources which you have used in your research. You will be allowed to work in small groups to carry out and collate primary research such as interviews or questionnaires, and your teacher will identify and record your individual contribution to such work. All other research should be carried out independently. In February of your Year 12, Booklet B will be issued in which you are required to answer set questions based on your own research and your own knowledge of the subject. You will be given one hour to complete the questions under test conditions, and you will be awarded up to 45 marks for your work in Booklet B. When you are completing Booklet B, you are allowed access to your research in Booklet A.

STARTING A BUSINESS

LEARNING OBJECTIVES

To develop knowledge and critical understanding of:

▶ the fundamentals of starting a business

▶ why businesses start and the resources required to maintain and grow them

▶ the various forms of business ownership

▶ the factors which influence the location of business

▶ business aims and objectives

▶ the impact that various stakeholder groups may have on businesses

▶ marketing options, elements of the marketing mix and market research methods

▶ the impact of e-business and m-business on potential growth strategies

▶ why businesses conform to quality assurance standards and health and safety legislation.

Starting up any business begins with an entrepreneur – a person who has the ability to spot an opportunity for a new business, has ideas and is prepared to take risks to make that business work.

Some well-known entrepreneurs are Richard Branson, who founded the very successful Virgin Group, and Bill Gates, who founded Microsoft. Two other young men in their twenties – Sergey Brin and Larry Page – had an idea, borrowed money and created Google, which is now valued at more than $70 billion.

There are many examples of smaller but successful entrepreneurs in Northern Ireland. Read about Shnuggle in the case study on this page.

▲ Adam and Sinead Murphy, owners of Shnuggle, pictured here with members of staff from UCI and NI

What it means to be enterprising

To be enterprising means to be able to spot a good business opportunity and to have the vision and drive to make that business succeed. In order to do this, the entrepreneur has to be prepared to take calculated risks.

Case study

Shnuggle was set up by husband and wife team Sinead and Adam Murphy in 2009, using their own experience to design clever baby products. They operate in the Ards Business Centre in Newtownards, Co. Down.

Sinead and Adam's story began when their first baby, Rose, was very ill. They had a traditional Moses basket for Rose but when she was sick this became unhygienic and impossible to clean. Sinead and Adam created a modern Moses basket which was hygienic and hypoallergenic.

Their business is now an international award-winning brand which has a presence today throughout the United Kingdom and in over twenty five countries worldwide. They currently employ six staff and have developed a further range of baby products.

In 2016 Sinead and Adam appeared on *Dragon's Den* asking for financial backing and the support of a Dragon. They were successful and Touker Suleyman joined them. Since then they have had two other offers of investment in the business so their future looks bright!

▲ Sinead and Adam created a more modern and hygienic Moses basket

So what are the characteristics of an entrepreneur?

- ▶ An entrepreneur contributes original ideas which give the business an edge over its competitors.
- ▶ An entrepreneur has to be a decision maker.
- ▶ An entrepreneur has leadership qualities and planning skills.
- ▶ An entrepreneur has self-confidence and a passion about their venture.
- ▶ An entrepreneur has the ability to work independently and develop their ideas.
- ▶ An entrepreneur is committed and willing to make personal sacrifices for the benefit of their business.
- ▶ An entrepreneur is a creative thinker and shows initiative.
- ▶ An entrepreneur has a vision of what the business could become and works single-mindedly towards that goal.
- ▶ An entrepreneur has the energy to work hard and make sure that the business achieves its full potential.
- ▶ An entrepreneur is willing to take calculated business risks.
- ▶ An entrepreneur is persuasive and able to encourage financiers such as banks to lend money to the enterprise.
- ▶ An entrepreneur can motivate others in the work team and inspire them with enthusiasm.
- ▶ An entrepreneur has determination and is not discouraged by failures and setbacks, but understands that many good business ideas do not succeed, perhaps because it is the wrong place or time.

Why the government encourages enterprise

The government is keen to encourage enterprise and to develop an 'enterprise culture' in Northern Ireland. It has set up various schemes to help entrepreneurs to succeed. Grants and advice are offered through Invest NI, and the Young Enterprise Scheme works with young people. People are encouraged to try their ideas in business and to establish their own businesses rather than be unemployed.

There are several reasons why the government encourages enterprise:

- ▶ It reduces unemployment.
- ▶ New ideas may succeed and provide fresh opportunities for employment.
- ▶ People are motivated and have a 'feel-good' attitude.
- ▶ Competition ensures a healthier business environment.
- ▶ Leads to economic development which generates wealth in the economy.

Nature and rewards of risk taking

Risk is about taking sensible or calculated chances. Not all chances will work out well – it is said that only one in five new products succeed in business. Although four out of every five products do not succeed, an entrepreneur will not give up but will keep working until they find a successful idea.

Activity

Have you got what it takes to be an entrepreneur? Answer the following questions truthfully to find out. The good entrepreneur's answers are given at the end.

1 What do you do if you find a task difficult?
   (a) Keep trying until you get it right.
   (b) Give up.
   (c) Ask for help.

2 Can you make decisions?
   (a) Always.
   (b) Never.
   (c) Depends on the circumstances.

3 If you won the lottery, which of the following would you do?
   (a) Tour the world.
   (b) Treat all your friends to the greatest party ever.
   (c) Invest it.

4 How single-minded are you? When you are working, are you:
   (a) easily distracted?
   (b) oblivious to everything around you?
   (c) able to concentrate – but only if you like the work?

5 How energetic do you think you are?
   (a) Very energetic at everything.
   (b) Energetic at the things I enjoy.
   (c) There are lots of things I can't be bothered with.

6 How well do you work with people?
   (a) I'd rather work on my own.
   (b) I love being in a team.
   (c) I must be the team leader.

Answers: 1(a), 2(a), 3(c), 4(b), 5(a), 6(c)

The nature of risk taking for the entrepreneur is:

▶ Losing money
The entrepreneur will have invested considerable sums of money in the new product or business. If the venture fails, that money is lost and could bankrupt the entrepreneur.

▶ Losing time
The entrepreneur will have invested long periods of time designing the new product or planning the new business. If the venture fails, that time is wasted.

▶ Personal stress, perhaps leading to health issues
The entrepreneur will experience worry that the new idea may not be successful and may become stressed by the long hours worked and lack of sleep.

The rewards of risk taking for the entrepreneur are:

▶ Making profits
A successful business with successful products can earn large profits for the entrepreneur. This usually leads to increasing sales, with further opportunities for profit making. There is also the possibility of selling the successful business for a large sum.

▶ Becoming famous
Successful entrepreneurs have become household names. For example, everyone recognises Alan Sugar, who owned Amstrad and sold electrical goods, and James Dyson, who designed a bagless vacuum cleaner.

▶ Satisfaction

Success brings a high level of satisfaction and sense of achievement. For some, the buzz and excitement make the risk worthwhile.

▶ Independence

Some people may want to be independent, to own their own business, make their own decisions and be their own boss. This independence is a reward for taking a risk.

Activity

▲ Perks of the business: a coffee shop

Imagine that you work in a local coffee shop full time and have done so for five years.

There are two other full-time staff serving customers and two others in the kitchen preparing food and washing up. The owner has just told you that he is retiring and has suggested that you should take over the coffee shop. He has also told you that he does not own the premises but that they are rented. Should you take over the coffee shop, or not?

1 Write down the risks you think you would face if you took over the coffee shop.

2 Now write down the rewards you would gain if you took over the coffee shop.

3 State your final decision, with reasons.

Checklist ✓

At this stage you should be able to:

○ describe what it means to be enterprising

○ identify and explain the key entrepreneurial characteristics

○ analyse why the government encourages enterprise

○ analyse the nature and rewards of risk taking.

Examination question

Identify and explain two characteristics of an entrepreneur.   [6 marks]

How to answer this question

Name one characteristic, e.g. is willing to take calculated risks.   [1 mark]

Explain in more detail what taking calculated risks means.   [2 marks]

Name the second characteristic, e.g. has leadership qualities.   [1 mark]

Explain how they might show leadership.   [2 marks]

Altogether there are four **resources** which are necessary in any business. They are:

Land	Labour
Capital	Enterprise

Land

A basic need in business is the land on which to place the business premises, houses, roads and farms. However, 'land' is used more widely in this economic sense and includes all natural resources – not only the surface of the land but also the oceans and all raw materials which are contained either on, above or in the earth. Such resources and raw materials would include oil, gas, trees, water, fish, wind, coal and minerals. Supplies of land are limited, which makes it a very valuable resource.

▲ A potential greenfield site

Labour

The term 'labour' refers to the human resource in the business – the workers who are employed to manufacture the product or provide the service for which the business has been set up. The labour used in the business may be physical labour or mental labour, depending on the nature of the business's final product. Supplies of labour with the appropriate skills are also limited.

▲ Construction workers are an example of physical labour

Capital

Capital is defined as 'wealth which is employed in the creation of further wealth'. It is the element contributed by capitalists – the owners and is a resource to business as it is used to purchase **non-current assets** (such as land, buildings, machinery, equipment and vehicles). Capital is always in short supply and capitalists will risk investing it only in safe business projects.

▲ Investing money may pay off

Enterprise

Enterprise has a special role in business activity. You learned in the previous section that enterprise is contributed to a business by people known as **entrepreneurs**. They develop a business idea, and acquire all the other resources of land, labour and capital. They are usually the **managers** and they play a most essential role in business, estimating future **demand** and ensuring that production is at the correct level to meet that demand.

It is the role of the entrepreneur to organise the capital, the land and the labour in the correct proportions to run the business successfully. For example, some businesses such as large factories require vast amounts of capital and land but, because they are heavily mechanised, they may require proportionately less labour. Other businesses such as large department stores may be very labour intensive. For this reason, they would use a large amount of labour but proportionately less land.

Examination question

Kennedy Systems is a large business producing electrical appliances. They employ well-trained staff and highly developed technology.

Name two resources which Kennedy Systems has used and explain how those resources would be used in the business.
(6 marks)

How to answer this question

Name the two resources which you think have been used.
(2 marks)

Explain how each of those resources would be used in a manufacturing business.
(Up to 2 marks for each resource)

Each of the people who contribute the resources has to be rewarded. The following table shows how:

Resource	Contributed by	Rewarded by
Land	Landlords	Rent
Labour	Employees	Wages and salaries
Capital	Capitalists	Interest
Enterprise	Entrepreneurs	Profit

Activity

Molly has come up with a good idea for a new, small business. She knows that the business would be successful but her difficulty is that she would need finance and premises. Some friends agree to join the business. Jack will fund the purchase of all non-current assets, Jamie has premises which he will rent to the business and Sean will work in the business.

Using the spaces provided, name the resource provided by each person and the rewards which he/she can expect.

Name	Resource provided	Reward
Jamie		
Jack		
Molly		
Sean		

How businesses use resources differently

A business would not be successful unless it has all four resources. A person might have adequate amounts of capital but unless that person has enterprise, he/she would not be able to start a business.

Equally, an entrepreneur may have great ideas for a successful business but unless he/she has land on which to start the business and labour to operate it, there will be no business.

On the other hand, a landowner may own large areas of land but without the ideas contributed by enterprise or sufficient amounts of capital, he/she would not have a business.

Checklist ✓

At this stage you should be able to:
- ○ explain the resources a business needs
- ○ analyse how businesses use resources differently.

Activity

Study each of the following businesses and state which resource(s) you think it would make most use of:

A large well-mechanised farm   ....

A young girl working on her own making jewellery   ....

An out-of-town supermarket   ....

A fisherman   ....

1.3 Business ownership

Why do businesses start?

Entrepreneurs usually start businesses because:

▶ they have a good idea for a product which they think will sell. This may have started as a hobby or personal interest.

▶ they wish to be independent and be their own boss rather than work for someone else

▶ they want to make money and keep the profits of the business for themselves

▶ they need a job and starting their own business keeps them in employment

▶ they need the buzz and sense of satisfaction which the venture gives

▶ they wish to provide a service to the community.

⌃ A bookshop owner

How do businesses start?

It is important that careful planning takes place beforehand if the business is to be successful. The entrepreneur will have to:

▶ decide on the product and produce a model or prototype

▶ decide on the best place to get the materials required

▶ design a business plan

▶ study the market to see if there are already similar products available

▶ research the price at which any competitors are selling the product

▶ work out the costs of production and a profit margin in order to decide on a selling price

▶ carry out **market research** which would show the type of people who would be likely to buy the product and what price they would pay

▶ research where the product could be sold to best advantage

▶ organise the necessary finance. This may be from personal savings or borrowing from friends or arranging a bank loan or **overdraft**

▶ advertise the product widely in the most economical way

▶ create a brand for the product that would make it 'stand out from the crowd'

▶ register the product and get a patent.

(You will find greater detail in the later section on the **marketing mix** in Unit 1, Section 2.2 and on the **business plan** in Unit 3.)

Different sizes of businesses

The business world is made up of organisations of varying sizes – from single ownership to large multi-national companies. Businesses are classified by the European Commission according to the number of employees they have and according to their annual turnover as follows:

Micro businesses

A business is described as micro if it has between one and nine members of staff and if its annual turnover is less than £1.7m. **Micro businesses** are very important in Northern

Ireland and represent the main growth area in business in the last ten years. It is estimated that as many as 95% of all United Kingdom businesses are micro businesses and that 75% of all United Kingdom businesses are owned by single **owners**.

Size Category	Staff Headcount	Turnover
Micro	1 to 9	Less than £1.7m
Small	10 to 49	Less than £5.6m
Medium	50 to 249	Less than £22.8m
Large	More than 249	Greater than £22.8m

⌃ A table showing how different sizes of businesses categorise staff and turnover

Small businesses

A business is described as **small** if it has between ten and 49 members of staff and if its annual turnover is less than £5.6m.

Medium-sized businesses

A business is described as medium-sized if it has between 50 and 249 members of staff and if its annual turnover is less than £22.8m.

Small and medium businesses (SME)

The term **SME** is a composite term used to describe all micro, small and medium-sized businesses. A SME would have fewer than 249 members of staff and its turnover would be up to £22.8m.

Large businesses

A business is described as large if it has more than 249 members of staff and if its annual turnover is greater than £22.8m.

Types of ownership in the private sector

Any business which is owned by private people is known as a private sector business.

Introduction to private sector businesses

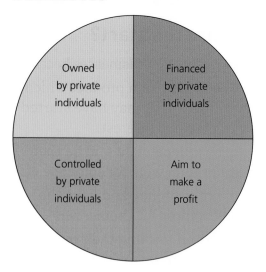

⌃ Features of private sector businesses

Some of these businesses may be small and owned by just one person – that person is called a **sole trader**. In some cases the business may be slightly larger and two or more people may have put money into it and perhaps joined together to work in the business. That is an example of a **partnership**.

Other businesses may be even larger and money would be needed from many people to keep them going. A large business would be organised as a **private limited company**, and the largest business of all would be organised as a **public limited company**.

There is one other type of business in the private sector – a **franchise**.

You will now study each of these types of business organisation in turn. At this stage, it is important for you to remember that **private sector businesses** are owned and controlled by private people who aim to make a profit from the money they have invested in the businesses.

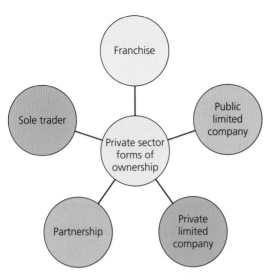

▲ A diagram showing different forms of private sector ownership

Sole trader

This is the most common form of business ownership. Sole traders are found in every town and district throughout Northern Ireland, running small shops as well as providing services such as hairdressing, plumbing, dressmaking, painting or electrical work. It is a popular form of business organisation because sole traders are their own bosses and own the businesses themselves. It is estimated that approximately 75% of all United Kingdom businesses are run by sole traders.

▲ A sole trader's shop in Clogher Co Tyrone

Sole traders' businesses are easy to form as they do not have to provide a lot of involved legal documentation before they can be established. All the sole trader has to do is to get a licence to trade from the local authority and perhaps planning permission if the building is to be altered. The business has to be registered for VAT with Revenue and Customs and then it is ready to open.

Sole traders provide the entire capital for setting up their businesses and usually work in their own shops or businesses. Their major aim in running the business is to make a profit and to expand. Depending on the size of the business, they may employ others to help with the work.

Sole traders are entitled to keep any profits made but also are responsible for losses incurred. They have unlimited **liability**, which means that if they do not have enough money in their businesses to pay their debts, they have to use their private funds to meet them.

Advantages of a sole trader

▶ The business is cheaply and easily formed without involved legal procedures.

▶ The owner can keep all the profits made in the business.

▶ The owner can make all the decisions and can make them quickly without having to call committee meetings.

▶ Because the business is usually small, the sole trader has very close links with the customers and employees.

▶ The financial affairs of the business do not have to be published, although tax authorities must have access to them.

Disadvantages of a sole trader

▶ The major disadvantage is unlimited liability. This means that if sole traders do not have enough money in their businesses to pay their debts, they have to use their private money to pay them.

This could have serious consequences because, in extreme circumstances, their cars, houses and other private possessions might have to be sold.

▶ Sole traders are responsible for all the losses in the business.

▶ Sole traders have to raise all their own capital.

▶ The amount of capital which sole traders have is limited, so their businesses are likely to be small.

▶ Because their businesses are small, banks are less willing to lend money to sole traders than they would be to large businesses.

▶ Being small, it is more difficult for sole traders to compete with the large business

organisations as they cannot take advantage of **economies of scale**.

▶ The business is very dependent on one person. The sole trader in a shop, for example, is expected to have expertise in sales, purchasing, advertising, accounting, window dressing, deliveries and stocktaking. This means they work very long hours.

▶ If the sole trader becomes ill or is on holiday, there is often no one to take over.

▶ The sole trader frequently does not have anyone with whom to discuss problems.

Usually the size of a business is determined by the capital available, but in some cases the owner has made a conscious decision to remain small.

Activity ✎

Read this short case study and answer the questions which follow.

▲ Poppy working in her new salon, Hair Line

Poppy is an excellent hairdresser who has been working at 'Best Cuts', a very good hair salon in Newcastle. She loves her job but has always dreamed of setting up her own salon.

For several weeks she had noticed an empty shop which had a notice in the window saying it was available for renting. She decided to go for it!

Her mother helped her to clean and paint it. Her father put up some mirrors, installed basins and electrical points and built shelves and cupboards. Poppy had saved enough to be able to buy dryers and other necessary items of small equipment. Her brother offered to lend her money, if necessary.

On 1 October Poppy opened her new business, which she named 'Hair Line'.

1 Outline the difficulties Poppy might have in her new business.

2 State the advantages which Poppy will have as a sole trader.

3 How might Poppy use extra money in the business?

Activity

Read about Anne in the following case study and answer the questions at the end.

▲ Anne making the finishes touches to a client's lunch

Anne runs a small catering business from home. She caters for business lunches in companies' own premises, dinner parties in private houses and small family parties to celebrate events such as birthdays, christenings and anniversaries. She likes to do all the buying and cooking herself but employs Rebecca and Emma sometimes to help as waitresses at the functions.

Anne has learned from experience that she can cater each week for a maximum of four lunches for twelve people each, as well as a maximum of two evening parties of approximately the same size. This calculation is based on the amount of freezer space she has, the size of her cookers and other kitchen equipment, and the room in her car for transporting her food.

She has built up a very good reputation and has as many customers as she can cope with. In fact, the quality of her catering is so high that she is having to refuse work and some customers are anxious to employ her for larger functions such as wedding receptions. Sometimes Anne wonders if she should expand.

1 Give details of two major items of expenditure Anne would have if she decided to take on extra work.
2 What risk would Anne take if she did decide to expand her business?
3 Name two advantages Anne would gain by expanding.

Examination question

A sole trader has unlimited liability. Explain what is meant by 'unlimited liability' and state why it is a disadvantage for the business owner. (4 marks)

How to answer this question

Define unlimited liability. (Up to 2 marks)

Describe one major disadvantage of unlimited liability. (Up to 2 marks)

Partnership

Partnerships are most frequently found in professional businesses such as doctors, dentists, veterinary surgeons, accountants, opticians and solicitors. Just think of the doctor, dentist or vet you go to – do they work on their own or in partnerships? If you are unsure, have a look at the nameplates outside their premises. If they show a number of names, then the business is probably a partnership.

▲ A name plate of a partnership

Partnerships are also commonly found in trades such as plumbers and electricians. They are popular in these businesses because expertise can be shared and each partner can take responsibility for one area of work.

A partnership consists of two or more people (partners) who jointly own a business. On some occasions an additional partner may be brought in to contribute capital but not to work in the business or to take any part in its organisation. This person is known as a '**sleeping partner**'.

The partners agree between themselves how they will run and organise their business. They are jointly responsible for any debts incurred in the business because their liability is unlimited. They have to provide the entire capital for setting up their business. Their aim is to make a profit and to expand and they are entitled to keep any profits made but also are responsible for losses incurred.

Advantages of a partnership

▶ There is more capital in the business than there is in a sole trader's business, which allows it to expand.

▶ **Specialisation** is possible as the partners may bring different skills to the business.

▶ The owners can share responsibility for decision making and discuss the problems which occur in the business.

▶ If one partner is ill or on holiday the business can carry on.

▶ The financial affairs of a partnership do not have to be published, although tax authorities must have access to them.

Disadvantages of a partnership

▶ As in the case of the sole trader, the major disadvantage in a partnership is unlimited liability. This means that if the partners do not have enough money in their business to pay their bills, they have to use their own private money. This puts their private possessions at risk. Each partner is liable in this way even if the debt was created by one of the other partners.

▶ If one partner is dishonest or inefficient, all partners are held liable for that partner's actions or decisions. It is important therefore that partnerships are formed only between people who know each other well and trust each other totally.

▶ The partners have to raise their own capital.

▶ When compared with a large company, the amount of capital in a partnership business is small.

▶ Partnerships have the same difficulty as a sole trader in borrowing money from banks.

- Because their capital is usually small, they cannot take advantage of economies of scale.
- There is the possibility of conflict between the partners.
- The death or bankruptcy of one partner may cause the break-up of the business. This is known as 'lack of continuity'.

A partnership involves a number of people and disagreements may occur, so partnerships are advised to draw up a **Deed of Partnership** to set out the rules.

Deed of Partnership

A Deed of Partnership states:

- how the profits and losses are to be shared
- the amount of capital which each partner will contribute
- if salaries are to be paid and the amount to be paid
- whether interest on capital is payable
- how the duties and responsibilities are to be shared
- how new partners might be introduced to the firm.

Case study

▲ Kieran washing a customer's car

Darren and Kieran were good friends who both loved working with cars. Even before they left school they had earned pocket money for themselves by washing cars in the large yard at the side of Kieran's home. They quickly built up a good reputation as very capable workers and their business was increasing all the time.

The boys realised that their hobby could be turned into a profitable business so,

soon after leaving school, they decided to open a car wash and valeting business in Coalisland.

Market research had shown that there was no local competition and they had proved that there was a demand for this service.

Darren had a substantial sum of money which he had inherited from an uncle and he was willing to invest some of it in the new business. Kieran was able to borrow £2,000 from his father and the boys were allowed to continue to use the yard at Kieran's house for a small rental.

They consulted a business adviser who helped them to plan the details of their business and also drafted their Deed of Partnership. Darren and Kieran thought the Deed was unnecessary since they were such good friends but the business adviser wisely insisted.

**Deed of Partnership between
Darren and Kieran**

Trading name of the business:

Coalisland Car Valet Service

The function of the business will be to provide the services of:

- Power washing and waxing all road vehicles
- Cleaning vehicles in preparation for Motor Vehicle Testing
- Valeting vehicle interiors

Business Capital:

- The total capital of the business will be £4,000
- Each partner will contribute £2,000

Share of Profits or Losses:

- All profits or losses will be shared equally by Darren and Kieran

Wages and Interest Payable:

- Each partner will be entitled to draw equal wages from the partnership as agreed annually between them
- No interest will be payable on capital

Banking

- The bank account will be in the name of Coalisland Car Valet Service
- Each cheque must be signed by both Darren and Kieran

The Duties of the Partners will be as follows:

- Darren will undertake all accounting and banking
- Kieran will undertake all purchasing of materials and machinery
- Both partners will share equally the work of washing, waxing and valeting

Dissolution of the Partnership

- The partnership may be dissolved by mutual consent between the two partners
- In this event, the assets will be shared equally between the two partners

Darren and ➤
Kieran's Deed
of Partnership

Activity

Read this short case study and answer the questions which follow.

Poppy's hairdressing business in Newcastle, 'Hair Line', has been very successful. She now employs two juniors to do shampoos and act as receptionists, and her own skills are in great demand as a hairdresser.

However, Poppy is annoyed at having to turn away customers because she is too busy. She knows there is enough work for two qualified hairdressers and has thought of employing another one to work with her. The difficulty is lack of space and she does not want to borrow money in case she could not repay it.

Poppy's friend, Charlie, also a qualified hairdresser, has discussed the possibility of forming a business partnership with her. Eventually they decide to go for it. They also decide to retain the name 'Hair Line', to make it a unisex salon, to keep the two juniors and to move to larger premises which are available in the town. They have agreed to contribute £10,000 each as capital.

1 Name any advantages which Poppy will gain by moving into a partnership.

2 What new problems may arise for Poppy in the new business arrangement?

Limited companies

It is legally possible to form a company with as few as one **shareholder** and one **director** and there is no limitation on how large it may become. While there are many small companies in Northern Ireland, there are also many which are extremely large. Businesses on this scale could not possibly raise the amount of capital required if they remained as sole traders or partnerships.

▲ Moy Park is an example of a limited company prominent in Northern Ireland

Shares and shareholders

In order to raise the vast amount of capital required in large public companies such as Moy Park, members of the public are invited to become members of the company and invest money in it. They do this by buying shares on the **Stock Exchange**. This makes them shareholders – or part-owners – in the company. From the company's point of view this has the advantage of providing large amounts of capital, while the shareholder benefits by becoming a part-owner of the company and being entitled to a share of its profits at the end of the year.

There are two types of shares:

▶ **Ordinary shares**. These shares are not guaranteed a dividend (share of the profit) at the end of the year. Whether they get a dividend depends on how successful the company has been during the year. Owners of ordinary shares are given voting rights in the company which gives them a say in the election of the Board of Directors.

▶ **Preference shares**. These shares are less common and are safer because they are guaranteed a fixed dividend out of the profits before any payment is made to the ordinary shareholders. Preference shareholders usually are not given voting rights in the company because their investment is not at as much risk.

Ownership and control of a company

Although the shareholders are the owners of the company, obviously it is impossible for them to run the company. The shareholders are entitled to attend the company's annual general meeting to elect a Board of Directors who run the business on their behalf. In practice, few shareholders actually attend the annual general meeting.

Although the Board of Directors has overall responsibility for the running of the company, they employ managers to undertake its day-to-day running. This situation is often referred to as a 'divorce of ownership and control', because the people who own the company do not control its running and the people who run it may not be its owners.

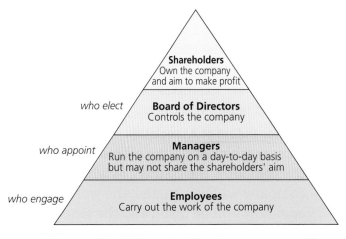

▲ A hierarchical triangle of business ownership

Main features of limited companies

Apart from the increased capital you have already learned about, companies have two other important advantages over sole traders and partnerships.

▶ **Limited liability** – The most significant feature of the limited company is that it has limited liability. This means that people who invest in a company cannot lose any money other than the amount they put into it. If the business should fail, the shareholders' liability is limited to the amount of their original investment – their private possessions cannot be taken. (Remember that sole traders and partners risk losing everything if their businesses fail.)

▶ **Separate legal existence (incorporation)** – A limited company is considered in law to be quite separate from its owners – it is said to be incorporated. Being incorporated gives people who are owed money by the company the right to sue the company without affecting the owners of the company. Equally the company could sue people who owe money to the company if necessary. This is very different from the situation of the sole trader or partners, who could be taken to court as owners of the business.

Forming a limited company

Setting up a limited company is a lengthy legal procedure and the company must be registered with the Registrar of Companies. The following documents are examples of those to be completed before trading may commence:

▶ **Memorandum of Association** – This has six clauses which state the official name of the company, the country in which the company will be situated, the work the company will be doing and the amount of capital with which the company is to start. The Memorandum also has a liability clause which states that members' liability is limited and an association clause which is a declaration by at least two people that they wish to form a company.

▶ **Articles of Association** – These show the voting rights of the shareholders, the method of election of directors, how profits will be divided, how meetings are to be conducted and the duties of the directors.

▶ **Certificate of Incorporation** – This is issued to show that the company has a separate legal existence from its owners and can act independently from them.

▶ **Prospectus** – Before shares can be sold, the company issues a Prospectus which gives details of the company's plans and its hopes for the future. Possible investors will read the Prospectus and use it to decide whether or not the company is a worthwhile investment.

▶ **Trading Certificate** – After the company has sold shares and raised enough capital to be able to trade efficiently, a Trading Certificate will be issued showing that the Registrar is satisfied that the company is in a position to begin trading. At that stage, the company may begin to trade.

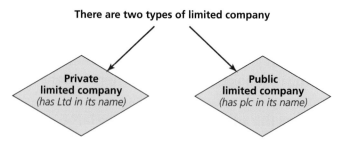

Private limited company

A private limited company is called 'private' because its shares cannot be bought by members of the public. Instead, shares in a private limited company are held by a small group of people (very often members of one family) who are able to keep control of the business. Shareholders in a private limited company may only sell their shares privately and with the consent of the other shareholders. Each year the shareholders are entitled to a share of the profits which is paid in direct proportion to the number of shares each one holds.

A private limited company is attractive to shareholders because they retain control of the business while at the same time enjoying the benefits of limited liability. This gives them all the advantages they would have had in a partnership but with the added security of limited liability. You can now see why the partnership is less popular to trading businesses. The official name of the company includes either 'Limited' or 'Ltd' to indicate that the liability of the owners is limited.

Advantages of a private limited company	Disadvantages of a private limited company
The amount of capital available is much greater than in sole traders and partnerships.	Some of the financial information of a private limited company must be available for inspection by members of the general public. This may give competitors valuable insights into the affairs of the company.
Because the business is on a larger scale, it is usually easier for it to borrow money.	Shares are not available for wider sale, so expansion may be difficult.
As a larger business, it can benefit from economies of scale.	The process of forming the company is more involved than it is in business organisations such as sole traders and partnerships.
It has limited liability.	
The business has a separate legal identity from its owners and may take legal action on its own behalf without involving the owners.	
There are a number of directors and managers in the business so responsibility and workloads are shared.	
There are opportunities for specialisation and **division of labour**.	
Control of the business is retained by a small group of shareholders.	

Examination question

Sandwich Limited has been in business for over ten years. Originally it was a partnership with only one shop in Belfast which prepared sandwiches to be delivered to local offices. Due to its success, the owners extended the premises and opened a coffee shop.

Five years ago the business became a private limited company and opened four new outlets. The company has gone from strength to strength and has a very good reputation.

1 Identify the main difference between a partnership and a private limited company. (1 mark)

2 Explain two reasons why this business decided to become a limited company. (4 marks)

3 Explain two aims which the business has now. (4 marks)

How to answer this question

The first question asks you to identify the main difference, so all you have to do is name the difference which you think is the most important one. No further explanation is needed when the command word is 'identify'.

The second and third questions ask you to 'explain' so you must give details of two reasons and two aims – if you simply name them, you will get half marks.

Public limited company (plc)

A public limited company is the largest type of private sector organisation. (Although its name is public limited company it is in the private sector because it is owned by private people.) Shares in a public limited company may be sold to members of the public – that is how it gets its name. Shares are bought and sold on the Stock Exchange all the time, but although ownership of the shares may change, the actual amount of capital in the business does not alter. The value of the shares rises and falls according to how successful the company is at that particular time and according to the general economic conditions in the country.

A public limited company may have thousands of owners, although the number of shares owned by each person may be quite small. However, the total capital in the company is very large. The liability of the shareholders is limited to the amount which they invested in the company and they have the confidence of knowing that they cannot lose more than that. Each year a dividend is declared and shareholders are paid a share of the dividend in proportion to the number of shares they own.

The official name of the company includes the initials 'plc' to indicate that the liability of the owners is limited.

Advantages of a public limited company

▶ Public limited companies are very powerful organisations with great influence in the market.

▶ Shareholders have limited liability.

▶ The capital available is very large, which gives the business all the benefits of easier borrowing and economies of scale.

▶ A public limited company has the resources necessary for growth and expansion.

▶ Because the business has a separate legal identity from its owners, it can take legal action without involving the shareholders.

▶ The business has continuity and shareholders may buy and sell their shares without affecting the business.

▶ Each director and manager has his/her own area of responsibility in the business, giving the benefits of specialisation and division of labour.

Disadvantages of a public limited company

▶ The shareholders are the owners of the business but the directors and managers make all the decisions. Therefore the owners of the company have no real say in its running.

▶ The formation of a public limited company involves a lengthy legal procedure.

- The financial information of a public limited company must be published for the information of the general public.
- In some public companies top management and employees feel out of touch with one another.
- Decision making in large companies is frequently slow because a series of meetings has to be held and numerous people have to be consulted.

Activity ✎

The following extracts from letterheads indicate the type of business ownership in each of the businesses. Study the letterheads and complete the answer for each business.

1

JONATHAN
Plumber and Electrician
88 Middle Street
CRUMLIN
Co Antrim

2
MARIE LONG & KIM SHORTT
Qualified Hairdressers
101 Top Road
DROMORE
Co Down

3

PREMIER PRINTERS LTD
PREMIER PRINTERS LTD
66 Low Avenue
MARKETHILL
Co Armagh

4
ALPHA MUSIC
MAKERS plc
15 Beta Drive
CASTLEDERG
Co Tyrone

1. Name the type of business ownership in each business.
2. How many people might each business be owned by?
3. What, in your view, is the greatest advantage of each type of organisation?
4. What, in your view, is the greatest disadvantage of each type of organisation?

Franchise

A franchise is really a **marketing** method and is an excellent way for someone to set up in business. This method gives the person the opportunity to sell a well-known set of products, but without the risks attached to opening as a sole trader and having to start from scratch.

Franchising originated in America and has become popular all over the world. It is a system through which successful business ideas can be hired out to other businesses. A franchise gives permission to the **franchisee** (person who is buying the franchise) to set up a business owned by the **franchiser** (person owning the franchise) using an established business name and idea.

The business can also use the established trademark and image. A franchise can be organised as a sole trader, partnership or limited company and a franchisee's liability depends on how the business is organised.

Franchises are expensive to buy as the franchisee has to pay a large sum as an initial fee as well as royalties which are calculated as a percentage of the annual income.

Here are some of the franchises operating in Northern Ireland.

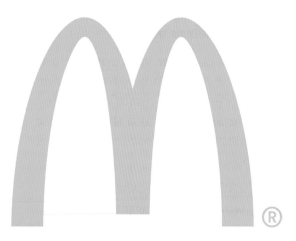

▲ McDonald's

▲ The Zip Yard

▲ Subway

Another of the well-known franchises in Northern Ireland is Benetton – you probably shop there yourself!

▲ Benetton

Just imagine that, at some time in the future, you are setting up a new Benetton shop in your local area. Very simply, you would reply to an advertisement and apply to Benetton for a licence to sell their goods and operate a business using their name.

Benetton would consider your application – for example, they have to be sure that you have the experience and qualifications to run one of their retail outlets and that the new outlet would not be too close to one of their existing shops.

If your application is successful, you (the franchisee) would pay an agreed sum of money as capital for the use of the Benetton trademark and image, and Benetton (the franchisor) would provide shop fittings, stock, premises and design. They would also train you in the techniques which they apply to selling their products.

You would be expected to buy an agreed percentage of goods solely from Benetton, to reach a certain sales target and to organise the business according to the Benetton guidelines. In addition, you would have to pay a royalty to the franchiser – this is really a share of the profit made and would be a set percentage.

Advantages of a franchise

The franchisee gains:

▶ from having reduced risks and capital investment

▶ the sole right to sell a well-known set of products and brand in that particular area

▶ increased sales as consumers know the quality of that particular established brand

▶ use of a brand name

▶ training provided by the franchisor

▶ the right to be his/her own boss in the shop

▶ the benefits of national advertising and **promotions**

▶ continuous support from the franchisor

▶ increased borrowing power from the bank because franchised businesses are usually profitable.

The franchisor gains:

▶ increased opportunities for expansion

▶ further benefits from economies of scale

▶ a percentage profit from all sales in that particular shop

▶ another retail outlet which is run without any increased capital investment

▶ by having the retail outlet run and managed for them.

Disadvantages of a franchise

The franchisee loses:

▶ any individuality. All shops are decorated and organised in the same way in order to be instantly recognisable by the public

▶ independence as he/she must organise the business according to the rules given by the franchisor. In many ways the franchisee could be seen more as a manager than an owner

▶ the right to sell the business without approval from the franchisor

▶ the right to buy stock from other sources which may be cheaper

▶ royalties which must be paid annually to the franchisor.

The franchisor loses:

▶ management of the day-to-day running of the shop. If the local service is poor, the reputation of the franchise is damaged.

Activity

The following people all want to set up in business and ask you to advise them which type of business ownership is best suited to their needs. Complete the table with the appropriate names.

Person	Individual needs	Suitable type of business organisation
Rob	I want to be my own boss	
Peter	I want to run a McDonald's fast food restaurant	
Brian	I want to operate a fleet of ten jets	
Simon	I want to go into business with my cousin	
Barbara	I need to have limited liability	
Ella	I want to be part of a really big business with lots of capital	
Tina	I would love to open up a little home bakery and do the work myself	
Alan	My two sisters and I could set up a dressmaking business. We work well together	
George	I dream of owning a leisure centre with my four friends but I do want limited liability	

Activity

Complete the following table to show details of businesses in the private sector.

	Liability (type of liability)	Ownership (number of owners)	Finance (source of finance)	Use of profits	Control and decision-making (who controls the business?)
Sole trader					
Partnership					
Private limited company					
Public limited company					

Checklist ✓

At this stage you should be able to:
- ○ explain why and how a business starts
- ○ identify and describe different sizes of business
- ○ identify and describe different types of private business ownership
- ○ evaluate the different types of private ownership
- ○ compare and contrast different types of private sector businesses considering ownership, control, finance and liability.

1.4 Public sector ownership

Meaning of public sector ownership

Any business which is owned by the country as a whole and run on behalf of the people is known as a public sector business. The government takes over the running and control of vital activities such as law and order or defence. Other activities such as education and the health service are also administered by government because it is important that every citizen has use of these services. If those services were left in private ownership, it could be that they would be too expensive and not everyone would have access to them.

▲ Parliament Buildings, Stormont

Some public sector enterprises are run by the central government of the country, either in Westminster or by the Northern Ireland Assembly in Stormont. Others, known as **municipal undertakings**, are run by local authorities (councils).

Although the government or local authorities run and control **public sector businesses**, they are owned by the country. The finance for public sector businesses is found by either central or local government, and their aim is to give a service for the people of either the country as a whole or for those who live in the local authority area.

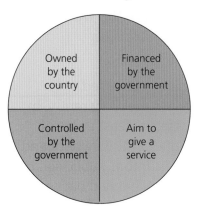

Owned by the country	Financed by the government
Controlled by the government	Aim to give a service

▲ Features of public sector ownership

Differences between public and private sector businesses

Public sector businesses differ from private sector businesses in several important ways:

Ownership

Private sector businesses are owned by private people but public sector businesses are owned by the country as a whole. There are no individual owners in the public sector.

Purposes and aims

Their purposes and aims are very different. Private sector businesses aim to maximise profits for their owners. In public sector businesses the aim is to give a service to the people and less emphasis is placed on profit making, although they are expected to break even.

Control

Private sector businesses are controlled by the people who own them or by directors and managers appointed to do so, but public sector businesses are controlled by the government or local authority.

Finance

Capital is raised differently. In private sector businesses, the capital is invested by private people but in public sector businesses the capital is either borrowed from the government's central funds – the Treasury – or taken out of the local rates.

Use of profits

The profits of the business are used differently and losses are met differently. In private sector businesses, at least some of the profits are distributed to the owners and they also bear the losses, but in public sector businesses, any profits are handed back to the government and their losses are offset by the Treasury.

This information is summarised in the following table.

	Private sector	Public sector
Ownership	Private individuals	Country or state
Purpose and aim	To make profit	To give a service
Control	Owners or Directors	Government or Local Authority
Capital	Raised by private owners	Comes from Treasury or from rates
Use of profits	Distributed to owners	Handed back to government or local authority

The most usual form of public sector ownership are **public corporations** which are run by the government, and municipal undertakings which are run by local authorities.

Public corporations

Public corporations are defined as government-controlled market bodies.

(A market body is one which produces goods and services for sale and at least 50% of its income comes from sales.)

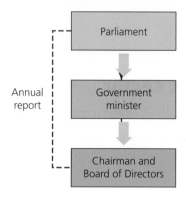

▲ Control of a public corporation

Examples of public corporations in the United Kingdom include British Nuclear Fuels, Royal Mint, Bank of England, British Broadcasting Corporation, British Waterways Board and the Civil Aviation Authority. These activities are too important to be left to private individuals.

There are several reasons why these industries have been taken over:

▶ Some services are essential and must be provided, but their costs are so high that a privately-owned firm would not be interested in them because they would not make a profit.

▶ In many cases the capital investment needed would be too great for any privately owned business to afford.

▶ It would be unsafe for private people to run dangerous industries such as the provision of atomic energy.

▶ Nationalisation (taking over by the Government) prevents large, powerful, privately-owned **monopolies** from existing and being able to set very high prices for their services.

▶ In some instances, the business was failing, so the government took it over in order to save jobs.

▶ Sometimes it would be wasteful to have several organisations duplicating services.

Aims of public corporations

The overriding aim of a public corporation is to give a service. Public corporations are expected to break-even but this is often not possible.

Control of public corporations

The government has overall control of the public corporation and appoints a government minister to take responsibility for it. The minister appointed would be the one whose department is most closely linked to the work of the corporation. The minister would oversee the appointment of a chairman and board of directors and they would become responsible for the day-to-day running of the industry.

The chairman of the board of directors must report annually to the minister who, in turn, presents the report in parliament where it is publicly debated and later published for the information of the general public.

Finance of public corporations

Public corporations are financed in the following way:

▶ Most of the money for public corporations comes through grants from the Treasury which is the government department responsible for the country's finance.

▶ In addition, the corporation may borrow from the Treasury.

▶ If the corporation makes profit from its activities, some may be **ploughed back** into the business.

▶ Public corporations get revenue from charging for the services they provide.

Advantages of public corporations

▶ The government ensures that the country's essential services are provided.

▶ The government is in a good position to plan the overall provision for the country.

▶ Services are not duplicated and resources are not wasted.

▶ Any profits made could benefit taxpayers by reducing the level of taxation.

Disadvantages of public corporations

▶ Public corporations are very large which can lead to inefficiencies.

▶ It is difficult to motivate employees in an impersonal organisation.

▶ The taxpayer has to meet higher tax payments if the corporation makes a loss.

▶ The running of the corporation could be politically influenced.

Activity

In the following table, link the first part of the sentence with its correct ending.

A public corporation is	to give a service.
Public corporations are financed	that it may be inefficient.
One advantage of a public corporation is	controlled by the government.
A disadvantage of a public corporation is	by the Treasury.
Public corporations aim	that services are not duplicated.

Municipal undertakings

The word 'municipal' refers to local government, so municipal undertakings are activities organised by the local councils.

There are eleven local councils in Northern Ireland. They are:

▶ Antrim and Newtownabbey Borough Council

▶ Ards and North Down Borough Council

▶ Armagh City Banbridge and Craigavon Borough Council

▶ Belfast City Council

▶ Causeway Coast and Glens Borough Council

- Derry City and Strabane District Council
- Fermanagh and Omagh District Council
- Lisburn and Castlereagh City Council
- Mid and East Antrim Borough Council
- Mid Ulster District Council
- Newry Mourne and Down District Council.

Each council has elected representatives who have been voted onto the council to represent the people and to work with the council staff to provide and maintain key services throughout the area.

The services for which local authorities are responsible may vary slightly from area to area, but all are expected to provide:

- refuse collection and disposal
- street cleaning
- health and environmental services
- parks and recreational facilities
- local housing
- parking areas
- maintenance of local roads.

In addition, they support:

- the arts
- tourism
- economic development.

▲ Street cleaning is an important service

Main sources of finance for municipal undertakings

Government grant

The government gives a capital grant to the local authority to assist it with essential building work. It is unusual for the government to finance the project any further.

Rates

Some of the money required to run local government enterprises comes from the rates. Rates are paid by each householder and each business in the area according to the size of their properties.

Charge for the activity

An entrance fee is charged to each person using the facilities provided by the council in the area – for example a swimming pool or leisure centre.

Activity

This activity is based on your own local authority. You should arrange for one member of your class to contact the local authority in order to find the necessary information. Alternatively, if you have access to the internet, you could find some information there.

Answer the following questions:

1 Give the name of your local authority.
2 Write down the address of its main office.
3 Find out the name of the Chief Executive of your local authority.
4 Make a list of the business activities your local council undertakes.

Social enterprise

What is **social enterprise**? The Social Enterprise Alliance defines it as:

> 'An organisation that marries the social mission of a non-profit programme with the market-driven approach of a business.'

A social enterprise is a business which has social aims and reinvests a large proportion of its profits into the community or back into the enterprise. It is set up to address social problems, improve communities or the environment. Its main aim is to improve human and environmental well-being. Unlike other forms of business, it does not have as its primary aim the need to make maximum profits for its shareholders or owners. A social enterprise makes its money in a socially responsible way and can be in any sector or any type of business. It competes alongside other businesses but uses business principles to achieve social aims and promote ethical trading.

A charity depends on donations to survive, whereas a social enterprise is self-sustaining.

The work of a social enterprise

To provide employment

Many social enterprises were originally set up to meet social needs such as unemployment in the area. A social enterprise provides employment for local people and often offers a more flexible approach to working which can be of particular benefit to groups of people who find it difficult to enter the world of work, such as the long-term unemployed, people with learning disabilities, minority ethnic groups or physically disabled people. A social enterprise is an ideal environment for such people to develop their potential. In other words, social enterprise helps people to help themselves.

To provide a sense of community

Groups such as the long-term unemployed, people with learning disabilities, minority ethnic groups, the homeless and the physically disabled can often feel isolated and find it difficult to fit into society. A social enterprise provides a social setting for such people and gives them a sense of community and of belonging to a group.

To solve an environmental problem

Some social enterprises were originally set up to solve an environmental problem. This may be a scheme to create a pleasant area such as a garden in a run-down district. People from the social enterprise work together on the project which gives them a sense of purpose and also brings them together in a group.

Fifteen

▲ The Fifteen restaurant

Fifteen is one of the most famous social enterprises and is a restaurant in London set up in 2002 by the celebrity chef, Jamie Oliver. It was established to help homeless, unemployed people who often had criminal records and problems with drugs or alcohol. The restaurant trains disadvantaged young people who are interested in becoming chefs. If they are committed to improving themselves and are hard-working they are given a year-long placement at the restaurant.

The restaurant is very successful and now has many outlets. Every year new trainees start the course. Those finishing the course go on further work placements or sometimes open their own restaurants.

Divine Chocolate

▲ One of the benefactors of Divine Chocolate

Divine Chocolate was **launched** in 1998 to produce chocolate which is Fairtrade, an affordable price and co-owned by a co-operative of 85,000 Ghanaian cocoa farmers called Kuapa Kokoo. The enterprise has been very successful and because Kuapa own 44% of the company, the profits are shared with the farmers who grow the cocoa beans. Customers are keen to buy the chocolate **products** in their shops not only because the goods are affordable but also because they know they are ensuring a fair deal for the producers in Ghana who otherwise would receive much less for their cocoa.

Jericho Foundation

The Jericho Foundation is a social enterprise which creates local jobs and helps the unemployed to be fulfilled, skilled and employed. One of the groups the Jericho Foundation works with is survivors of human trafficking – people who have been brought to this country and made to live in very poor conditions. The Jericho Foundation aims to rescue them from such conditions and turn their lives around.

Examination question

Define the term 'social enterprise' and explain two advantages of a social enterprise.   (6 marks)

How to answer this question

Write the meaning of the term (up to 2 marks) and then give details of two advantages of a social enterprise (up to 2 marks for each advantage). You can give advantages from either the point of view of the people who organise the social enterprise or from the point of view of people who are helped by the enterprise.

Examination question

Analyse two differences between the private and public sectors.   (6 marks)

How to answer this question

You are expected to consider each difference by comparing two aspects of each sector.
(3 marks for each difference fully compared.)

Checklist

At this stage you should be able to:

○ explain the meaning of the term 'public sector'

○ compare and contrast public and private sector organisations in terms of ownership, aims, control and finance

○ explain the meaning of the term 'social enterprise'

○ analyse how a social enterprise aims to deliver a range of outputs including economic e.g. employment, social e.g. community spirit, and environmental e.g. sustainable business practice.

1.5 Business location

Getting the location of a business correct is vitally important and can make the difference between success and failure.

Factors influencing location of business locally and nationally

Several different factors influence the location of a business. Although much of the decision of where to situate a business depends on the type of business being opened, other factors need to be considered as well. Think about Colin's problem in the following case study:

Case study

▲ Colin's service station

Colin has always wanted to run a service station, and now has the required capital. Three sites are available for him to buy and he could afford any of them. He simply wants to go to the site where he would sell the most fuel and small goods such as newspapers, magazines, drinks and confectionery and has no other considerations in mind. The sites are:

▶ On the M1 motorway where drivers have to travel approximately forty miles to the next service station unless they leave the motorway.

▶ In the small seaside town of Castlerock which has a small population but has sizeable numbers of visitors during the summer months.

▶ In the very busy city of Newry which is situated on the main Belfast to Dublin route, has a large population and is a good commercial centre. However Newry is situated on the border with the Republic of Ireland, where fuel is sometimes cheaper than in Northern Ireland.

Activity

Complete the following table to list the advantages and disadvantages of each site.

Site	Advantages	Disadvantages
On the M1		
Castlerock		
Newry		

Now give Colin your opinion on the best choice of site for his proposed business stating the most important reason.

I would advise Colin to locate in:	
Because:	

In your consideration of Colin's problem, you have looked at the type of business he hopes to run and then decided on the location where he would achieve the highest sales revenue. However, decisions about location are never as straightforward as this, and other factors have to be considered.

The other influences on location which you have to study in the GCSE Business Studies specification are shown in the following diagram:

▲ Forestry in Fermanagh

Some of Northern Ireland's traditional industries were originally started in places where a supply of the raw materials was available. However in some cases, the supply of those raw materials has been exhausted for many years and the industries continue with imported materials. (See the Case Study on Belleek Pottery later in this unit.)

It is therefore the case that closeness to raw materials was more important in past centuries than at present because transport systems are more developed now.

Proximity to raw materials

In examples of manufacturing businesses where the raw material is heavy, it makes economic sense to place the business near the source of the raw materials. For instance, timber firms frequently locate in heavily forested areas and quarrying businesses will locate where the stone is found in the land.

Proximity to markets

As in the case of closeness to raw materials, closeness to markets is now less important than it once was for manufacturing businesses. Good transport systems have meant that goods can be moved to the market more easily.

However, closeness to markets is of great importance in the case of retail businesses and service industries. Shops and offices need to be located centrally in towns and cities which are popular with shoppers and where they are obviously going to get customers. Services such as doctors, dentists and solicitors also need to be situated where people can easily get to them.

Shopping Centres are popular locations for shops. They usually have one major retail store as the anchor store and a series of other smaller outlets and boutiques. The large store attracts large numbers of shoppers and all the other retail outlets in the Centre benefit from the passing trade.

For example Marks & Spencer is the anchor shop in Sprucefield in Enniskillen but all the other shops in Sprucefield are also busy because of the large numbers of visitors.

▲ Marks & Spencer

Availability and price of land

A major consideration is the availability and the price of land. The cost of land varies greatly from area to area, and the success of the new business could be seriously affected by this capital cost.

The cost depends on:

▶ how central the site is. Sites in the centre of towns are the most expensive to buy or rent and also have a higher rates valuation. In addition, they are usually smaller so are suitable for use by **retailers** rather than **manufacturers.**

▶ the area of the country in which it is situated. As a general rule, land becomes more expensive near large towns or cities. It is cheaper to buy or rent in more remote areas or in areas which are considered to be less prosperous.

▶ the competition for the site. Having a number of parties interested in the site will increase its price considerably.

▶ the availability of land. Land is a very scarce resource and planning restrictions are rigid.

Other factors also have to be considered regarding the suitability of the land.

▶ At some time in the future the business may wish to expand, so the business has to be sure that there is available land for future expansion.

▶ Whether the land must be purchased or is available for renting is also relevant.

▶ The amount of the rates payable to the local authority will also influence new businesses.

▲ A digger preparing land for development

Government influences

The influence of the government is very significant in the location of business. Some parts of the country suffer greatly from unemployment as a result of the decline of traditional industries and from the movement of some companies away from Northern Ireland to countries where labour is cheaper. The Government tries to cure employment black spots and to even out wealth and resources throughout Northern Ireland.

In order to do this the government has programmes to:

▶ encourage businesses to locate in certain areas by providing in advance factories at reduced rates in those areas

▶ organise local trade fairs and also take local business people to foreign countries to set up trade stands at fairs in order to promote their businesses

▶ offer financial incentives such as inward investment grants and tax relief to foreign companies to set up in Northern Ireland

▶ set up Industrial Estates and Business Parks

▶ offer advice to existing businesses and to those entrepreneurs wishing to set up a business.

Communications

A good **communication** system influences a business to choose its location. Businesses need to be in areas where information is easily transmitted. It is important for a business and its customers to be able to be in quick and clear communication.

▲ There are many forms of communication

Transport infrastructure

A sound infrastructure of good roads and/or a reliable rail network encourages a business to choose to move to an area. Having these in place would assist the business to deliver goods more quickly to its customers and would also help it to receive its deliveries more easily.

Closeness to a seaport or airport may also be important, depending on the type, size and weight of the product being made, and on whether or not raw materials have to be imported.

The cost of transport is a major consideration. If the business is a manufacturing business requiring heavy and bulky raw materials from another country, it is more economical to locate the business near a seaport in order to reduce costs of transporting over land. Similarly, if the finished product is a heavy one and is mostly exported, a location near the port would further reduce costs.

However, Northern Ireland is a very small country and therefore the distance to be travelled overland is relatively small to any part of the province. The consideration of transport overland in Northern Ireland is much less important for this reason, than it would be in a large country such as Canada, for example.

▲ Large sums have been invested in roads in Northern Ireland

Parking

Available car parking facilities are very important for retail businesses, but most particularly for those selling groceries or goods.

There is also the added fact that town centre parking is expensive and limited. These are the main reasons why large out-of-town retail centres such as Sprucefield outside Lisburn are so popular.

Car parking facilities are also important for manufacturing businesses in order to accommodate the large number of employees, delivery vehicles, visitors and trade representatives.

▲ A shopping centre car park

Activity

Match the businesses named on the left with their most suitable locations from the list on the right-hand side.

Business	Location
A chemical factory	At the entrance to a hospital
A toy shop	In a centre of population near several large towns
A leisure centre	In a remote area but convenient to farms
A newspaper and confectionery shop	In an area far away from houses
An abattoir	Attached to a hotel
A hospital	In the middle of the orchard county
An apple juice factory	In a high street
A flower shop	Beside a bus station

Examination question

L&L Flowers is a flower shop which wishes to expand by opening another flower shop. Discuss three factors which might influence the location of the new flower shop. (6 marks)

How to answer this question

Choose factors which would apply to a flower shop. 3 of the marks will be given for naming three appropriate factors. You are asked to discuss each of the factors so you would be expected to give a reason why each factor would influence the location of the new shop. This would gain the remaining 3 marks.

Case study

▲ The Belleek Pottery

The world famous Belleek China is manufactured in the small village of Belleek which is situated on the banks of the River Erne and on the border between Counties Fermanagh and Donegal.

In 1849, John Caldwell Bloomfield inherited the Castlecaldwell estate which included the village of Belleek. This was shortly after the potato famine in Ireland and the new landlord, concerned about his tenants, was anxious to find work for them. A geological survey of the area revealed the presence of feldspar, kaolin, flint, clay and shale – the necessary raw materials for the production of pottery.

In 1858, using his own capital plus that of two wealthy friends who were interested in the project, John Caldwell Bloomfield opened a pottery on a site at the side of the village where the river would provide power to drive a mill wheel. He used his influence to get the Railway Service to build a railway to Belleek so that coal could be brought in to fire the kilns and also provide a method of transport for the finished product to be taken to markets.

The new pottery provided a much needed source of employment for local people. However, experienced potters were also required and they were brought to Belleek from Stoke-on-Trent – one of the most famous and established pottery areas.

The Belleek Pottery became very prosperous and by 1865 it had established a steady market throughout Ireland and England as well as America, Canada and Australia.

Belleek Pottery continues to operate on the same site, although obviously its structure and methods have had to be updated. A major capital investment, partly funded by the Industrial Development Board in 1983, made this possible. The building has been modernised, all the kilns are now powered by electricity and the water wheel is no longer in use.

Activity

Read the case study on Belleek Pottery Ltd and answer the following questions:

1 What was the major reason for locating the pottery in Belleek?

2 Name three other influences for choosing the site in Belleek.

3 Give details of two reasons why china is still manufactured in Belleek.

Checklist ✔

At this stage you should be able to explain the following factors that influence the location of businesses:

○ proximity to raw materials

○ proximity to market

○ availability and price of land

○ governmental influences

○ communications

○ transport infrastructure

○ parking.

When entrepreneurs start up new businesses, they will have aims and objectives which they set out in order to give a focus to their activities. These aims then become their targets and they can judge their progress against their stated aims.

In order to be successful, the business's aims have to be SMART:

- ▶ Specific
- ▶ Measurable
- ▶ Attainable
- ▶ Realistic
- ▶ Timed

Mission statement

The business's aims are usually summarised in a short statement known as a **mission statement**. This statement sets out the purpose of the business and how the business will carry out its activities. The mission statement shows members of the public what the business stands for and what its guiding principles are.

Activity

Study the following selection of mission statements and answer the questions.

> McDonald's® Brand vision is 'To be the best quick service restaurant experience'. Being the best means providing outstanding quality, service, cleanliness, and value, so that we make every customer in every restaurant smile.
>
> And our brand mission 'Is to be our customer's first choice, when it comes to, top quality products, outstanding service / cleanness and great value for money'.
>
> Accordingly our operations have been aligned around a strategy called the Plan to Win centering on five basics for an exceptional customer experience – People, Products, Place, Price and Promotion.
>
> We are committed to improving our operations and enhancing our customers' experience, through our commitment to our people development & growth, giving back to the community in which we do business and delivering quality, service and cleanliness at the highest standards to all our customers.
>
> You can help achieve this vision by being the best, embracing and reflecting our values in how you conduct yourself in everything you do.

CULLODEN
ESTATE AND SPA

Through our commitment to excellence, we will guarantee that every visit to the 5 star Culloden Estate and Spa in Belfast will be a special occasion.

Built for a Bishop....Fit for a King

The Culloden Estate and Spa, the flagship of Hastings Hotels, Northern Ireland's leading hotel Collection, is renowned as one of the finest hotels in Ireland.

We enhance the magnificence and splendour of the Culloden by:

- the warmth, friendliness and professionalism of our dedicated team;
- continually investing in the quality of our guests' comfort and staff development;
- anticipating and exceeding our guests' expectations

1 What do McDonald's expect of their members of staff?

2 What would you, as a customer, be entitled to expect in a McDonald's restaurant?

3 The Culloden Hotel is a five-star hotel. In what way does the hotel's mission statement convey its high quality?

Business aims

The aims of each business will be different according to the size and type of the organisation, although there are usually some general aims and common ideas in most of them. The usual aims are detailed here.

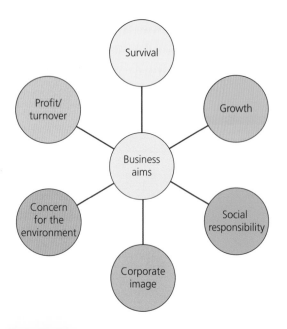

Survival

When a business first opens it takes some time for it to become established in the market. During the period when it is becoming established it is unlikely to be in a profit-making position and its basic aim, at the early stage, would simply be to survive.

There are other times when established businesses may have difficulty in making sales revenue and even staying in business. This would occur at times when the country's interest rates are high making it difficult for customers to borrow money to purchase goods. The result is that consumers are able to buy fewer and less expensive goods.

At such times the business simply aims to survive and stay afloat until economic conditions improve. In order to do so, the business may reduce prices as low as possible to hold on to their customers or it may reduce other expenditure as far as possible.

Profit and turnover

One of the most basic aims for a business is to make profit and turnover (sales) and to improve on the profit levels and turnover of previous years. Everyone involved in the business benefits – the owners and shareholders get larger returns on their investments, customers will have an improved variety of goods on offer in the business, while employees have job security and their morale is improved. In addition, making profit is the best way of guaranteeing the business's survival and it also has other benefits for the business since it allows it to expand in the future and to take advantage of economies of scale.

However, businesses have to be careful that, in trying to maximise profit and turnover, they do not price their goods so highly that consumers leave and take their custom away. This would cause the profit levels and turnover to fall and the custom would go to competitors instead.

The most successful business is one which is able to price and sell good quality items at prices which are fair. This will retain customers who will return to the business, thereby ensuring that it makes further profit.

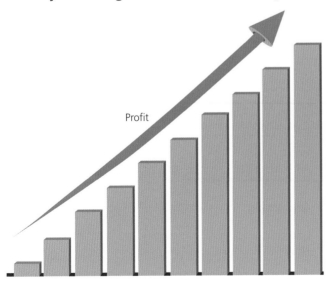

▲ A graph showing rising profits and sales

Growth

If a business is successful, it will aim to grow and expand its market into new areas by opening more branches, by taking over other businesses, or by extending its range of products. A business would have several reasons for wishing to expand in these ways.

By opening new branches the business would have access to a larger market which would normally lead to increased sales and profits. Extension of the range of products, if successful, would also lead to increased sales and profits. Higher profits lead to greater job security for employees and to greater consumer confidence in the firm.

Another method of **business growth** is to eliminate competitors – either by merging with them, taking them over or causing them to close. With a competitor no longer in the market, the sales in the surviving business would increase.

Corporate image

A good corporate image is very important to a business and is one of its aims. This means that the business wants to be thought well of by its customers, by other companies and by members of the general public. This would give it a good reputation in the community for good service and value.

In order to enhance and maintain its corporate image, a business will make sure that it treats its customers fairly and with respect, and it will provide a number of customer services such as wheelchairs, a restaurant or a crèche. It will have well-trained staff who are helpful to customers and it may also contribute generously to the local community and have a high profile there.

Concern for the environment

Concern for the environment and global warming have become major issues for all of us. All responsible businesses are aware of their responsibility to reuse and recycle. For example, all large supermarkets have either stopped using plastic bags or at least have limited their use by charging customers for them and introducing 'bags for life'. Some businesses place great emphasis on caring for their local environment and enhancing the area surrounding their premises. In order to do this they landscape their grounds attractively and plant trees around their buildings which provide food for birds. As far as possible they will use natural light and natural ventilation in order to save energy.

Most businesses also use recycled paper and packaging materials and are careful that effluent and chemicals from their places of work do not contaminate local rivers and lakes.

▲ More and more people are investing in bags for life

Social responsibility

Businesses aim to be responsible socially in their local communities. Caring for the environment is one way in which they do this. In addition, they work with the community providing as much

local employment as possible. Other examples are that they work with local schools taking part in career meetings and competitions. Locally they sponsor community events such as marathons, and allow charities to organise collections in their premises. They will provide special facilities for the disabled, such as special opening sessions especially at busy times.

Activity ✎

Match the most appropriate aim to the businesses listed, giving a reason for your choice. The first one is done for you as an example.

Description of business	Appropriate aim	Reason
Small boutique just starting up for the first time	Survival	As the business is new it will take some time to become established.
Large popular supermarket		
Factory situated in an area of natural beauty		
Hospital		
Hotel which is proud of its reputation for high quality		
Farmer who has been badly affected by poor weather		
Hairdresser who is well established and has regular customers		

Activity

The following list gives details of a number of businesses and names one aim which is important to each business. You are asked to complete the third column to show how that aim would affect the activities of that business. The first one has been done for you.

Description of business	Aim of business	How the business activities would be affected
Large grocery shop	Concern for the environment	Would plant trees in its grounds Would provide litter bins
Social enterprise	Public service	
Travel agency – during a recession	Survival	
International car manufacturer	Growth	
Small business which undertakes painting and decorating work	Profit improvement	
Up-market fashion store	Corporate image	

How the aims of a business may be in conflict

On occasions a business may find that its aims may be in conflict with one another. Keeping one aim can sometimes cause tension between the **stakeholders** or even with another aim. For example:

▶ Shareholders are most interested in profit improvement and may be unhappy about some of the profits being given to a worthy cause such as the Developing Countries. On the other hand, the donation to the Developing Countries would meet the business's social responsibility aim.

▶ Managers may aim to expand the business premises which would mean a reduction in profit in the short term. Shareholders may oppose this temporary loss of profit.

To illustrate this point let us consider the following business.

Case study

A large meat processing factory is situated near a residential area of a major town. The factory is prosperous, profits are good and it provides employment for over one hundred local people. However, the local residents are unhappy because heavy traffic to the factory is causing dangers for the children and is damaging the surface of the road past their houses. They also complain about a bad smell coming into their houses from the factory.

The factory is due to be extended because it is so successful. The directors also have plans to install new processing machinery which would eliminate the smell. The residents formed a pressure group and have asked their MLA and the Local Authority to help them to ensure that the factory does not get planning permission for the extension.

It seems impossible to satisfy all the people concerned!

Activity

Consider each of the following courses of action and complete the spaces to show one group who would be in favour of the action and a second group who would be opposed to it.

Action	Those in favour	Those opposed
The factory closes and moves to a different area		
The factory expands on its present site and installs the new processing machinery		
The factory stays as it is		
The factory spends a large sum of money widening and improving the road		

If you were the Managing Director of this factory, state which action you would recommend to your board, giving your reasons.

Comparison of public sector and private sector aims

The aims of businesses in the private sector and businesses in the public sector are very different. In general, the differences are as follows:

Sector	Aims
Private sector – Sole trader Partnership Franchise Private Limited Company Public Limited Company	To create and improve profit To grow and expand To give customer satisfaction To have a good corporate image
Public sector	To provide a service To break even
Social enterprise	To contribute to the community To relieve social problems

Activity

In the following table, name the sector (public, private or social) to which each person belongs and state an aim which he/she would have.

Business	Sector	Aim
A small shopkeeper trading near a large supermarket		
A public limited company		
Divine Chocolate		
A man owning a small business and working on his own cleaning windows		

Why aims and objectives are helpful to businesses

Having aims is helpful to a business because they:

▶ define what a business is and what it aspires to be

▶ serve as a guide for the business's activity in the future

▶ provide targets for the business to achieve

▶ act as a standard against which the business may compare its progress.

Ethical issues associated with business aims

Obviously the majority of businesses wish to make profit – that is the basic reason for being in business. However, they also aim to deal fairly and honestly with their customers, employees and suppliers. That is their ethical duty.

Quite apart from morals and ethics, would you ever go back to a business which had treated you dishonestly by giving you shoddy goods and refusing to change them, or by giving you less change than you were entitled to? Of course not, and businesses know that customers will return to them if they are treated fairly and honestly. Businesses do not pursue the aim of profit creation at the expense of these issues and will be willing to reduce their profit a little for that reason.

Ethical issues in business aims fall under the following headings:

Environmental issues

Businesses share the responsibility of caring for the environment. For this reason, they landscape their grounds, plant trees, provide litter bins and encourage people to use them, use recycled paper and packaging, sell biodegradable products in their shops and do not provide free plastic bags.

Employee working conditions

Businesses pay their employees fair **wages** – minimum wage levels are laid down in legislation but good employers will pay the Living Wage rates. Most businesses see their employees as their most valuable resource and provide good working conditions.

Equality

Businesses aim to treat all customers equally and give the best service to everyone. They aim to treat male and female workers equally in terms of pay and conditions. They also aim to treat able and disabled persons equally in terms of the working environment and working conditions.

Social responsibility

Many businesses refuse to trade in goods which have been made in countries where workers are exploited and many businesses sell 'Fair Trade' products. For example, the Body Shop has always refused to sell any product which was tested on animals.

Examination question

Banland Leisure Centre operates in the public sector. Explain one way in which the aims of Banland Leisure Centre differ from the aims of a similar business in the private sector. (4 marks)

How to answer this question

State one aim of the public sector leisure centre (2 marks) and then explain one aim of the leisure centre in the private sector, showing the contrast between them. (2 marks)

Checklist ✓

At this stage you should be able to:

- ○ describe and explain the business aims and objectives of survival, profit and turnover, growth, corporate image, concern for the environment, social responsibility
- ○ analyse how the aims and objectives of a business affect its activities
- ○ analyse how, on occasions, these aims may be in conflict
- ○ compare and contrast the aims and objectives of private and public sector organisations
- ○ analyse why aims and objectives are helpful to businesses
- ○ analyse the ethical issues associated with business aims.

1.7 Stakeholders

Stakeholders in a business are people who affect, or may be affected by, the actions of that business. Stakeholders may be individuals or groups of people.

The following are the main stakeholders in business:

Owners

The owners of a business are those who have invested money in it. They may have contributed the total capital for the business, as in the case of a sole trader or a partnership. In a small business, the owners may also manage and run the business.

Owners have the greatest interest in the progress of the business since a large part of their money is invested in it and, in the majority of cases, the owners depend on the business for their livelihood.

The reward which owners get from the business is in the form of profit but they also risk having to bear any loss incurred in the business.

Shareholders

Shareholders are those people who invest money in a business which is a limited company. Their investment is in the form of shares and this makes them part owners of the company. Shareholders do not take any part in the management of the company although they are entitled to attend the annual general meeting and vote for the Board of Directors.

The reward which shareholders receive from the business is in the form of a dividend which is a share of the annual profit. If the company is not in a profit-making position, the shareholders risk losing their shares.

However, they have limited liability which means that their loss is limited to the amount they invested in the shares.

Directors

Directors are appointed to the Board of a limited company and their function is to be responsible for the overall running of the company. Directors make the policy decisions and have the ultimate power in the company. It is usual for a company to have a managing director and a number of other directors, each of whom looks after a certain area of the business's operation, for example, sales, finance or production.

The reward which a director receives from the business is in the form of a **salary**, although it is possible for directors also to be shareholders in which case they would also receive a dividend.

Managers

Managers are the second layer of authority below the directors and they have responsibility for the day-to-day running of the business. Managers oversee the work being done in the company and the workers and **supervisors** report to them.

Managers are rewarded with a salary and they have a great interest in the success of the business since their employment depends on it.

Producers

Producers of raw materials or goods to a business also have a stakeholding in it and want to see it succeed. This is because producers do not want to lose any of their customers but want to ensure that they are prosperous and able to pay their accounts.

Farmers selling vegetables to a grocery shop would be an example of one of its producers. Producers are rewarded by high levels of sales revenue which adds to the profits of their own businesses.

Consumers

All businesses consider consumers (customers) to be of the greatest importance. Quite simply, without consumers (customers) the business ceases to exist. The business depends on consumers for its income and needs them to purchase its goods or services. Therefore, businesses spend a lot of time and money on customer service to ensure that their customers are satisfied with both their product and their service.

Consumers have a stake in a business since it probably is situated in a convenient place for them to shop in and they will support it if it supplies goods at suitable prices. They also have an interest in seeing that the business succeeds because it gives them a greater number of businesses to deal with which improves the competition and the variety of goods on offer.

> 'If you don't take care of your customers, someone else will.'

Lenders

It is probable that the business will have borrowed money at some stage either to start the business or to keep it running. Banks are major lenders to all sizes of business but, in the case of a small business such as a sole trader, the lender may be family or friends. All lenders, whatever the size of their loans, are stakeholders and are interested to see the business succeed so that they have confidence that the business will be able to repay their loans.

Employees

Employees who work in the business are important stakeholders since they rely on that business for their livelihood. They are interested in the success of the business so that they have job security and are sure of their wages to maintain their own households.

Pressure groups

▲ Greenpeace

Pressure groups may be formed by any group of people wishing to exert influence on the activity of the business. This makes the group a stakeholder in the business. A trade union is one pressure group and represents the interests of the workers in the business and negotiates with management on their behalf. The trade union has an interest in seeing a business succeed because it ensures the safety of its members' jobs. If the business loses profit or fails altogether it will have to make workers redundant. Those workers would then depend on the trade union to try to save their jobs or to find work for them elsewhere.

Another active pressure group is Greenpeace whose interest is environmental. Its members may lobby a business if it has plans to engage in some activity with which they do not agree, such as cutting down trees.

The Community

The local community indirectly is a stakeholder in a business and therefore wishes to see general business prosperity in its town. If businesses are successful, there is full employment in the area so workers have more money to spend. This has a multiplier effect on other businesses such as hotels, restaurants and leisure centres. General morale in the area is improved and crime may be reduced.

Activity

Name the stakeholder who is most likely to have said the following:

1 I want the business to succeed so that they will continue to buy my products.

2 We want our members to have secure jobs in that business.

3 I want to make profit from my investment in the business.

4 I want the business to succeed because my job depends on it.

5 If the business fails there would be less wealth in the area.

6 I want the business to remain open because it is convenient for me to use.

How the aims of stakeholders may differ

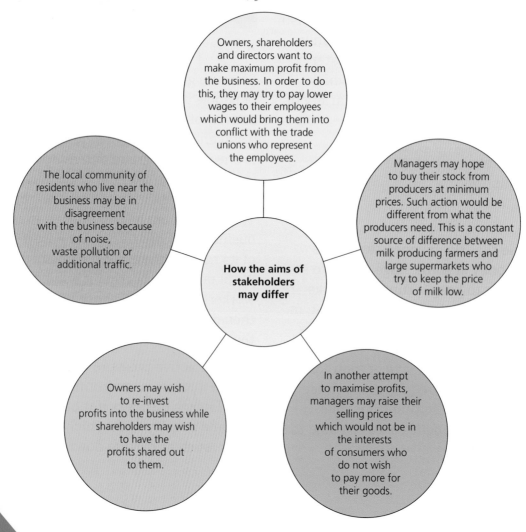

Activity

Complete the following table to show why each stakeholder would have an interest in a business.

Stakeholder	Interest
Owners	
Shareholders	
Directors	
Managers	
Producers	
Consumers	
Pressure groups	

Examination question

Identify two different stakeholders in an airport and explain their interest in that business. Analyse how the aims of these two stakeholders may differ.　(10 marks)

How to answer this question

Firstly identify one appropriate stakeholder (1 mark) and then explain that shareholder's interest in the airport　(2 marks)

Identify a second appropriate stakeholder (1 mark) and then explain that shareholder's interest in the airport　(2 marks)

Show how the aims of these two stakeholders are different　(4 marks)

It is very important to choose stakeholders which would be suitable for an airport.

Activity

In the following word search, find the words shown in the list. The words can be read in straight lines, horizontally, vertically or diagonally, either backwards or forwards. There is no overlap of words in the grid.

| stakeholder | shareholder | dividend | employee | lender |
| owner | director | manager | community | producer | consumer |

S	U	K	C	O	N	S	U	M	E	R	H	J	D
Z	T	X	C	B	V	N	M	L	O	P	I	U	I
M	F	A	G	W	Q	C	M	M	B	E	R	T	R
A	Q	A	K	S	V	V	C	X	Z	W	Y	P	E
N	R	C	B	E	M	S	D	F	S	Y	C	L	C
A	R	Q	W	X	H	C	V	B	N	V	O	K	T
G	E	W	E	Q	E	O	A	P	V	K	M	V	O
E	D	V	R	F	R	Y	L	G	R	H	M	B	R
R	N	W	T	W	E	U	I	D	C	S	U	M	K
W	E	K	I	V	S	T	Y	B	E	D	N	P	I
H	L	J	D	C	Q	W	L	U	A	R	I	R	H
M	C	N	S	E	M	X	W	A	M	A	T	B	V
D	I	V	I	D	E	N	D	Q	W	T	Y	R	C
I	P	O	H	B	D	E	H	V	U	O	J	A	F
Z	K	X	V	X	B	R	J	F	R	W	C	I	U
E	E	Y	O	L	P	M	E	E	L	V	T	K	Q
W	R	I	L	R	K	N	D	A	T	E	W	G	R
U	A	P	P	R	O	D	U	C	E	R	I	O	E
F	Q	E	B	G	N	E	S	T	G	L	V	W	N
R	G	S	T	V	N	C	R	Y	N	A	E	S	W
S	H	A	R	E	H	O	L	D	E	R	C	E	O

Checklist ✓

At this stage you should be able to:

○ describe and explain the following groups who have an interest in business:
- owners
- shareholders
- directors
- managers
- producers
- consumers
- lenders
- employees
- pressure groups
- the community

○ discuss how the aims of stakeholders may differ.

What is marketing?

The Chartered Institute of Marketing defines marketing as follows:

> 'Marketing is the process responsible for identifying, anticipating and satisfying customer requirements profitably.'

To put it more simply, it is how a business can increase its sales, its reputation and its profit by making its goods more attractive to consumers. Marketing finds out what products or services consumers want either now or in the future and provides those products or services to them at a price which leaves a profit for the business. You can see that marketing is about much more than simply selling!

Modern marketing focuses very clearly on consumers and always looks at the business from their point of view. It asks what consumers really need and if the business is meeting that need. Market-driven businesses will change the product or service to suit the consumer.

Purpose of market research

In order to understand consumers' opinions, the business must collect information from them, and from people who may become consumers in the future, to find out whether they like the business's products and will buy them.

The business will collect information on whether the product will be bought, on the type of consumer who will buy it and how often they will buy it. They will also find information on the price that consumers would pay and about the area those consumers live in. This collection of information is called market research.

Businesses are market-driven – they need to sell their products – and therefore consumers' opinions are most important to them.

They spend large sums of money on market research finding out about their market because:

▶ the information ensures that they are providing the products which consumers are most likely to buy

▶ it enables them to price the products at an acceptable level for consumers

▶ it can show if the packaging is attractive to consumers

▶ it indicates the type of people who would be their target market

▶ it shows the area in which sales are likely to be more successful

▶ sometimes it gives information about competitors

▶ it makes the business aware of any changes in consumers' tastes

▶ having all this information gives the business confidence to develop the most appropriate marketing strategy

▶ it can also prevent the business from making expensive mistakes.

Activity

▲ Rory washing a customer's windows

Rory is a Year 12 student who will be leaving school in June after he has finished his GCSE examinations. He is planning to set up a window cleaning business in his home town.

Make a list of the information Rory would need about the market before he sets up his business.

Methods of market research

Secondary/desk research

Secondary research is also known as '**desk research**' which gives a clue how it is worked. Secondary/desk research is done by using published statistics, data and other information which had been collected previously. This makes secondary/desk research very suitable for use by smaller businesses as it is cheaper and less time consuming.

Secondary/desk information may come from government publications, from external sources such as newspapers, trade journals, government publications or the internet. Information may also come from the business's internal sources such as its own sales and financial records.

This diagram shows the various ways in which secondary/desk research can be done.

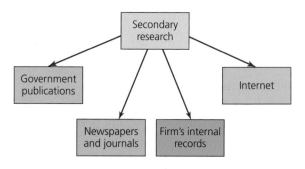

Advantages of secondary/desk research

▶ The information is cheap to obtain.

▶ The information is available immediately.

▶ If the information is from a reliable source it will be well researched and accurate.

▶ The data available covers a wide range of sources.

Disadvantages of secondary/desk research

▶ The data is unlikely to have been collected for exactly the same purpose as the business requires so may not meet the firm's needs exactly.

▶ The information may be out-of-date.

▶ The information is available to all other businesses in the market.

Primary/field research

Primary research is also known as '**field research**'. It is the collection of original information by the business and is carried out by making direct contact with consumers and members of the public who may become consumers.

Advantages of primary/field research

▶ The business can design the research in the best way to discover the particular information it needs.

▶ The business can be sure that the information gathered is up-to-date.

▶ The information can be analysed easily.

Disadvantages of primary/field research

▶ Designing the research, gathering the information and analysing it can be slow.

▶ It is specialised work so businesses often employ specialist researchers and this can be expensive.

This diagram shows the various ways in which primary/field research can be done.

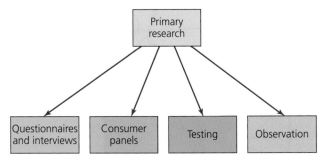

Questionnaires and interviews

This is probably the most common method of primary/field research. You may have been stopped on the street or in a shop yourself and asked questions about a certain product.

Questionnaires can be conducted by telephone or by post as well as face-to-face.

Advantages of questionnaires and interviews

▶ The questionnaire is designed to find out exactly the information the business requires.

▶ Information is taken directly from the people who are, or will be, the business's consumers.

▶ The questioner can help the member of the public to understand the questions.

Disadvantages of questionnaires and interviews

▶ Some people resent being stopped and questioned on the street or telephoned at home.

▶ Sometimes people misunderstand the questions and give misleading responses which makes the results less accurate.

▶ It is a slow method and can be expensive, especially for smaller businesses.

▶ Postal questionnaires are not always returned.

▲ A company gathering data through using questionnaires

Observation

As its name suggests, this method of primary/ field research involves watching or observing the reactions of people to products. For example, people may be **observed** making their selection of goods in supermarkets.

Advantages of observation

▶ It is not costly for the business.
▶ Consumers need not even be aware it is happening.

Disadvantages of observation

▶ It is less accurate and is open to misinterpretation.
▶ It is not suitable for all products.

Consumer panels

The use of consumer panels involves taking responses from people who sit on panels and give their opinions on given products or other consumer information. Panel members are paid and have been selected for their expertise or knowledge in this area.

Advantages of consumer panels

▶ Very detailed information can be gathered.
▶ The panel members are skilled and impartial.

Disadvantage of consumer panels

▶ It is an expensive method so is suitable only for large companies.

Testing

Testing involves members of the public being given samples of the product and being asked for their opinion of it. This is frequently used in supermarkets when a new variety of a food such as cheese is being launched on the market.

Advantages of testing

▶ Tests are straightforward to organise.
▶ Consumers' first-hand opinions are given.

Disadvantages of testing

▶ It may not test a cross-section of the public.
▶ It is not suitable for all products.

▲ People taking part in a soft drink testing

Activity 🖉

Let's return to Rory who plans to set up a window cleaning business. He now needs you to advise him how he might find the information he needs about the window cleaning market in his home area.

Write down the names of the methods he should use and tell him how to find the information he needs.

Activity

Complete the following list to show the best method of primary/field research to use to collect information on each of the products:

1 A new flavour of cheese ....
2 Detergent ....
3 Television programmes watched ....
4 A new soft drink ....
5 Trainers ....
6 Golf balls ....
7 Baby wipes ....
8 Computer software ....
9 Bathroom tiles ....
10 Cars ....

Sampling

Sampling is a part of primary/field research. Instead of asking opinions from a large number of people, this method questions a selection – or sample – of people. For accuracy of results, it is estimated that any sample should consist of approximately 2,000 people. The people questioned would be chosen as being representative of the population as a whole.

Sampling has the advantage of being manageable for the business which would find it impossible to survey everyone. It is also within its financial means and time limitations.

Methods of sampling

There are several methods by which sampling can be done. The two most commonly used are **random** and **quota sampling**.

Random sampling

A random sample is where people are randomly selected and asked for their opinions on a product. The random sample may be taken as every tenth person who walks down the street or every fiftieth name in the telephone directory, for example.

There is a possibility that some of the people questioned may not be familiar with the product or even be interested in it. For instance, there is not much point in questioning a very young girl about walking sticks or non-drivers about cars! Therefore the results of random sampling are of most use where the product is one which nearly everyone uses – chocolate bars, for example.

Advantages of random sampling

▶ Personal opinions are given by those surveyed.
▶ Everyone has a chance of being chosen.
▶ Random surveys are easily organised and are cheap.

Disadvantages of random sampling

▶ Results are not very accurate unless a very large sample is used.
▶ The method is unsuitable for some products.
▶ It does not necessarily reach the most appropriate people.

Quota sampling

Quota sampling is where **interviews** are held with a set number of people who fall into pre-determined categories and reflect the type of product. For example, a quota sample might consist of 50 per cent males and 50 per cent females or one-third teenagers, one-third middle aged people and one-third elderly people.

As in random sampling, these people's views are taken to reflect the views of everyone in their gender or age group.

It is important that the sample also reflects the composition of the people in the area, so, if there were more elderly people living in the area than teenagers, then the sample should contain more elderly people than teenagers.

Advantages of quota sampling

▶ Results are more accurate than in random sampling.

▶ It is more likely to reach the appropriate people.

▶ Personal opinions are given by those surveyed.

▶ Everyone in the particular category has a chance of being chosen.

Disadvantages of quota sampling

▶ The composition of the population in the area must be known in order for the correct proportions to be interviewed.

▶ The method is unsuitable for some products.

Activity

Westways High School is considering the formation of a chess club. You have been asked to undertake a quota sample of both boys and girls from all year groups in order to find out their level of interest in the new club.

The following table of information showing the school population has been supplied to you. The information gives the total number of boys and girls in each year group and the percentage which that represents of the total school population of 500 pupils. It has been decided to exclude Year 14.

YEAR	BOYS	% BOYS	GIRLS	% GIRLS	% TOTAL
8	45	9	48	9.6	18.6
9	35	7	40	8	15
10	40	8	30	6	14
11	45	9	45	9	18
12	50	10	50	10	20
13	35	7	37	7.4	14.4
TOTAL	250	50	250	50	100

⌃ Table: Population of Westways High School

1 Which method do you think is the best one to carry out this survey? State your reasons for your choice.

2 Write three questions you would ask the pupils.

3 State whether you agree or disagree with excluding Year 14, giving your reasons.

Market segmentation

Market segmentation is a very useful method by which businesses may study their market. Market segmentation is the selection of the groups of people who would be most interested in a particular product so that the product may be targeted at them. Targeting the correct segment of the market is vital to the business if it is to achieve sales.

This method involves dividing the market for a product into different groups and types of consumers. Examples of the groups are given in the list below. While all groups differ from one another, members of groups are seen to share tastes and to have similar spending patterns. For example, most teenagers share tastes in clothes and music while the majority of wealthy people tend to go to the same restaurants and drive similar cars.

Markets are commonly segmented according to:

Age

Each age group has its own choice of product. Think of the differences in preferences in music and clothes as examples. Do your parents like the music you listen to? Does your granny like your clothes?

Gender

In some products males and females choose differently. For example, research has shown that males and females have different tastes in the cars they buy. Females are more influenced by the shape, colour and appearance of the car while males tend to be more influenced by its performance.

Ethnic/cultural background

Each race or ethnic grouping of people has its own taste in food, music and clothes. Their religions also may have different requirements which they will want to observe.

Region

Consumers living in different areas of the country, or in different countries, like different foods and clothes and often have different hobbies.

Socio-economic class

This classification looks at the occupation of the head of the household and places the occupations in different bands. Obviously the occupation will determine the level of income of the household which, in turn, will determine the type of products they buy and their spending patterns.

There are several ways in which to classify the population socio-economically but the UK Office for National Statistics has produced the following classification for the 21st century.

Group	Description
1	Higher professional and managerial workers
2	Lower professional and managerial workers
3	Intermediate occupations
4	Small employers and non-professional **self-employed**
5	Lower supervisory and technical workers
6	Semi-routine occupations
7	Routine occupations
8	Long-term unemployed

Examination question

Chocoholics Limited is a company which manufactures chocolate products. The company plans to put a new flavour of chocolate bar on the market. Explain two ways in which the company should segment its market. (4 marks)

How to answer this question

Name two segments of the market which are likely to buy the new chocolate bar (2 marks) and then explain why you have chosen those two segments (2 marks).

Activity

In the following word search, find the words shown in the list. The words can be read in straight lines, horizontally, vertically or diagonally, either backwards or forwards. Some letters may be used twice.

marketing	field	research	secondary	primary	interview	observation
questionnaire	sampling	random	quota	segmentation	testing	consumer

r	a	n	d	o	m	w	v	c	f	s	q	a	q	w	e	t	y	u	i
e	z	x	c	v	b	n	m	j	i	a	s	u	d	f	g	h	o	j	n
s	e	c	o	n	d	a	r	y	e	j	k	l	o	p	o	i	b	u	t
e	j	w	q	w	e	r	t	y	l	t	r	i	p	t	i	k	s	l	e
a	c	o	n	s	u	m	e	r	d	l	k	j	h	g	a	f	e	d	r
r	a	s	m	a	r	k	e	t	i	n	g	t	y	u	i	k	r	r	v
c	m	z	n	b	v	c	x	z	l	k	j	h	g	f	d	s	v	d	i
h	n	j	t	e	s	t	l	n	g	t	y	p	p	o	i	h	a	g	e
l	k	j	h	g	f	d	S	a	p	o	i	u	r	y	t	r	t	e	w
q	u	e	s	t	i	o	n	n	a	i	r	e	g	i	f	d	i	t	r
s	e	g	m	e	n	t	a	t	i	o	n	h	y	z	m	x	o	v	c
m	n	b	v	c	x	z	s	d	l	y	w	q	f	h	u	a	n	k	l
z	x	a	t	y	p	n	l	e	o	l	k	j	d	f	t	y	r	p	r
v	m	k	l	p	r	t	o	s	a	m	p	l	i	n	g	z	d	y	t

Examination question

Surebuys plc is a large supermarket. It uses primary/field research to identify the needs of its customers.

1 Define 'primary/field research' and identify two ways in which it could be collected by Surebuys plc. (4 marks)

2 Explain the terms 'random sampling' and 'quota sampling'. State, with a reason, which would be more suitable for Surebuys plc. (6 marks)

How to answer this question

In Part 1, write an explanation of primary research (2 marks) and then name two ways by which Surebuys plc could collect information using primary research – no explanation needed of the ways. (2 marks)

In Part 2, write an explanation of random sampling (2 marks) and an explanation of quota sampling (2 marks). Then decide which is more suitable for Surebuys and explain the reason for your choice (2 marks). You should take into consideration the size and type of business.

Checklist

At this stage you should be able to:

- ○ explain the term marketing
- ○ explain the purpose of market research
- ○ describe and explain the main methods of market research
- ○ describe and explain the main methods of sampling
- ○ discuss the most appropriate method of market research and sampling for particular circumstances
- ○ explain market segmentation
- ○ analyse and evaluate the results of market research.

Introduction to the marketing mix

The marketing mix describes all the key activities which are used in marketing a business's products. This is frequently referred to as the four Ps – Price, Promotion, Place and Product.

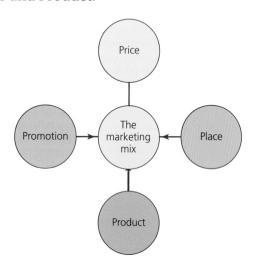

▲ A baker and his mix

It is important for a business to put on the market a PRODUCT which will be desirable to consumers. It must be available at a PRICE which consumers can afford and in a PLACE where the target market will be shopping. In order to attract consumers to the product, PROMOTION – perhaps in the form of advertising – is necessary.

The idea of the marketing mix is the same idea as when mixing a cake. A baker will alter the proportions of ingredients in a cake depending on the type of cake he/she wishes to bake. The proportions in the marketing mix can be altered in the same way and differ from product to product.

A new brand of detergent, for example, would be marketed very differently from a new range of expensive jewellery.

The new detergent would be advertised widely in popular newspapers and on television, possibly with introductory offers and demonstrating how clean it makes the washing. Expensive jewellery will be advertised in expensive glossy magazines and on television in a way which portrays luxury.

The marketing mix will also vary at different times throughout the life of a product. The price would be lowered or advertising might be increased at times when sales are falling off. A business will manipulate the four elements of the marketing mix in whatever way it has to in order to keep ahead of its competition.

In this section and the next three sections you will study the four main elements of the marketing mix in turn.

Price

Pricing policies

There are a number of pricing policies which a business may adopt. You will be examined on the first three policies only:

- **skimming**
- **penetration**
- **competitor-based**
- cost-based
- destruction
- psychological
- price wars.

The choice of policy depends on:

- the type of product being marketed
- the competition in that market
- the price which people would be willing to pay
- the costs of production which must be covered.

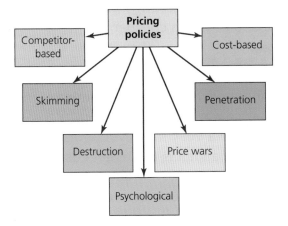

Skimming pricing

Skimming is most often used in the case of new products when there is little competition in the market. This strategy sets a relatively high price initially in an attempt to 'skim' the market – like skimming the cream off the milk! Some people would be willing to pay the higher price because the product is new and unique and few other people would own it. Later on, other businesses will enter the market setting up competition so, in order to maintain sales, the price would be reduced.

The high initial price gives the impression of high quality and is justified by the manufacturers because the product usually would have had high costs in research and development. The danger of skimming is that some people will be deterred by the high price and prefer to wait until the price falls.

Pricing of mobile phones is an excellent example of skimming. When mobile phones were first produced they were very expensive and few people owned them. Initially they were something of a status symbol. Later they were produced in large numbers by a variety of manufacturers and the price fell to such an extent that today most people own a mobile phone.

Penetration pricing

Penetration pricing is where a low price is set at the beginning in order to gain entry by a new business to an existing market, and where the price increases when the place in the market has been secured.

Penetration pricing would be used by a new business trying to break into – or penetrate – a market where other competitors already are well established. This pricing strategy is suitable for a **competitive market** and can only be used in the short term.

In order to attract consumers to the new store, and away from the competitors, they have to be attracted by low prices. The basic idea is that, once the consumers have been attracted by the lower prices, they will become regular consumers. It is at that stage that prices would be raised.

This method of price setting ensures sales, at least in the short term. It is possible, however, that the price has to be set so low that profits may be minimal.

Competitor-based pricing

Competitor-based pricing is when a business simply accepts the price which its competitors are charging for a product and then prices its product at the same level or slightly lower in order to gain some advantage over the competitors.

Competitor-based pricing would operate in a market where there is strong competition and involves close monitoring of competitors and any changes they make to their prices. This strategy is operated for products such as washing powder, where customers will buy their favourite brand in whichever shop offers it at the lowest price.

Supermarkets such as Tesco and Asda watch each other's prices very closely. If you shop in one of these supermarkets and buy a product which is cheaper in the other, you will be refunded the difference in the prices.

Cost-based pricing

Cost-based pricing, also sometimes referred to as 'cost-plus pricing', involves working out the business's **total costs** and then adding on a percentage profit. The business also has to consider the total number of items which it plans to produce and sell.

The calculation is simple:

Cost-based Price = Costs + Profit

The big advantage of cost-based pricing is that the business is guaranteed to make a profit on its sales since it has covered its costs. However, the danger is that the business may not be able to sell the expected quantity of the product perhaps because competitors are offering the same goods at a lower price. Therefore, in operating cost-based pricing it is vital to be aware of competitors' prices and what the market will bear.

Destruction pricing

Destruction pricing is also known as 'destroyer pricing'.

It is a ruthless strategy which is designed to destroy competitors' sales or even drive them out of business altogether.

This method operates by reducing the price of an existing product or selling a new product at an artificially low price. Sometimes this new low price may be below cost level so the business would be sustaining a loss for a period of time. Once the competitors have been driven out of the market, the prices would be raised again.

If the competitor is a small business it would be unable to reduce its prices in this way and may be forced to close. This has been the fate of so many of our corner shops and village stores in Northern Ireland because they simply could not offer goods at the same price as the supermarkets.

Psychological pricing

This pricing policy is commonly used and is where an item is marked at £19.99 instead of £20, for example. It is meant to give consumers the idea that they are getting a bargain as the price seems to be much cheaper.

Price wars

In very competitive markets such as the grocery market, businesses sometimes engage in **price wars** in which prices of some goods are cut to a very low level in order to secure sales. The idea is to attract customers to their particular supermarket to buy the marked-down goods and encourage them to buy other goods while they are there.

Price wars are not popular with businesses, however, even though they often happen. They are risky because advantages gained over other businesses are short-lived and rival businesses tend to respond by slashing prices even further.

If pursued long enough, price wars would cut profits seriously and, in the end, only the consumer benefits by the low prices.

Read the following extract from the report of the British Retail Consortium (BRC) chief executive:

We are now in the fourth year of falling shop prices which is great news for consumers. This is as a direct result of the intense competition in the retail industry with consumers having access to more choices and greater ability to compare prices than ever before.

▲ With lower prices, customers are able to fill up their trolley

Activity

Seven pricing policies are described in the column on the left. Link each description to the appropriate name in the column on the right.

Description	Pricing policy
This policy tries to put other firms out of business	Psychological pricing
This policy is based on the prices charged by competitors	Destruction pricing
This policy charges a high price at the beginning and reduces it later	Competitor-based pricing
This policy cuts prices very low in order to take sales away from competitors	Cost-based pricing
This policy prices goods at £9.99 instead of £10	Penetration pricing
This policy sets a low price at the beginning and increases it later	Skimming
This policy is based on the costs incurred in making and selling the goods	Price wars

Activity

Study the following situations and name the pricing strategy which is being described in each example.

1 A new hardback book is published at £30. Two months later it is sold in paperback for £10.
2 Several stationery companies in Belfast keep lowering their prices for computer paper to take sales away from each other.
3 A new supermarket in Lisburn opens selling a particular chocolate bar at 50p. Existing supermarkets in the town lower their prices of the chocolate bar to 40p.
4 A bicycle manufacturer introduces a new model at a low price in order to attract sales.
5 A chemist shop in Lurgan researches the price of particular brands of toothpaste in all local outlets and then charges the same prices as they are charging.
6 A florist in Lisnaskea sets her prices to cover her total costs plus a little profit.

Factors which affect price

Price has to be carefully worked out for every item put on the market. Several factors have to be considered.

Demand

The business has to estimate the demand for the product and price accordingly. Demand will determine how much consumers will pay. If the demand is high, a higher price may be charged and if demand is low then the price will also be low. Demand will be low in times of recession when many people are unemployed but will rise when there is more money in the economy. (See the section on Demand at the end of this section.)

Cost of production

The producer has to calculate the total costs incurred in manufacturing the goods. These costs would include factory overheads and raw materials.

The retailer has to calculate the costs incurred in offering the goods for sale such as transport charges, wages to sales staff and shop overheads.

The price charged to the consumer has to be set at a level which would cover all these costs.

Need to make a profit

The overall aim of any business owner is to make a profit from the business, so the goods must be priced at a level which not only covers the total costs but also leaves a margin of profit for both the manufacturer and the retailer.

The owners would expect the level of profit on their investment in the business to be at least as much as the interest they could have earned if they had invested their money elsewhere. A healthy profit margin also encourages other investors to buy into the business.

The highest level of profit, however, will not necessarily be made by charging the highest prices, since this could discourage sales.

Competition in the market

We have already seen in this section how competitors' prices are monitored in order to increase sales. The aim in business is to set the price at a level which would encourage customers away from competitors.

To do this, the price has to be slightly lower than that charged by the competition if the goods are exactly the same.

Price which the market can bear

It is most important that the business is sensitive to the price which customers can afford and are willing to pay. This is linked to the type of product and to the area in which it is being sold.

If the goods being sold are luxury items they would be targeted at a wealthier market, as that particular market could bear a higher price. Goods being sold in a shop in a less well-off area will have to be priced at a level which the customers there could afford. Obviously, better quality items would be sold at higher prices than those charged for items of a poorer quality. Whatever the circumstances, the price charged has to be the one at which the highest level of sales would be made.

Seasonality

The demand for certain items rises at particular times of the year. For example, the highest sales of toys are made in November and December for the Christmas market. At these times of greatest demand the price is at its highest and falls immediately after the event. This is why it is possible to buy Christmas cards very cheaply in January.

The red rose you bought for your girlfriend or boyfriend for St Valentine's Day was very expensive, but the next day the price would have been considerably lower!

Quantity of inventory in hand

At times when there is a surplus of goods in the shop, a retailer will hold a sale in order to reduce the inventory. The price charged to the consumer is lowered in order to clear the goods.

This also happens with airline tickets which can be bought much more cheaply immediately before the date of the flight. In this case, it is better for the airline company to sell the remaining seats at a reduced price rather than fly with a half empty plane. In business, this is referred to as 'under-used capacity'.

Relationship between price and demand

Demand is 'the quantity of a product which will be bought by consumers at a given price'.

The price of a product has a very great influence on demand. In general, as price increases, demand decreases and as price decreases, demand increases.

The relationship between price and demand is best illustrated graphically with price on the vertical axis and quantity demanded on the horizontal axis.

Activity

Seven factors which affect prices are described on the left. Link each one to the appropriate factor in the column on the right.

Description	Factor
The price is set so that the owners make some money for themselves	Demand
The price charged has to cover all costs of production and selling the goods	Seasonality
A high price can be charged when a lot of consumers want to buy the goods	Price the market could bear
The price depends on the time of the year	Cost of production
The price depends on how much people can afford to pay	Need to make a profit
The price depends on what other businesses are charging for the same goods	Quantity of inventory in hand
The price is determined by how much of the goods the business has	Competition in the market

As price decreases, demand increases. This fact can be shown on a demand line which always slopes downward to the right.

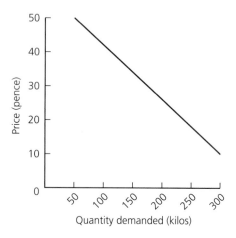

Quantity demanded (kilos)

This graph illustrates demand for a certain item:

▶ 50 kilos are demanded at 50p per kilo

▶ 300 kilos are demanded at 10p per kilo.

Activity

Study the above graph showing demand.

1 Read off the number of kilos which would be demanded if they were priced at 40p per kilo.

2 Find out how many kilos would be demanded if the goods were priced at 30p per kilo.

3 What do your answers prove about the relationship between price and demand?

There are many factors which cause a change in the demand for products:

▶ **The price being charged for the goods** – Usually the higher the price being charged, the lower the demand for the goods.

▶ **Customers' tastes and fashion** – People buy what they like or according to the prevailing fashion. If a product becomes very fashionable and popular, demand will increase.

▶ **Level of income** – Customers usually buy what they can afford. As income increases people would not necessarily buy more goods but they probably would buy better quality goods.

▶ **Price of other goods** – Some goods act as substitutes and can be bought instead. For example, if potatoes were very expensive, people might eat rice or pasta instead. Other goods are complementary goods which means they are often used together. For example, if the price of fish fell, people would eat more fish. This might cause extra demand for potatoes because fish and chips usually go together.

▶ **Advertising** – Increased advertising, if successful, would cause an increase in demand.

▶ **Credit rates** – At times when the lending rate is low, people will be able to borrow more from banks and building societies and demand for goods will increase as they buy more goods.

Successful businesses are those which can satisfy consumer demand and can get the right product to the right place at the right time and at the right price.

▲ It's a balancing act

Activity

Anton is a butcher who has a large stock of beef in his shop. Unfortunately there has been a recent health scare which has put some people off buying beef.

1 Advise Anton on ways to increase demand for beef.

2 What else might Anton do in order to increase trade generally in his shop?

Checklist ✓

At this stage you should be able to:

○ explain the term 'marketing mix'

○ explain and discuss a range of pricing policies

○ evaluate pricing policies for given circumstances

○ analyse the factors which affect price

○ analyse simple demand curves to explain the relationship between price and demand.

Examination question ↻

a A new washing-up liquid is being launched. Explain two factors which would affect its price.   (4 marks)

b Identify and discuss a suitable pricing strategy for the washing-up liquid.

   (3 marks)

c Explain the relationship between price and demand.   (2 marks)

How to answer this question

a This is a straightforward question. Choose two factors and explain them in detail.   (2 marks for each factor)

b Identify one strategy (1 mark) which would be appropriate for a washing-up liquid and explain the strategy (2 marks).

c It would be helpful to include a diagram when explaining the relationship between price and demand.   (2 marks)

The second part of the marketing mix is the product – possibly the most important element of all. If there is no product there is nothing to market.

Let's be clear, before we go any further, what exactly 'product' is. Products are not only goods but may also be services.

> A product may be defined as the commodity which the business is offering for sale.

A car is the product of a company such as Ford, a holiday is the product of any hotel or travel agency, a band's product is a concert, an operation or other treatment would be a hospital's product while legal advice from a solicitor is also a product.

Before the product is put on the market, research and development takes place, market research is carried out on the product and it would also be tested, particularly in the case of mechanical or scientific products. Research and Development takes a long time for expensive products such as cars, and could last as long as ten years. By contrast, it would last a very short time in the case of fashion items where the producer would be anxious to get the product ready for the market as quickly as possible while the fashion lasted. Research and Development is expensive for the producer and no income is being received.

Product life cycle

All products have a lifespan. Some products, such as mustard, seem to have a very long lifespan while other items are crazes for a period of time but tend to go out of fashion equally quickly.

▲ Mustard has been sold in various forms in its life cycle

However, even products such as mustard have had to change over the years in order to maintain their places in the market. For example, originally mustard was manufactured in powder form. Later it was developed in its ready-made form and, even later, a variety of flavours were added to give us the range of mustards we can buy today.

The concept of the lifespan of a product is illustrated by the **product life cycle** which shows the path of a product from the very beginning through to its withdrawal from the market. This identifies five separate stages in the life cycle of a typical product:

1 **Introduction or launch**
2 **Growth**
3 **Maturity**
4 **Saturation**
5 **Decline**

Stage 1 – Introduction or launch

In the introductory/launch stage of the life of a product, emphasis is placed on marketing and promotion in order to make the public aware of the product and to create a desire to buy it.

At this point, sales would be slow at the beginning for all goods but would increase rapidly for low cost goods such as detergents if the marketing activity had been successful. In the case of high-fashion goods, sales would also be fast because people would want to have the item as quickly as possible. Sales would be slower for expensive products such as cars, because most people would not spend so much money on a product until it has proved its reliability.

The product would still not be in a profit-making position at this introductory/launch stage because sales would not yet be great enough to cover the costs incurred in research and development.

If the product is in the introduction/launch stage the business needs to make sure that it is being offered for sale in the most appropriate place and that the most appropriate pricing policy – either skimming or penetration – is being used. At this stage, the business will also decide to advertise widely to create an awareness of the product. The product will be made in low quantities at this stage until sales have improved.

Stage 2 – Growth

At this stage, sales grow rapidly as most people would have become aware of the product, many would have tried it and it would be starting to achieve a degree of customer loyalty.

At the **growth** stage, sometimes prices can be reduced, especially if other producers start to provide competition by putting similar products on the market.

The increased sales would put the product into a profit-making position at this stage as the income from sales covers the initial costs of research and development as well as marketing.

If the product is in the growth stage, less advertising would be required because sales are growing, but the business would decide to produce in greater quantities in order to meet the demand. **Competitive pricing** would also have to be introduced if other producers had brought similar products to the market. At this growth stage, a forward looking business would consider marketing abroad and would be exploring opportunities through the internet.

Stage 3 – Maturity

At the **maturity** stage, sales levels would be maintained but not increasing and the product would have an established place in the market. However, the competition becomes very intense at this stage and it is more difficult to increase the volume of the product's sales any further. In an attempt to do so, the product will be advertised intensively once again. Because sales would not be increasing the business would stabilise production levels because it would not want to have excessive inventory.

The maturity stage is usually a lengthy one in household products but would last for a very short time in fashion items as the next new craze takes over.

Profits at this stage are at their highest because sales have stabilised. Nevertheless, an astute business would realise at this stage that it needs to begin to research and develop a second product to have ready to replace its first product when it reaches the later stages in the cycle. Alternatively, it might take the opportunity to slightly alter minor aspects of the product and re-launch it as 'new' or 'improved'.

Stage 4 – Saturation

The **saturation** stage is the highest point in the life of the product. Although competition is intense, there are unlikely to be any new competitors at this stage.

Sales have been pushed as far as possible and new customers cannot be found. Some may be attracted to the product because of decreased prices or extra advertising. The business might decide to engage in **sales promotions** such as offering free gifts or 'buy one get one free'. At this stage, the weakest products will drop out of the market which may prolong the saturation stage of the others for a period of time. Profits would still be good at the maturity stage but not growing.

Stage 5 – Decline

The **decline** stage is the final stage in the life of a product. Sales have fallen to such an extent that they are not covering the manufacturing costs and the product is therefore unprofitable. The appeal of the product at this stage is only either to those who have a loyalty to the product, or to those who are slow to try new ideas. The business would try to extend this stage as long as possible but at least until the remaining inventory had been sold.

Further advertising or price reductions would not be successful and would be offered only if large inventories remained, in which case strategies such as 'buy three for the price of two' would be used to clear them. The product should be withdrawn from the market when this stage is reached. However, this decline stage can be lengthy for some products. For example, Horlicks is less widely used now than previously and less advertising is done. However, the product still has a good place on the market because there is still a sufficient number of customers to sustain it.

Other, short-life products – like last year's high fashion – simply cannot be sold at any price, and so their decline stage is exceptionally short. The business which has prepared for this stage will have a second product ready for introduction to the market to replace the declining product.

▲ Horlicks has a sustainable customer base

Illustration of the product life cycle

The product life cycle is illustrated on a graph. Remember that the length of the different stages will vary according to the type of product being manufactured and sold. For this reason, the shape of the graph will be different for various products.

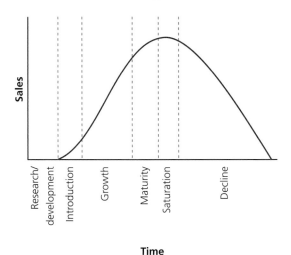

▲ Typical product life cycle of detergent

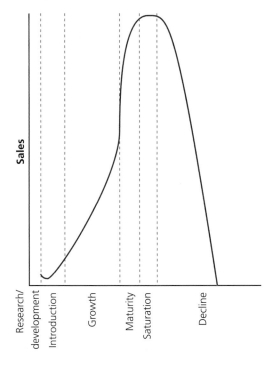

▲ Typical product life cycle of a high-fashion item

Activity ✎

For the following products place each of them in each of the five stages of the Product Life Cycle: the latest mobile phone, computers, Corn Flakes, Horlicks and fax machines. Now write their names on the curve of the Product Life Cycle below at the stage you think is most appropriate.

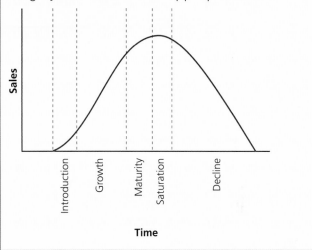

Strategies used to extend the product life cycle

Businesses aim to prolong the life of their products as long as possible in order to maximise profits. This is frequently done by making minor alterations to the product which makes people want to have the latest variety or model. For example:

▶ Sales of Flash cleaners have been expanded by introducing a variety of Flash for the bathroom, for the kitchen, etc.

▶ Popular drinks such as Coca-Cola and Club Orange have introduced 'lite' varieties so that people on diets would continue to buy them.

▶ New, updated editions of books are introduced to maintain sales when previous editions are becoming out-of-date and sinking into the decline stage.

▶ Car manufacturers bring out new designs to their cars on an annual basis, sometimes only involving minor modifications. In each of these cases, the new model or 'improved formula' product is re-launched to persuade **consumers** to buy it.

▶ In other cases, packaging of the product is altered to give an updated appearance to the product while promotion and advertising are obvious methods by which to extend the product's life cycle. This is done at stages in the product's life when sales need to be stimulated.

▶ A price reduction is another strategy frequently used to encourage sales and combat competition. In other cases, manufacturers may reconsider the place in which they are selling the product and may decide to introduce it to the export market in order to improve sales.

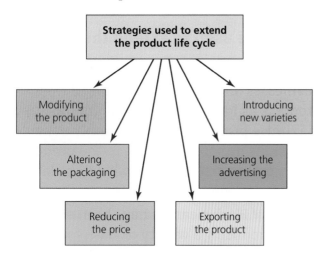

Examination question

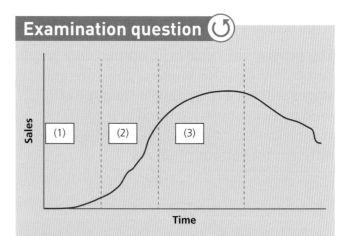

The diagram above shows the product life cycle of a car. Name the stages marked 1, 2 and 3.

Analyse two extension strategies which could be used to extend the life cycle of the car.
(9 marks)

How to answer this question

Name the three stages (3 marks). Then choose two extension strategies which would be suitable for a car and give details of them (up to 3 marks for each strategy).

Activity

The following products have reached the saturation level of the product life cycle. How would you extend their lives and prevent them going into the decline stage?

1 A window cleaning cream which has had a very reliable reputation for a long time but is losing out to newer competing products.

2 A high-fat chocolate bar which is no longer popular because of a recent healthy living campaign.

3 A computer which is very cheap but is very limited.

4 A fizzy drink which has been packaged in the same way for fifty years.

Legal constraints on products

The government has imposed a number of legal constraints which are designed mainly to protect consumers from faulty or unsafe products. However, it is recognised that the law also acts as a useful framework for business and, in the vast majority of cases, businesses are anxious to treat customers fairly and to produce goods which are of high quality. They want to deal with complaints in a proper manner because poor quality goods or poor service gives the business a poor reputation and ultimately affects sales.

Nevertheless, it is impossible for the law to cover every eventuality. Consumers still need to exercise common sense and caution when buying goods. If a stranger offers you a brand new, very modern car with luxurious extras for £1,000, your common sense should tell you to walk away from what is obviously an illegal deal.

This is summed up in the Latin words 'caveat emptor' which means 'let the buyer beware'. This is exactly what the buyer should do by taking time to read the small print on packaging for example.

On 1 October 2015, The Consumer Rights Act came into force. It strengthened and modernised previous laws and also included legislation on the supply of services and of digital goods.

Consumer Rights Act, 2015

This Act states that:

▶ Goods supplied by a business must be 'of satisfactory quality'. This means that goods must be properly and safely manufactured and should not be faulty or damaged at the time of sale.

▶ Goods must be fit for the purpose for which they were supplied or for any specific purpose the consumer made known at the time of sales, e.g. a waterproof coat must keep out the rain.

▶ Goods must be as described. They must match any description given to the consumer or any models or samples shown at the time of sale on the packaging, e.g. the contents of a tin of biscuits, must be like the illustration on the outside of the tin.

▶ The supply of services such as dry cleaning, work done by professionals, travel services, car repairs, fitting kitchens, double glazing, for example, is also included. The services must be given with reasonable care and skill, at a reasonable price and completed within a reasonable time frame. If the service is unsatisfactory, the service provider has to re-do the work at no extra cost.

▲ A waterproof coat must keep out the rain

▲ This tin should contain the type of biscuits illustrated

▲ All food businesses need to be registered

The Act also covers the supply of digital goods such as online film and games, music downloads and e-books etc. These goods have the same rights as all other goods.

Consumer Protection Act, 1987

The Consumer Protection Act, 1987 is designed to protect consumers from products that do not reach a reasonable level of safety. Any product not achieving the level of safety which consumers are entitled to expect is said to be defective.

Any person injured by a defective product is entitled to sue the producer or manufacturer for damages. However, if unsafe goods have been supplied, under the terms of this Act, an offence would also have been committed even if no one were injured by those goods.

In the case of foreign goods which were imported to this country, the consumer may take action against the importer, or against any business which had branded the goods with its own name. **Wholesalers** or retailers are not liable under the terms of this Act.

The consumer is expected, as in the case of the previous Act, to use the product responsibly. Warnings and instructions given with the product should be obeyed, and the product should be used with reasonable care. Therefore, if the manufacturer could show that the product became defective because of the way in which the consumer used it, then the consumer would have no right to claim against the manufacturer. Any action against a manufacturer must be taken by a consumer within three years of the injury.

This Act also allows local councils to seize unsafe goods and suspend the sale of suspected unsafe goods. It also prohibits misleading price indications.

Activity

What would you do if you were in the following situations?

1 I bought a shirt but when I arrived home I changed my mind. I took it back to the shop the next day but the staff would not give me a refund. Can they do this?

2 I had new taps supplied and fitted on my bath by a plumber but they drip all the time. What should I do?

3 My new toaster has never worked properly. The shop manager told me to send it back to the manufacturer as the fault had nothing to do with the shop. Is this correct?

4 Recently I bought an electric cooker privately from a neighbour. What are my rights?

Checklist ✓

At this stage you should be able to:

○ demonstrate knowledge of the product life cycle

○ discuss the strategies used to extend the product life cycle

○ demonstrate knowledge of the Consumer Rights Act, 2015 and the Consumer Protection Act, 1987.

The third part of the marketing mix is promotion. This is another commonly used term but could you define it?

> Promotion is the process by which businesses inform customers about their products and encourage them to buy those products.

Promotion is a very important element of the marketing mix because even the best products will not be sold if consumers do not know about them.

Promotion is important not only at the introduction of a new product, but as an on-going process throughout its life, because consumers need to be reminded about it if sales levels are to be maintained.

Promotion also keeps the name of the company and the name of its product(s) at the forefront of customers' minds. This creates an image for the company and also helps to keep it ahead of its competitors.

Activity

Study the above information, then copy and complete the following statements to show what effective promotion does for a company.

1 Promotion is important at the .... of a ... product
2 Promotion makes .... aware of .... products
3 Promotion keeps customers .... about products
4 Promotion maintains .... for the company
5 Promotion creates an .... for the company
6 Promotion helps to keep the company ....

Methods of promotion

There are many methods of promotion but the most usual are advertising, sales promotion, **sponsorship** and **public relations** (PR).

Advertising

Advertising is an important aspect of promotion and one in which companies invest large sums of money. They do this in order to:

▶ introduce a new product to the public and encourage sales

▶ remind the public about an existing product and boost its sales

▶ target a new segment of the market thereby increasing their market share

▶ provide information about products or events.

Types of advertising

There are three types of advertising and each one has a different function:

1 **Informative advertising** – This type of advertising is purely factual and its intention is to give information. Advertisements about forthcoming events, advertisements giving technical information or advertisements recalling products because of faults are all examples of **informative advertising**.

2 **Persuasive advertising** – As its name suggests, the intention of **persuasive advertising** is to persuade members of the public to purchase the advertised product. This type of advertising aims to convince people that the product being advertised should be selected in preference to the goods produced by rival companies. It also aims to convince them that the quality of

their lives would be improved if they were to buy that particular product.

3 **Generic advertising** – The word 'generic' means 'applied to a large group or class; general not specific'. **Generic advertising** is, therefore, advertising for a whole industry or a particular type of goods regardless of where the product is sold. Advertising encouraging people to drink more milk or eat more meat are examples of generic advertising.

Activity

Which type of advertising is described in the following examples?

1 A doctor is telling everyone about the new opening hours at his surgery.
2 Advertising which encourages members of the public that potatoes are good for them.
3 A new perfume is being advertised in the glossy magazines.

Hoardings and posters

Hoardings are large boards situated at the side of the road. They have an immediate visual impact on passing traffic and can be seen at a distance. To be effective, they must be large, and therefore are limited to short messages which can be read quickly. This advertising method has no control over its audience so it must be designed to appeal to all tastes and age groups. It is most suitable for advertising goods which are bought by the majority of the population.

In cities, large, brightly-lit neon signs are commonly found as modern replacements of hoardings. These neon signs are expensive to maintain and therefore are used only by large multi-nationals, such as Coca-Cola. Neon signs on point-of-sale fridges now frequently replace posters and are also used by companies such as Coca-Cola.

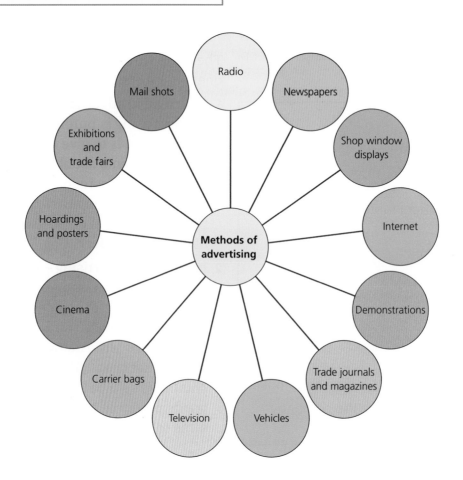

Television

This is the most expensive type of advertising, costing approximately £1,000 per viewing second according to the time of day. It reaches a wide audience and is highly effective because it can be glamorous and entertaining.

Seeing the product on television has an important visual impact. Times of advertising are altered to suit the audience, so toys, for example, are advertised during the day or early evening to target children.

Radio

Radio is the advertising method which probably has the widest audience because the radio is listened to at all times of the day and in a wide variety of places. It is cheaper than television advertising and different stations can be used to target different sectors of the market.

Cinema

This type of advertising can reach only those members of the public who visit the cinema. It is therefore more restricted than either radio or television advertising. Cinema advertising is frequently locally based and is often used by shops in the area.

Internet

The internet is the fastest growing and most recent form of advertising. Advertisements on the internet have a world-wide audience and can be reached at any time. They are capable of giving vast amounts of information which can then be saved or printed by the consumer. It is possible for the consumer to link with the advertisers in order to get further information. On the other hand, the internet cannot be accessed by anyone who does not have the necessary equipment.

Newspapers

Newspapers are bought by the majority of the population so this form of advertising is capable of reaching a wide audience. All newspaper advertising is expensive. It is important that the advertisers choose the appropriate newspaper to reach their target market because different sectors of the public read different newspapers. For example, readers of *The Sun* would have no interest in *The Times* or vice versa.

Newspapers can also cater for small classified advertisements about items for private sale. They may cover a local area – such as the *Portadown Times* – or have a province-wide readership – like the *Irish News*, the *Newsletters* or *Belfast Telegraph*.

▲ Northern Ireland newspapers

Magazines and trade journals

Specialist trade journals are good for advertising items such as specialist equipment, since the target market for that equipment is likely to read the journals. For example, *The Lancet* is a journal which is read by the medical profession. Magazines are bought by most people and their vast range caters for all interests and age groups. Advertising in magazines can be accurately targeted at the appropriate age group and is, therefore, very effective.

Exhibitions

Exhibitions are attended by large numbers of visitors and are aimed at a certain sector of the market. For example, the Ideal Home Exhibition is held every September in the King's Hall, Belfast and attracts a large number of exhibitors showing household furniture, materials and equipment. People visit the exhibition to view the latest trends in house design.

The annual Motor Show shows the latest models of cars and encourages the motoring public of Northern Ireland to order them.

Demonstrations by experts

This is a very effective method of advertising and is favoured by food manufacturers or manufacturers of kitchen utensils, for example. An expert is employed to give demonstrations using the product. The idea is then got across to the public that the product must be excellent if the expert uses it.

Mail shots

The term 'mail shot' covers all leaflets sent to people's homes. Mail shots are often used to inform people within a targeted area about the opening of a new store or about local special sale events. There is no guarantee that the mail shots will be read, and some people resent being sent what they consider to be junk mail.

Vehicles

Advertising on vehicles can be very effective because it may be seen by a large number of people in different parts of the country. This method is cheap if the business's own vehicles are used.

Advertising on public transport vehicles – such as buses – is popular but this must be limited to matters of interest in the area serviced by the public transport vehicle. As with hoardings, the message must be limited to a few words.

Shop window displays

These displays are very effective in attracting the passing public to enter the shop and make purchases. If the window display is good it will give the impression that the goods inside the shop are also good. One advantage of this method of advertising is that customers are likely to act immediately. On the other hand, the display is limited to people who are in that immediate area.

Activity ✏️

Identify and write down the most appropriate methods of advertising to use in the following circumstances:

1 A small shop, with very little money to spend on advertising, has a very attractive range of new clothes in stock. Few people know about the new range.
2 A village grocery shop has decided to remain open to 10 pm on six days per week.
3 A new household gadget is being launched on the market by a large company.
4 Your family has bought new furniture and wishes to advertise your old furniture for sale.
5 A large well-known ice-cream manufacturer wishes to improve sales of all types of ice-cream throughout the country.
6 A local jewellery business wants to tell the public about its excellent stock.
7 A craftsman, who makes wood carvings, is famous locally for his original designs and excellent workmanship. He would like to expand his market.
8 Organisers of a charity dance would like to make people aware of the event.
9 The government wants to encourage people to travel by train.
10 A school is advertising the dates of its open nights.

Carrier bags

Advertising on carrier bags is very cheap but less effective now than when carrier bags were given out freely by businesses. Bags are seen by large numbers of shoppers in the area of the shop.

Sales promotion

Sales promotion is an overall term covering all methods which are used to persuade the customer to purchase the product. The diagram below illustrates the various types of sales promotion.

Special offers

These are very commonly used. Examples are buy-two-get-one-free, or get 10% extra free. The customer is attracted by the low price and sales for the shop are increased.

Discounts

This is where a discount of 10% or half price for example, is given off the total price. Again the customer is attracted by the low price and buys the product.

Loss-leaders

This is another form of price reduction found in larger shops. The price of one or two items is reduced to a very low level (even to the level of making no profit on those items). These low price goods attract customers in, and the shop hopes to encourage them to buy other, full-price goods while there. Bread is sometimes offered as a **loss-leader** in supermarkets.

Price reductions

In this case the price of the product is reduced for a short period of time. The low price encourages people to buy that particular product which improves its sales.

Money-off coupons

Sometimes coupons are printed on the packaging of a product offering the next purchase of the product at a lower price. Coupons sometimes are sent in the post or can be cut out of newspapers. Customers save the coupons and have to buy the product again to take advantage of the offer. In this way, sales of the product are doubled for the company.

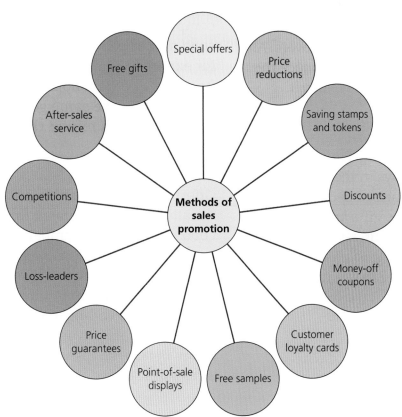

Competitions

Customers are sometimes encouraged by producers to buy a particular product by printing entry forms for a competition on the packaging or including a leaflet at the point of sale. The prize is usually very worthwhile – a luxury holiday or a car – and this encourages people to buy the product.

Customer loyalty cards

Customers' cards are swiped at the check-out point and the totals of their purchases are recorded electronically. Each purchase earns points and the points can later be exchanged for cash or air miles. Such cards encourage customers to return to the same store in order to build up their points. The Marks Spencer Sparks Card is a form of **loyalty card**.

Free samples

Free samples of some products are given of items such as food, cleaning materials or make-up. Customers are sometimes asked to sample foods in shops. Some products occasionally have free samples of another product attached, and sometimes magazines have free samples of make-up attached to their front covers. All these samples are designed to introduce the product and encourage people to buy it.

Free gifts

Some products contain small free gifts enclosed in their packaging. For example, Kellogg's gave small toys in their cereals at one time but were criticised because of the safety factor. Other free gifts are obtained by collecting a certain number of tokens printed on the packaging. Sales are improved because customers have to buy more of the product in order to collect the tokens and get the gift.

▲ A Sparks card

Point-of-sale displays

Special displays are sometimes mounted in the shop to encourage shoppers to buy that particular product in that shop. An area is allocated to the product and special display stands erected to draw attention to the product. For some products such as small kitchen appliances, the display may also include a demonstration showing the benefits of those particular appliances.

Price guarantees

Customers are encouraged to shop with companies which offer price guarantees such as 'our prices cannot be beaten'. Tesco, for example, challenges customers to find its goods in other shops for less money. If they can find the same goods at a cheaper price, Tesco will refund the difference in the two prices.

After-sales service

Offering an excellent after-sales service is usually an encouragement for customers to choose a particular company when buying an expensive item such as a computer. This gives the customer confidence that assistance would be available if required. For this reason, customers are willing to pay a higher price rather than take advantage of special offer prices in large shops which do not have an after-sales service.

Activity ✎

Name the sales promotional method which you would recommend in each of the following examples and explain your choice of method.

1 Sales of fish have fallen off since a recent health scare about chemicals being dumped at sea.

2 A new cereal is being launched on the market by a well-known company which already markets many varieties of cereal.

3 A new luxury car is being launched. The car is very expensive.

4 A cheese manufacturer wishes to improve sales of all types of cheese in order to beat the competition.

5 A small computer retailer is generally having difficulties because people are buying from the large retailers which have a larger variety and can sell at cheaper prices.

Sponsorship

It is quite common for businesses to sponsor sporting events, charity events or school events. All of these activities portray the business as being public spirited and interested in its local community. The business donates the funds necessary to run the event and, in return, the players wear kit displaying the company logo. The company name also is usually emblazoned around the sports field. This provides wide publicity for the business, especially if the event is being televised.

Public Relations (PR)

Any activity under the heading of public relations is one where the public's awareness of the company is raised and the company is seen to be generous. Creating a good impression in this way creates a loyalty with members of the public who will then be more likely to buy from the business.

Examples of public relations activities are where companies donate sizeable sums of money to charity or perhaps contribute cash or products towards famine relief or a war-torn area.

How social media promotes business activity

Social media brings businesses into the 21st century and is accelerating business through the use of innovative technology. The modern era of social media began in 2002 with the growth of the world-wide-web. It comes in many forms, such as social networks, media sharing sites and social book-marking. The growth of community websites such as Twitter, Instagram, Facebook, Google and Linkedin means that many businesses feel under pressure to have a social media presence.

Social media is a new set of channels through which to market products. It boosts business marketing in the digital age and presents businesses with a great opportunity to increase their market share figures. It is used extensively to advertise and promote businesses and large organisations such as Dell, IBM and Burger King use it to convey their place in the market and their friendly customer relations. It is estimated that 39 per cent of companies now use social media services as their primary digital tool to reach customers and numbers continue to grow.

The advantages of social media are:

▶ It allows for two-way communication with consumers to market products whereas traditional media such as television and newspapers are static and only allow for one-way communication. Therefore it gives an important customer service.

▶ It is an excellent marketing tool, enabling businesses to reach potential consumers directly.

▶ It drives sales and is important in product promotion.

▶ It makes customers aware of the company brand.

▶ It has global reach and a blog or tweet or YouTube video can be viewed by millions almost for free.

▶ It helps consumers to discover products and services and also offers them support and answers to questions.

▶ It allows businesses to stay on top of what competitors are doing and to keep in touch with its own consumers.

▶ It gives businesses information on business opportunities and trends.

▶ It enables businesses to learn from customers and manages enquiries.

▶ It gives the business a very up-to-date image.

It has some disadvantages:

▶ Dissatisfied consumers can protest strongly and possibly damage the image of the business.

▶ Because social media is conversational, there must be someone online at all times in the business to interact with its online audience.

Case study

Before the car manufacturer Ford launched its Fiesta model, it gave one hundred cars to people who used social media and asked them to record their impressions of the car on social channels. As a result, videos of the car generated 6.5 million views on YouTube and Ford received 50,000 requests for information about the car.

When the car was finally launched in 2010, 10,000 cars were sold within the first six days!

▲ The Ford Fiesta model car

Legal constraints on promotion

The government aims to protect consumers and to ensure that there is fair and honest trading in our fast-changing society. One area in which protection is needed is the area of promotion, so that consumers are not deliberately misled by false advertising and promotional offers which are not genuine value for money. The Trade Descriptions Act was among the earliest pieces of legislation and still is the major tool used to guarantee fair practice in promotional activities.

Trade Descriptions Act, 1968

The Trade Descriptions Act prohibits manufacturers, retailers or service providers from giving false or misleading descriptions for the supplying of goods or services. This covers all information given on the goods about:

▶ their quantity or size
▶ their method of manufacture or testing
▶ the place and date of their manufacture
▶ the people who manufactured them.

The scope of the Trade Descriptions Act is very wide and includes all forms of services as well as all types of goods. For example, some farmers were prosecuted for falsely describing their cattle as coming from a BSE-free herd.

In addition, this law ensures that prices are genuine. If products are described as 'reduced' in a sale, they must have been on sale at the higher price in that shop for at least twenty-eight consecutive days in the previous six months. Otherwise, sale bargains may only be described as 'special purchases' which indicates that those products were bought specially to offer to customers at a lower price. Sometimes the quality of special purchases is not as good as that of the regular stock, and the law ensures that consumers are made aware of this possibility.

The Trade Descriptions Act also states that the country of origin must appear on the packaging of all imported goods. Descriptions may either be written, pictorial or oral, and any breaches of the Trade Descriptions Act may incur fines or imprisonment.

Other constraints on promotion

In addition to the legal constraints on promotion, several bodies have been established to give further protection to consumers. In some cases these bodies have been set up by the government, while in other instances, they are independent.

Advertising Standards Authority (ASA)

The Advertising Standards Authority is an independent body set up to monitor all advertisements which are not broadcast.

The Advertising Standards Authority regulates all advertising in:

▶ magazine and newspaper advertisements
▶ radio and television commercials (not programmes)
▶ internet advertisements e.g. banners
▶ commercial e-mails and SMS text messages
▶ posters, leaflets, door drops, circulars and brochures
▶ cinema commercials
▶ advertising on smartphones and tablet apps
▶ advertising on CD ROMs, DVD and video
▶ sales promotions such as special offers, and prize draws
▶ direct mail addressed to you personally.

The basic principles of the Advertising Standards Authority are to make sure that all advertisements are:

▶ legal, decent, honest and truthful
▶ prepared with a sense of responsibility to consumers and to society
▶ in line with the principles of fair competition.

The basic function of the Advertising Standards Authority is to ensure that the public is not misled or offended by advertisements. In order to fulfil this function, the ASA carries out spot checks on approximately ten thousand advertisements every week and will ask the company either to withdraw or amend any advertisement which does not comply with its principles.

The majority of advertisers are so anxious not to offend the ASA's principles that many of them seek the Authority's advice before publication, which saves them the possible expense and bad reputation caused by having to withdraw an advertisement later.

If a company does not withdraw or amend its advertisement, the ASA does not have any legal power to make it do so. The ASA's main sanction is to ask publishers to refuse more space for an advertisement until its terms have been upheld. In the case of continued offences, the ASA will refer an advertiser to the **Office of Fair Trading (OFT)** who can legally prevent similar advertisements being published in the future.

The Advertising Standards Authority also deals with complaints from members of the public who have felt misled or offended by an advertisement. On average the Authority deals with 12,000 complaints per year.

Ofcom

Ofcom (Office of Communication) is an independent organisation which regulates the communication industries in the United Kingdom. Ofcom was formed in 2003 and took over the previous duties of the former Independent Television Commission. Its duty is to protect consumers from harmful or offensive material on television, radios and the airwaves over which wireless devices operate.

Its basic principles are to make sure that all communication:

▶ adheres to rules on taste and decency
▶ is impartial
▶ does not give offence or cause harm
▶ supports market growth and competition
▶ sets high technical standards.

So, broadly speaking, its function for broadcast communication is very similar to the function which the Advertising Standards Authority has for advertising media.

Activity

Answer the following questions:

1 What are the major principles of the Advertising Standards Authority?

2 How does the Advertising Standards Authority carry out its function?

3 Why do companies often seek the advice of the Advertising Standards Authority before they publish an advertisement?

4 What is the major difference between the work of the Advertising Standards Authority and the work of Ofcom?

Checklist

At this stage you should be able to:

○ describe and explain the four main methods of promotion
○ evaluate each method of promotion
○ explain how social media can be used to promote business activity
○ identify and justify the most appropriate methods of promotion in particular circumstances
○ demonstrate knowledge of the legal constraints on promotion.

2.5 Marketing mix – place

This section is about getting the goods to the place where they are going to sell most successfully. This means that manufacturers must study carefully where to sell their products as well as how to get them, in good condition, to that place. To do this, the business must consider the most appropriate **channel of distribution** to use.

Parties involved in distribution

There are four parties involved in distribution – manufacturer, wholesaler, retailer and consumer. It is important to make sure that you understand the roles of all four before you study the various channels of distribution.

Manufacturer/producer

The manufacturer or producer is the creator of goods in large quantities. In the example of goods such as furniture, cars etc. the manufacturer would be a factory owner. A farmer is also a producer – producing goods such as fruit, vegetables and meat. Similarly a fisherman is also a producer.

Wholesaler

The wholesaler is the link between the manufacturer and the retailer. The wholesaler purchases goods in bulk from the manufacturer and transports them to warehouses where they are stored. The goods are then available for sale to retailers in smaller quantities. This process is often referred to as 'breaking bulk'.

The wholesaler provides a useful service for small retailers. Because of this service, retailers do not have to provide very large storage facilities nor do they have to buy and pay for large quantities of goods at one time. Instead they can visit the local wholesaler on a regular basis and restock when necessary. In some cases the wholesaler offers a delivery service and often credit facilities (allowing the retailer to pay later).

Wholesalers also provide important services for manufacturers, saving them the numerous transactions which they would have if they had to deal directly with retailers.

The diagrams on the following page illustrate this point. One diagram shows the number of transactions required between four manufacturers and six retailers, while the second diagram shows how these transactions are reduced by using a wholesaler.

Large retailers such as Tesco, Lidl, Sainsbury, Asda and Marks & Spencer deal directly with manufacturers, store their goods themselves and distribute the goods daily in their own lorries to their branches. They do not require the services of a wholesaler as they act as their own wholesalers. The traditional wholesaler is only used for small scale retailers. Examples in Northern Ireland are Holmes Cash and Carry in Cookstown, Newtownards and Coleraine and Musgrave in Belfast.

Retailer

The retailer is the final seller of the goods to the consumer. Retailing is most frequently done in shops which may range in size from very large supermarkets to very small village shops. Whatever the scale on which they operate, they all provide a similar service to the consumer. The retailer makes the goods available for the consumer at a convenient place and also further breaks bulk of the products so that the consumer is able to buy small amounts.

Without a wholesaler

| Manufacturer A | Manufacturer B | Manufacturer C | Manufacturer D |

| Retailer E | Retailer F | Retailer G | Retailer H | Retailer I | Retailer J |

With a wholesaler

| Manufacturer A | Manufacturer B | Manufacturer C | Manufacturer D |

WHOLESALER

| Retailer E | Retailer F | Retailer G | Retailer H | Retailer I | Retailer J |

Consumer

The consumer is the final user of the product. The consumer would buy small, usable amounts of the product for a household and replace them frequently.

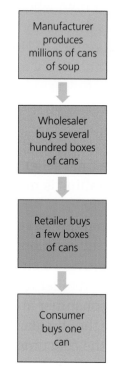

▲ How bulk is broken (using canned soup as an example)

Activity ✎

Refer back to the diagrams on this page which illustrate the number of transactions which would be made with and without a wholesaler.

1 What environmental advantages would there be in having fewer transactions?

2 Name one social cost of closing wholesalers.

Channels of distribution of goods and services

Channel of distribution is the way in which the goods are passed from the manufacturer to the consumer.

The choice of channel of distribution depends on the:

▶ **Type of goods** – if the product is a very specialised one, the manufacturer and consumer are likely to want to be directly in contact with each other. For example, a shipping company would be in direct contact with its ship-builders and a house builder would be in direct contact with the person who owns the house.

- ▶ **Value of the goods** – generally the rule is that the more expensive the product is, the fewer are the places which sell it. This maintains the expensive and elite image of the product. For example, Rolex watches are sold in only one shop in Northern Ireland – Lunns in Belfast.
- ▶ **Life span of the goods** – if the product is perishable, it must be distributed widely so that people can get it quickly. Fresh fruit and vegetables would be in this category, and therefore are usually sold directly from producer to the retailer or even to the consumer.
- ▶ **Costs involved** – the most cost-effective method has to be found. If the channel of distribution involves high costs, it would be unsuitable for low-cost goods.
- ▶ **Demand for the goods** – if the product is one which is used regularly by everyone, it must be distributed widely and be available immediately. For example, people expect to be able to buy items such as shampoo almost anywhere.
- ▶ **Competition for the goods** – manufacturers need to beat the competition, and therefore they would distribute their products to the same places as are chosen by their competitors.

There are three channels of distribution in common use:

1 **Traditional** – from the manufacturer to the wholesaler to the retailer to the consumer.

2 **Modern** – from the manufacturer to the retailer to the consumer.

3 **Direct** – from the manufacturer to the consumer.

Channel 1 – Traditional method from the manufacturer to the wholesaler, to the retailer, to the consumer.

Channel 1 is the traditional channel of distribution and involves the product being passed through two middlemen before it finally gets to the consumer. The product is first sold by the manufacturer in large quantities to the wholesaler, then it is sold by the wholesaler to the retailer in smaller quantities, and lastly, it is sold by the retailer to the consumer in single units.

This channel of distribution is still widely used, particularly by small retailers who avail of the storage, bulk-breaking, credit and delivery services of the wholesaler. However, this method is being replaced in the case of large retailers by the modern method.

Channel 2 – Modern method from the manufacturer to the retailer to the consumer.

Large companies such as Marks & Spencer, Asda, Sainsbury, Tesco, Currys or Computer World all buy directly from manufacturers. They have the financial reserves necessary to do this, and their orders are so large that manufacturers find it easier to deal with them directly. Because these firms deal with the manufacturers directly, placing very large orders, they earn large **discounts** and, as a result, they are able to sell the goods at a lower price to the final consumer.

Manufacturers feel that sometimes they can push sales of their products more forcefully if they deal directly with retailers rather than through a middleman. They also are now in more direct contact with retailers because they see the retailer as being close to the consumer, and this puts them in a better position to hear the views of consumers.

Channel 3 – Direct method from the manufacturer to the consumer.

This channel distributes goods directly from the producer to the end-user. It is suitable for certain types of business – for example, businesses selling fresh produce, and businesses selling very exclusive, and therefore very expensive, goods.

Craft industries often receive orders for items such as individually designed pieces of furniture, for example. The customer would have designed the item and then would liaise directly with the craftsman who has the skill to produce it.

Exclusive dress designers, such as Dior, also work in this way, directly consulting with their clients who are often film stars or royalty. Farmers often sell fresh fruit and vegetables at market stalls directly to their customers, and garden centres also sell their plants and flowers using this method.

▲ A farmer selling his fresh, locally grown produce

Changing trends in the distribution of goods and services

Looking at the three diagrams illustrating the channels of distribution will show how distribution has been simplified.

The present trend in home shopping is likely to continue because the majority of women continue with their careers and have less time to shop. Mail order catalogue companies remain popular for their convenience of home shopping and credit facilities. Many of the high street shops such as Next or Debenhams also have mail order services.

Shopping via the internet is very popular, especially with its increased security.

Increasingly, the trend is for large retailers to act as their own wholesalers and buy their goods directly from the manufacturers. Price savings made in this way allow the supermarkets to pass on these benefits to consumers in the form of lower prices. This stimulates trade even further for the retailing giants but causes greater difficulties for small retailers who cannot compete with the price reductions offered by the supermarkets.

Nevertheless, there will probably always be a place for small shops because of their long opening times, the convenience of their location and their personal customer service.

Activity

Maureen runs a restaurant in Tandragee. She has added a successful sideline to her restaurant by selling ready-made meals in shops in Tandragee, Richhill, Armagh and Portadown.

Maureen has carried out some market research and is certain that there would be a very good market for her ready-made meals among the elderly people in the area. Her plan is to sell complete dinners each day to the elderly people living in the local folds and sheltered accommodation.

Her accountant is unsure about cutting out the retailer and starting into direct selling to the consumer.

Maureen needs your help to persuade her accountant about the benefits of direct selling, and asks you to state the arguments she should use.

Examination question

Explain one advantage and one disadvantage for a company of using a wholesaler to distribute its product. (4 marks)

How to answer this question

You are not told what the product is, so you can choose any general advantage and any general disadvantage of the traditional method of distribution.

(1 mark for each advantage and disadvantage and 1 mark each for the explanation)

Checklist ✓

At this stage, you should be able to:
- describe and explain traditional, modern and direct channels of distribution.

Competition

Competition in business is rivalry between businesses. It is a situation where businesses are competing against one another for a share in the market, and where they employ all kinds of tactics to discourage their customers from going to other businesses, while also encouraging the customers from other businesses to come to them. Competition in modern business is at a very high level and makes businesses monitor each other's activities closely.

Competition can be very healthy as it encourages businesses to keep improving their services in order to out-do their competitors. This results in greater efficiency which gives customers greater selection and better products. Greater competition causes prices to fall – if there were no competition at all, businesses could charge what they liked.

Competition has the following benefits for consumers:

▶ businesses are forced to offer good products and good service otherwise consumers will not return

▶ businesses are forced to keep prices down, otherwise consumers will go to buy their goods elsewhere

▶ businesses will offer a wider range of products in order to be ahead of the competition.

Strategies used to manage competition

1 Pricing

▶ Businesses will keep their prices at the same level as, or slightly lower than, their competitors.

2 Product

▶ They will expand their range of goods.

▶ They will make sure the quality of their products is, at least, as good as their competitors' products.

▶ They will make sure that they have the required products in stock.

3 Effective customer service

▶ They will try to beat the competitors by providing a better service.

4 Promotion

▶ They will advertise widely.

▶ They will use promotional offers such as special discounts.

Impact of competition on the marketing mix

Impact on product

▶ Quality of products will be kept high to attract customers away from the competitors.

▶ Range of products has to be greater than that of the competitors.

Impact on price

▶ Competitive pricing strategy will be used.

▶ Prices cannot be higher than the competitors' prices.

▶ Special offers will be introduced in order to attract consumers.

▶ Products must be priced appropriately for the social area.

Impact on promotion

▶ Constant advertising is required to attract and retain customers.

▶ Promotional offers such as discounts and special offers are used.

- Good customer service is very important to retain existing customers and attract new ones.
- Attractive packaging will be used.

Impact on place

- Products must be available in the store when required, otherwise the customer will go to the competitor for them.
- Products have to be available in a convenient place for consumers.
- Products must be placed in an appropriate cultural or social area.

Examination question

Analyse the impact which competition has on the elements of the marketing mix.

(8 marks)

How to answer this question

You should closely examine how each of the elements (price, place, promotion and product) are affected by competition. The effect on each element will be given up to 2 marks.

Customer service

> Customer service is the provision of service to customers before, during and after a sale.

A business which values good customer service will place great importance on the training of staff and will communicate with customers to get feedback from them on the service they have been given. They will spend a lot of time and money on customer service to ensure that customers are satisfied with both their product and their service. Customer service is extremely important and is the reason why customers return to the business. They know that if something goes wrong they will be treated fairly, that their enquiries and complaints will be taken seriously and that they will be met with courtesy and consideration. If the customer has a complaint, it will be dealt with promptly and effectively and the customer will recommend the business to others. On the other hand, they will also tell others if the complaint has been handled badly.

Customer service is the responsibility of every employee in the organisation. Everyone from part-time students working on the shop floor to the managing director must provide customer service and create a good impression.

Case study

Sir Tim Leahy one-time Chief Executive of Tesco plc understands how important customers are. His motto is: 'Follow the customer, if they change, we change.'

Perhaps that is why Tesco plc is one of the most successful retailers in the United Kingdom. Another business executive is quoted as saying 'If you don't take care of your customers, someone else will.'

Customer service is important from the point of view of the business as well as of the customer because it promotes sales and ultimately profits. Quite simply, without customers the business ceases to exist.

▲ Good customer service makes the customer feel valued leading to more sales

How businesses provide good customer service

▶ They make the customer feel valued, is aware of their needs and try to meet those needs.

▶ They listen seriously to customers' views and act on them.

▶ They rectify situations where complaints have been made and exchange goods if they are faulty.

▶ They provide high-quality, reliable and safe products.

▶ They provide information and advice about products so that customers can make informed decisions.

▶ They provide after-sales service such as immediate delivery.

▶ Their employees are well-trained, skilled and are helpful.

▶ Assistance is available for disabled customers.

▶ The business environment is clean and welcoming, and signage is clear.

▶ Disabled facilities are available conveniently.

Effective customer service is important for a business because:

▶ it gives a business a competitive advantage over other businesses

▶ it will be rewarded with customer loyalty – the customers will remain with that business

▶ if the business deals with complaints effectively, customer loyalty is further strengthened

▶ this will improve sales and profit levels

▶ good service will attract new customers

▶ it will make the employees more efficient

▶ it will improve communication in the business.

Consider the two following stores.

'Good Store'	'Super Store'
'Good Store' is a typical large chain-store which sells the full range of groceries, cleaning materials, newspapers, books and magazines, DVDs, flowers, make-up and pet foods. It also has a bakery section, a butchery counter and a coffee shop.	'Super Store' is another typical large chain-store which sells the full range of groceries, cleaning materials, newspapers, books and magazines, DVDs, flowers, make-up and pet foods. It also has a bakery section, a butchery counter and a coffee shop.
It is difficult to find any assistants in the aisles and if you do find them, they are either chatting or are too busy stacking shelves to help you to find items. Very often they block the aisles with boxes they have brought from the storeroom.	Assistants are positioned in all aisles and are trained to look after customers and to help them to find items. Shelf stacking is done early in the morning or at other less busy times. The coffee shop is bright and clean and remains open throughout the day. Cleaning is carried out at night.
The coffee shop closes two hours before the shop and cleaners begin to clean at that time.	The shop has ten check-out points and they are all open all the time. Customers have loyalty cards where points are added every time they make a purchase.
The shop has ten check-out points but usually only five are open.	In addition, the store has a packing service for disabled customers and assistants will take their trolleys to their cars if requested.
The assistants are not helpful and do not know how to deal with complaints.	Prices are the same in both stores.

So which one would you go to? Of course, you would rather go to 'Super Store'. But what is the difference between the two stores? We know that the prices are the same in both stores, the range of goods is the same in both stores and the facilities are the same in both stores. The difference is the customer service – what it does in addition to offering its basic product or service.

Activity

In order to analyse the different ways in which organisations provide customer service, you should observe a business organisation in your local area.

1 Make a list of the examples of good customer service you see in that business.

2 Suggest ways in which their customer service might be improved.

Checklist ✓

At this stage you should be able to:

○ analyse strategies that a business may use to manage competition

○ analyse the impact that competition has on the marketing mix

○ analyse the different ways business organisations provide customer service.

Examination question

Foyle Leisure Centre is a large, popular Leisure Centre. Explain three ways in which the Centre might provide customer service.   (6 marks)

How to answer this question

Choose and explain three methods of customer service but make sure that they apply to a leisure centre. Up to 2 marks for each method.

2.7 International trade

International trade is the selling and buying of goods to and from foreign countries

It is impossible for any country to be totally self-sufficient and to be able to meet all its own needs. This is the reason why international trade is actively encouraged by the government.

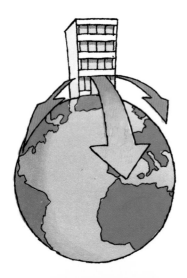

▲ A farmer harvesting coffee beans in Colombia

Activity

Have a look around your kitchen cupboard or your supermarket shelves and find out where these products came from:

orange juice   coffee   tea

bananas   asparagus   strawberries

Advantages of international trade

▶ **Increased market and profits** – Through international trade, a business can sell its goods in increased quantities. This situation leads to increased profits for the business.

▶ **More employment** – Increased sales lead to higher levels of production in the business. This situation gives employment to a greater number of people.

▶ **Economies of scale** – Increased production creates opportunities for economies of scale. This ultimately results in higher profits for the business.

▶ **Greater variety** – International trade increases the variety of goods available for consumers. This generally creates a better standard of living in the country. For example, the climate in Northern Ireland is unsuitable for the cultivation of citrus fruits, tea or coffee and, without international trade, these goods would not be available in Northern Ireland. Martin Luther King had this in mind when he once said: 'Before you've finished your breakfast this morning, you'll have relied on half the world.'

▶ **Political reasons**. The government encourages international trade because it establishes and develops good relations with other countries.

Disadvantages of international trade

▶ **Competition** – When a business enters the international market, it will meet stiff competition because there are so many more producers trying to sell their goods. To succeed, a business's marketing and product have to be better than those of its competitors.

▶ **Production** – Increased markets and increased production may require capital investment and **recruitment** of additional staff. Financial arrangements would have to be made available to undertake this. The business has to be aware of its capacity for production. If this capacity is exceeded, it will have to make sure that the increased investment would be economical and viable.

▶ **Distribution** – Distribution on an international scale is much more difficult than for a business which is marketing and selling to the domestic market only. Secure packaging and efficient transport systems all have to be in place. Unless the business is using the internet, it may need to employ agents in the foreign country or else set up a base there.

▶ **Documentation** – Businesses trading internationally have to be familiar with the documentation required for sending goods abroad. Within the European Union documentation has been simplified, but the problem remains in trade with other countries outside the European Union such as America or the Far East.

▶ **Language** – Businesses which trade internationally must have at least some members of staff who are capable of speaking, writing and translating the language of the country in which the marketing is taking place.

▶ **Currency** – Businesses need to be familiar with the currency of the foreign country and be able to sell their products in that currency. Within Europe, this problem has been eased somewhat since many European countries have adopted the Euro as its single currency.

▶ **Promotional activity** – Increased promotional activity may be required abroad and the promotional material may also have to be modified to suit the foreign country.

▶ **Cultural differences** – Exporters have to be conscious of the values and traditions of the country to which they are selling. It is vital that those values and traditions are respected.

Activity

Technoland is a business which produces computer games. It has decided to market some of its games abroad.

1 Give two reasons why it should market its products abroad.

2 Advise Technoland of two disadvantages it may experience in international trade.

Examination question

Evaluate the advantages and disadvantages of international trade for a local business. (8 marks)

How to answer this question

For a total of 8 marks you would be expected to thoroughly examine two advantages and two disadvantages of international trade which should be taken from the perspective of a local business. Up to 2 marks for each advantage and disadvantage would be given.

How the marketing mix would be affected by international trade

Marketing mix element	How that element is affected
PRODUCT	▸ May have to change to suit the legal, traditional and cultural requirements of the foreign country. For example, some Indians do not regard black clothes as fashionable, as is the case in this country. ▸ The religious culture of a country needs also to be respected. In McDonald's restaurants in Israel, Big Macs are served without cheese in order to separate meat and dairy products as required in kosher restaurants in order to fulfil the requirements of Jewish law. ▸ Must suit the technical set-up in the foreign country. For example, electrical sockets are different in the UK from many other countries. ▸ Units of measurement may differ in the foreign country.
PRICE	▸ Needs to reflect what the market in the foreign country would be willing and able to pay. It would be impossible to set a price for a product and sell it at the same price in every country. McDonald's are found throughout the world offering the same products for sale. The price of those products varies according to what local people could spend, and also according to the price charged by their competitors in that country. ▸ Has to be set at a level to cover taxes and duties. ▸ Has to be set at a level to cover transportation costs. ▸ Has to consider exchange rate variations. ▸ Has to be quoted in the appropriate currency.
PROMOTION	▸ Advertising must be global. ▸ Promotional material must be in appropriate language. Foreign language must be understood for the correct translation of instructions on the packaging of the product. ▸ Must consider any possible cultural differences, for example, illustrations must not be offensive. ▸ Must use a style suitable for the foreign market.
PLACE	▸ Product must be available in places where the target market would be able to buy it. ▸ Suitable transportation must be arranged for the movement of goods overseas. ▸ Secure packaging has to be used to protect the product. ▸ Insurance costs are high because of the risk of loss or damage to the goods. ▸ Climatic conditions are very different abroad and this results in variations of trading hours. For example, it is too hot to work in the afternoon in Italy and shops are closed from 1.00 pm to 5.00 pm. Contact has to be avoided with Italian businesses during those times.

Activity

Match the parts of the sentences in the following table appropriately.

Knowledge of a foreign language is needed	must be respected in international trade.
Prices vary throughout the world	differences in trading hours.
Local traditions, beliefs and customs	particularly in electrical goods.
Climatic conditions cause	to suit the religion of the other country.
Products may have to be modified	to suit the local economies.
Technical specifications differ throughout the world	to understand the transaction taking place.

Examination question

A local business is planning to sell its products abroad as well as to the home market. Explain how international trade would affect the four elements of the marketing mix. (8 marks)

How to answer this question

Each element of the marketing mix (price, product, promotion and place) should be examined to show how it would be affected by international trade. The effects may be either positive or negative. Two marks would be given for the effect on each element.

How transport methods and E-Business affect place

E-Business offers businesses of all sizes the possibility of worldwide trading. Local businesses can now be connected to consumers in over 100 different countries, allowing them the chance to be literally in more than one place at the same time.

Recent surveys have estimated that there are 4.7 billion people online worldwide. Just think of the vast opportunities all those people give businesses to expand their markets! The internet enables everyone to sell directly to the public, bypassing all the middlemen.

All types of products are traded via the internet although the most suitable products are small items such as books and videos, low-cost items which people will take a risk on buying, or hard-to-find, unique items such as crafts products.

While the overall trading opportunities are immense, transport of products to a worldwide market can be a problem.

Implications for transport of international sales are as follows:

▶ Products have to be delivered in safe condition, cheaply and on time. Small or light items can be posted using either surface mail or air mail. Larger, heavier items must be either shipped or taken by aeroplane to their destination.

▶ Matters involving customs and excise, import and export regulations and shipping laws must all be observed.

▶ E-Business sales must be accompanied by appropriate transport methods if the goods are to reach their destination safely.

Implications of the global market for business in the local economy

Every business, no matter how small, can now think of the whole world as being its marketplace if its product is the type of product which is demanded in other countries. The present situation has been thought of as a second industrial revolution.

Many of Northern Ireland's businesses are small. Previously those smallest businesses had a narrow market base and would not have considered exporting to be a viable option. The **global market** now presents that opportunity.

It also presents massive competition from businesses around the world. The business which can overcome the competition will survive and its market will continue to expand. This will result in increased employment and further opportunities for expansion. The business which cannot overcome the competition will fail and result in redundancies for its employees.

However, it may be beyond the scope of small businesses to respond positively to the competition. For this reason, **mergers** of businesses into larger units may be the answer to the need for increased capital in order to take advantage of economies of scale.

Globalisation has been made possible partly by:

▶ **The lifting of import controls between countries**. This makes it easier for local businesses to sell their products abroad.

▶ **The advances of technology** in general but especially due to the continuing development of the internet. It is estimated that the internet population is doubling each year, and now the internet is available in nearly every home throughout the developed world. Other components of technology are also developing continually.

Northern Ireland is a small country and, as part of an island on the extreme western side of Europe, it is geographically remote. These facts present difficulties for businesses in Northern Ireland which do not have to be considered by businesses in other, more central locations. Technology succeeds in reducing the effects of that remoteness and offers connection with potential customers all over the world.

The global market provides many challenges for local businesses, but it also presents definite opportunities. The questions now are 'How are those opportunities being grasped?' and 'How can the difficulties be overcome?'

The main implications of the global market for the local economy are as follows:

▶ **The need for the cultivation of a wide vision** – The Report by the Economic Development Strategy Review Group 'Strategy 2010' recommends that students should have skills in a variety of languages and should have opportunities to participate in international exchanges. The Report also stresses the value of town twinning arrangements which develop opportunities for exports and joint ventures as well as other inward investment projects and links. These are seen by the Review Group as being ways of widening the vision of Northern Ireland's population.

- **The need for training and practical experience** – Training and practical experience of export marketing is required in order to be able to avail of marketing opportunities abroad.
- **The need to be able to use the available technology competently** – Local businesses need to be using modern technology fully, and at an equal level to any of the other regions of Europe. The practical implications of this fact are capital investment in technology accompanied by training in the use of technology.
- **Stiffer competition for businesses in Northern Ireland** – This could result in the closure of some manufacturing companies and the redundancy of employees. On the other hand, stiffer competition could have beneficial results for businesses in Northern Ireland. It could be fought with the use of advanced technology and skills, and could result in increased trading and employment. The outcome of competition is largely determined by how globalisation is regarded and the degree to which it is welcomed. To beat international competition, businesses need to have a unique product of high quality. The product should be priced below the level of competitors with special inducements and a good personal service.
- **The opportunity for Northern Ireland to trade equally with all other countries** – Using modern technology, communication is equally easy throughout the world. Trading opportunities are equally available everywhere.

The greatest opportunity for businesses is that of expanding their markets throughout the world.

To be able to grasp that opportunity, businesses have to be prepared in advance. If those trading opportunities are taken up, they will result in Northern Ireland having more investment and employment which will lead to improved living standards and a growth in national wealth.

In order to make use of the opportunities of international trade, the business has to:

- research the market abroad to see if its product has to be modified
- decide on suitable forms of transport for the goods
- provide the type of packaging required
- understand the documentation required for sending goods abroad
- ensure that its employees are trained for the extra commitments
- train some staff to speak the foreign language required
- research the political, cultural, religious and legal systems of the foreign countries concerned
- make sure that its machinery and equipment are capable of coping with increased demands
- put in place a pricing policy below the level of the competitors
- make provision for the return of goods
- make sure that the quality of the product is of the highest possible standard
- offer special inducements with the sale
- supply the goods in the shortest possible time
- offer a personal service.

The role of the European Union (EU)

The European Union is an economic and political union of a total of twenty-eight member states (at the time of writing).

The full list of members

- Austria
- Belgium
- Bulgaria
- Croatia
- France
- Czech Republic
- Denmark
- Estonia
- Finland
- Italy
- Germany
- Greece
- Hungary
- Ireland
- Netherlands
- Latvia
- Lithuania
- Luxembourg
- Malta
- Slovenia
- Poland
- Portugal
- Romania
- Slovakia
- Spain
- Sweden
- United Kingdom
- Cyprus

The United Kingdom, following a referendum, is in the process of leaving the European Union but this process is likely to take some years to complete.

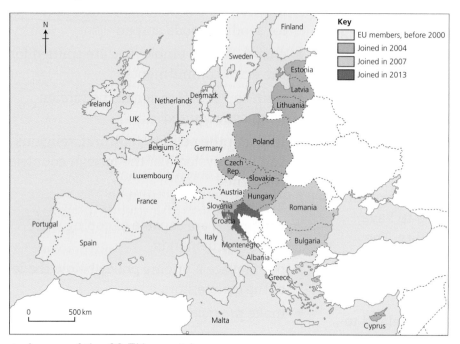

▲ A map of the 28 EU countries

Altogether there are approximately 500 million citizens in the European Union and the area generates an estimated 30% of the world's trade. A variety of languages are spoken by the member states and a variety of currencies used, although many have adopted the Euro. The European Union's aim is to promote social and economic progress among its member states.

All member states are represented in the European Union Parliament from where Directives (Community laws) are issued. Directives outline the objectives which the EU wishes to achieve and are binding on all member states, but it is up to the government in each country to choose how to implement those directives in that particular country.

Membership of the European Union provides better trading opportunities for businesses in those member states and opens up a wide market of potential customers and suppliers. It is easier to trade in this market than other overseas markets as many of the trading practices, regulations and standards apply throughout the European Union. This is largely due to the introduction of the Single Market.

The Single Market

The Single Market freed up the trade of goods and services and the movement of people between EU countries. The aim is that doing business with other EU countries should become more like doing business within your own country. The Single Market also intended to provide better opportunities for the people of the European Union by providing full employment and lead to improved standards of living and sustained economic development.

The Single Market set up the following four freedoms:

1 Freedom of movement of people and labour
▶ Citizens of any part of the European Union can live and work in any other part of the EU.
▶ Professional qualifications should be recognised in any area of the EU.
▶ Social Security benefits would be transferable between EU countries.

2 Freedom of movement of goods
▶ Companies can sell their products anywhere in the European Union and consumers can buy where they want.

▶ There are no quotas or tariffs.
▶ Standards of goods have been made the same to ensure that they are acceptable throughout the EU.
▶ Administrative procedures and taxation have been simplified.
▶ Custom duty is not charged on goods moving between EU countries.
▶ Consumers benefit from a wider range of products in the market.
▶ Increased competition should also make goods cheaper for consumers.
▶ The major disadvantage of this freedom is that competition would become much greater and inefficient companies would suffer a loss of market share.

3 Freedom of movement of capital
▶ Currencies and capital can flow freely between any areas of the European Union.
▶ EU citizens can use financial services in any EU country.
▶ Foreign exchange controls were eliminated.

4 Freedom of movement of services
▶ Professional services such as banking, insurance or advertising can be offered in any European Union country.

Activity: Discussion point

Although a decision has been made for this country to leave the European Union, opinion is still divided whether or not this is a good idea.

Divide your class in two. Choose a reporter in each group. One half to report back three points in favour of leaving the EU and the other half to report back three points in favour of staying in the EU.

Examination question

Explain the role of the European Union (EU).   (6 marks)

How to answer this question

For a total of 6 marks you would be expected to explain three roles of the EU.

Checklist ✓

At this stage you should be able to:

○ explain the advantages and disadvantages of international trade to a business

○ explain how the various elements of the marketing mix of a business would be affected by international trade

○ discuss the implications of the global market for business in the local economy

○ explain and evaluate the role of the European Union (EU).

2.8 E-Business

E-Business (electronic business) is the online transaction of goods and services, and the transfer of funds through digital communications.

E-Business involves carrying out business over the internet and operates by linking computer systems between buyer and seller. Most people are familiar with electronic transactions between a business and a consumer (B2C). Amazon.com is a popular example. E-Business may also take place between businesses (B2B).

Using modern technology, trading opportunities are available throughout the world. However, E-Business has opened up those same opportunities for every other business as well, and this results in a situation of increased competition. Where there is competition, businesses have to compete to persuade consumers to buy their goods or services. The reality is that only the best survive.

This section gives details of the advantages and disadvantages of E-Business for both businesses and consumers. You will notice that sometimes these will be similar for both groups.

▲ Amazon's website helps them with their customer-centric reputation

Advantages of E-Business for a business	Disadvantages of E-Business for a business
Business can be conducted at any time – even when the store is closed.	Competition is increased.
The business can buy and use products and services from a range of international sources.	An attractively designed website and an efficient electronic system are essential.
E-Business provides opportunities for increased sales revenue on a world-wide basis.	Efficient packing and reliable transport systems must be in place.
It expands the market from regional to global.	E-commerce is not suitable for perishable goods.
It leads to increased productivity.	Consumers dislike buying very expensive goods, such as jewellery, without seeing them.
It increases turnover and profits.	The business must be aware of differing cultures of customers.

It allows the business to become better known.	The business must understand different legal requirements in other countries.
Payment for the goods is made immediately.	The business needs to be able to cope with many languages.
Payment is more secure than by cheque.	Payment providers, e.g. PayPal, usually charge commission for their services.
Transactions can be processed very quickly.	
E-Business allows the business to access a greater range of customers.	
E-Business is excellent for specialist markets where customers would be few.	
Overhead costs are reduced – e.g. sales can be made from warehouses instead of high street premises where rates are high.	
Marketing costs are reduced.	
Fewer sales personnel are required for E-Business, saving wages.	
Processing errors are less likely to occur.	
It is easy to deal with repeat orders as all details are stored on computer.	
Direct communication with customers can be made by email.	
It saves having to print catalogues and update price lists regularly. Instead web pages are easily edited.	

Advantages of E-Business for customers	Disadvantages of E-Business for customers
It is possible to log-on to the internet at any time of the day or night.	Lack of trust of payment system is the greatest disadvantage.
It is possible to access the websites of businesses throughout the world.	Security issues and fear of personal information being wrongly used by hackers.
Gives a greater choice of goods so consumers can 'shop around' between businesses which allows them to research and compare prices and the range of goods.	Customers must have debit/credit cards for payment.
Customers are not charged according to the distance they are from the business.	Customers must be linked to the internet and understand the technology.
Websites give maximum information about products.	If goods are required immediately, it is necessary to buy from a shop.
This leads to better customer satisfaction.	There are some poor websites which may offer poor value.
It is very convenient to shop from home and time is saved by not having to visit shops.	There is no guarantee of product quality.
Transactions are almost immediate unlike via a catalogue which takes a longer time.	E-commerce is not suitable for perishable goods.
Goods are generally cheaper as business expenses are reduced.	The customer is unable to handle the goods before purchase and has to rely on an image in E-Business.

Repeat orders are easy as information can be stored on computer.	Returning goods can be difficult.
Direct communication with the business can be made electronically.	Some customers dislike the lack of personal contact.
Electronic price lists are up-to-date.	A few websites require special software not common in standard systems.
	Some customers may find the use of foreign currencies confusing.

How E-Business supports international business

▶ E-Business allows home businesses to purchase supplies and raw materials from international sources. These may be cheaper.

▶ E-Business opens an international market for home businesses who can market their products abroad and become known internationally.

▶ E-Business gives businesses a competitive advantage by opening up a global market and an international range of customers.

▶ Through E-Business, consumers have access to a wider choice of products and are likely to purchase from foreign businesses as well as from the domestic market.

▶ Through E-Business, products manufactured in this country are offered for sale on a world-wide scale. This increases productivity and sales revenue.

▶ E-Business provides excellent promotional opportunities for products on an international scale.

Activity

Match the parts of the sentences appropriately in the following table.

E-commerce increases competition	to have a credit card for payment.
Security issues in e-commerce	sales staff are not required.
In e-commerce a customer needs	perishable goods.
Wages are saved in e-commerce because	to have an attractive website.
In e-commerce it is necessary	greatly concern customers.
E-commerce is not suitable for	which is a disadvantage for a business.

Examination question

Beechgrove Ltd is a company which sells stationery and small items of office equipment. The company is planning to use E-Business and sell its goods on the international market. Describe three advantages and three disadvantages for Beechgrove Ltd of using E-Business.
(12 marks)

How to answer this question

This question divides into two parts. Firstly, you should describe three advantages for a company selling this type of goods.
Name each advantage and say why it would be an advantage to Beechgrove Ltd. (2 marks for each advantage fully described.) Next you need to describe three disadvantages for this particular company.
Name each disadvantage and say why it would be a disadvantage to Beechgrove Ltd. (2 marks for each disadvantage fully described.) Be careful that the advantages and disadvantages are from the point of view of the business.

Checklist

At this stage you should be able to:
- ○ explain the term E-Business
- ○ analyse the advantages and disadvantages of E-Business for a business
- ○ analyse the advantages and disadvantages of E-Business for customers
- ○ discuss how E-Business supports international business.

2.9 M-Business

M-Business (mobile business) refers to new business services and business models using mobile technologies such as smartphones.

The huge growth of mobile technologies has created new opportunities for businesses to connect with, and provide services to, their customers. Mobile technologies include smartphones, tablets and other portable devices connected to the internet, for example, smart watches.

The majority of the UK population have smartphones. In many developing countries mobile phones are the main way that users access the internet. The growth in the use of mobile technology is made possible by faster and smaller hardware, and better mobile networks. M-technology is growing very fast and expanding beyond the developed world – it is estimated that there are 4.7 billion mobile subscribers globally which is 65 per cent of the world population.

Features of Mobile Business

Mobile technologies have several key features that make M-Business different from other online business activities:

▶ Mobile technologies are, as the name suggests, technologies that are mobile or portable. This allows businesses to connect with, or provide services to, their customers and potential customers wherever they are and at any time, for example, by sending a delivery notification or special offer to a customer's phone.

▶ Mobile technologies are also location-aware. This means that the customer's mobile device knows its location and

communications can be targeted to that place. Knowing where a customer is can help businesses tailor their messages or services. It also makes delivery services more accurate.

▶ These features are changing how businesses provide their services. They are also leading to the development of new businesses that can only exist using mobile technology.

Uses of mobile technology in business

Mobile commerce

Businesses can sell directly to their customers online and through mobile apps on a customer's phone. Making their products and services easily available to mobile customers creates new opportunities for businesses. Some stores provide their staff with mobile devices to process sales or handle customer feedback. E-commerce sales on mobile devices makes up a growing percentage of all online sales. A retailer also might use mobile devices to check, update and manage his/her inventory levels.

Mobile payments

Many businesses now also accept payments via mobile devices in their physical stores through their point-of-sale (POS) systems. Some businesses are experimenting with technologies that allow customers to make purchases by scanning the barcode of a product.

Mobile marketing and communications

Mobile technologies allow businesses to communicate with their customers easily, for example, by sending notifications to customers' smartphones. Mobile devices also allow customers to communicate with businesses. For example, they can provide immediate feedback on their shopping experience or make a customer service enquiry.

Mobile banking

It is simple for bank customers to check their bank balances and make payments using an app. As more customers use mobile banking there is less need for bank branches which can save banks money. It is also convenient for customers as they can have access to their account information on their phones.

Transport and delivery services

New transport services are combining mobile payments with location-based technology. You can book and pay for a taxi service, or order a takeaway meal using a smartphone app and have it delivered to your exact location.

Games

Mobile games now earn more money than any other type of mobile app. They are more convenient for users than console or PC-based games and can be played on the go. A new generation of mobile games blends digital images with real-world locations.

Apps

There are millions of apps available for smartphone users. Many of these apps use the unique features of smartphones and provide services that could not exist in any other way. Examples include mobile games, fitness trackers or messaging apps.

Mobile ticketing

Mobile ticketing allows customers to use their mobile devices to search, order and pay for tickets for activities such as events, hotel rooms and travel. Mobile ticketing can reduce costs for business by eliminating the need to issue printed tickets. For many customers, mobile tickets are more convenient than having to print and remember paper tickets or reservations.

Mobile ticketing at Translink

▲ mLink allows customers to buy tickets with ease

Translink runs Northern Ireland's public transport network including railways and buses. In 2012, Translink introduced mLink, a mobile app that lets customers buy and use mobile train tickets on their smartphones. In 2015, the service was expanded to include mobile tickets on Metro bus services.

The following tables show advantages and disadvantages of M-Business to a business, and advantages and disadvantages of M-Business to customers.

Advantages of M-Business to a business	Disadvantages for M-Business to a business
Businesses can communicate with their customers immediately, wherever they are.	Businesses may have to invest in new hardware and software in order to make use of mobile technology. For example, they may need to install new point-of-sale systems to accept mobile payments or develop new business apps to provide mobile services.
Businesses can accept new forms of payments, giving customers more options.	New competition. Many existing businesses will have to compete with new businesses that deliver services mainly using mobile technology. This can be a disadvantage for existing businesses. For example, a mobile-only bank does not have to pay for bank branches in the same way that an existing bank does.
Businesses can develop new services that are more convenient, helping them to attract new customers.	Businesses have to adapt frequently to new innovations such as new smartphone designs, new mobile devices and new software. Mobile devices are usually smaller than desktop or laptop devices. This changes the way information is presented on-screen. Many businesses will have to update their website.
Businesses can reduce the cost of doing business, for example by using mobile ticketing which is useful in the business world for booking flights and arranging business trips.	Design or online advertising to suit mobile devices.
	There may be additional costs associated with staff training to use M-Business.
	There are new security needs. Businesses that accept mobile payments or communicate with their customers via mobile apps will need to consider additional security measures to protect their data and their customers' data.

Advantages of M-Business to customers	Disadvantages for M-Business to customers
Mobile services can be more convenient.	Mobile data use can be expensive.
Customers can access information about products and services on their devices, making them more informed consumers.	There may be increased security risks when using mobile technologies.
Mobile technologies can offer new services that did not exist before.	Constant communication from businesses can be unwelcome as some businesses sell their databases to third parties.
Mobile communications can make it easier to communicate with businesses.	

Examination question ↻

Chris is a friend of yours who owns and runs a retail shop. He is unsure about M-Business. Explain two advantages which M-Business would have for his business. (4 marks)

How to answer this question

You should give details of any two advantages of M-Business which could be applied to a retail shop. (Up to 2 marks for each advantage.)

Checklist ✓

At this stage you should be able to:

- ○ explain the term M-Business
- ○ describe and explain a variety of uses of mobile technology for business
- ○ analyse the advantages and disadvantages of M-Business for a business.

3 Business operations
3.1 Types of production

The term 'production' refers to the creation of either goods or services. For example, the teachers in your school are involved in production – producing the service of education and the workers in a factory are also involved in production – producing cars or whatever that factory makes.

Production may be divided into three types – primary, secondary and tertiary. You are already familiar with these three words in connection with school. You started your education in a primary school – that was the first stage. You are now at the secondary level of education – the second stage. If you continue to university, you will enter the tertiary level – the third stage.

Similarly, each industrial and business activity falls into a primary, secondary or tertiary stage.

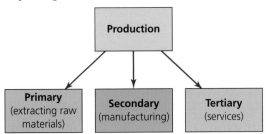

Primary production

Primary production is the sourcing of raw materials from the ground or from the sea. It is also using the earth's resources to grow items such as crops, fruit, flowers and trees.

Primary production includes farming, fishing, mining, quarrying, forestry and oil drilling.

Examples of primary production in Northern Ireland:

⌃ Forestry in Fermanagh

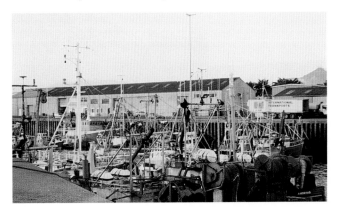

⌃ Fishing in Kilkeel

Farming is particularly important in Northern Ireland and there are 3.5 times more people working in agriculture in Northern Ireland than in the rest of the United Kingdom. Fishing is also important in Northern Ireland and Kilkeel is one of its major ports. Quarrying is important in the Sperrins where there are deposits of rock, sand and gravel which are quarried and used in the construction trades and road making. Forestry is carried out throughout the Province particularly on land which is unsuitable for farming.

Secondary production

Secondary production takes the raw material produced by the primary industries and works on it to manufacture finished goods. For example, wood produced by a primary industry would be manufactured into tables and chairs by a secondary industry. The world famous Bushmills Distillery in Co Antrim is a good example of a secondary industry, as it takes the primary product of barley and processes it to make Irish whiskey. Belleek Pottery is another example of secondary production as it takes clay and makes it into fine china.

▲ Bushmills Distillery

Tertiary production

Tertiary production provides services to all the other industries and to members of the public. These services include the selling of goods, and commercial services such as banking, marketing, insurance and transport. It also includes all professional services such as entertainment, hospitality, education, legal, religious and medical services. Tertiary jobs are usually centred in towns.

▲ A bank is an example of a tertiary service

Activity

State which type of production each of the following workers are involved in.

Occupation	Primary, secondary or tertiary
Insurance agent	
Fisherman	
Furniture manufacturer	
Teacher	
Farmer	
Shopkeeper	
Market gardener	
Solicitor	
Coal miner	

Examination question

Identify the type of production in each of the following:

a Extraction of raw materials from land or sea.

b The provision of services such as banking.

c The conversion of raw materials into finished goods. (3 marks)

How to answer this question

This question asks you to identify, therefore all you should do is write down the three names for a, b and c. No explanation is necessary in a question asking you to 'identify' so don't spend time unnecessarily.

Each stage of production is dependent on the other two in order to get the finished product to the consumer – this is known as the chain of production.

The production of Tayto Crisps in Tandragee in County Armagh illustrates the chain of production very well and shows how all three stages of production work together and are required in order to get the crisps to the consumer.

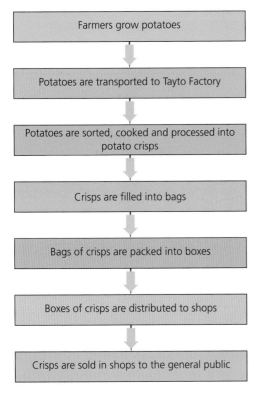

▲ The chain of production of crisps

▲ Tayto Crisps brand

Activity

The stages involved in manufacturing potato crisps are listed here. Beside each stage, in the spaces provided on the right-hand side, write down whether it is primary, secondary or tertiary.

Farmers grow potatoes ....

Potatoes are transported to the Tayto Factory ....

Potatoes are sorted and processed into crisps ....

Boxes of crisps are distributed to shops ....

Crisps are sold to the general public ....

Changing trends across the types of production

The modern trend in employment is for a move away from the primary and secondary sectors towards employment in the tertiary sector. This trend, known as **de-industrialisation**, is affecting most developed countries, including Northern Ireland. The tertiary sector continues to grow and it is estimated that 80% of all people employed in Northern Ireland are working in the tertiary sector.

There are several reasons for the changes in employment trends across the sectors:

▶ In the primary sector, farming has become more mechanised and fewer people are needed to work the modern machinery than in previous years when work was done manually. Jobs in the secondary sector have also been lost because of mechanisation.

▶ The agriculture industry has had difficult times because prices offered for its goods have been reduced. Milk and potatoes are examples of goods which are sold cheaply in supermarkets, making it difficult for farmers.

▶ There is little raw material in Northern Ireland apart from trees for the timber industry and stone for quarrying. Fewer people are needed therefore in the primary industries.

▶ Many traditional industries in Northern Ireland have closed down because they cannot compete with foreign goods coming on to the market at cheaper prices. This has hit the clothing industry especially. Manufactured goods are imported cheaply from countries such as Japan, China, Malaysia and Taiwan.

▶ The standard of education is high in Northern Ireland so many young people choose to follow professional careers rather than work in the primary and secondary sectors.

▶ People are spending more on leisure activities so entrepreneurs have moved into that market

▶ There is now more demand for services such as education, personal banking, insurance for property and cars, investment and legal advice, therefore increasing numbers of employees are needed in these areas.

Activity

1 On a computer, create a table with four columns and twenty-two rows.

2 In the first row, label the four columns – occupation, primary, secondary, tertiary.

3 In column 1, rows 2 to 21, write the occupations of twenty people you know well – members of your family or other close friends.

4 In columns 2, 3 and 4, classify each occupation as primary, secondary and tertiary by ticking the appropriate list.

5 On row 22 total the number of occupations in each of the three sectors.

6 Study your results and say whether they reflect the trends described in this section.

Examination question

Identify a changing trend across the types of production and explain two reasons for that trend.

(5 marks)

How to answer this question

You are asked here for one trend (change) in types of production which you should name (1 mark). Then go on to explain two reasons why that trend has occurred (2 marks for each reason fully explained).

Checklist ✔

At this stage you should be able to:

○ distinguish between the main types of production
○ classify businesses according to their type of production
○ understand the changing trends across the types of production
○ discuss the reasons for the changing trends
○ discuss the changing nature and importance of the types of production.

3.2 Methods of manufacturing

There are four methods of manufacturing, and the method chosen by any business depends very much on the type of product being made and the quantity which is required. Although you will study each of these methods separately, it should be understood that, in practice, very often a business may use a combination of the methods for some of its work.

JOB	BATCH
PROCESS	FLOW

▲ The methods of manufacturing

Job manufacturing

Job manufacturing is where one single item is completed at a time and is often produced to the customer's individual specification. Each product is unique and a long time would usually have been spent on it. For this reason, goods produced by this method are expensive to buy.

Job manufacturing would not be suitable for most factories as it is too slow but would be found in craft and designer shops where emphasis is placed on the handmade, high quality, interesting and individual character of the product.

Examples of goods made by the job manufacturing method are:

- craft goods
- luxury cars
- designer clothes
- double glazing
- stained glass windows
- landscape gardening
- house plans
- antique furniture.

Advantages of job manufacturing

- Each piece is made to the customer's exact requirements.
- **Job satisfaction** is high for the worker as he/she is producing a quality item.
- Quality of the goods is very high.
- The design is flexible and can be changed.

Disadvantages of job manufacturing

- The products are very expensive.
- The work is very time consuming.

Read the following example of job manufacturing:

Case study

Joan is a talented dress designer in Ballynahinch who especially enjoys designing and making wedding dresses. She works alone in a large room at the back of her house. Although her dresses are expensive, they are in great demand because they are expertly handmade and unique. Each bride comes to her with a vague idea of the design of the wedding dress she would like, and Joan draws the final design and makes the dress to suit the customer's individual requirements.

Joan gets tremendous job satisfaction from her work, and produces only one dress at a time so that it gets her full attention. Very often she changes little details of the dress during its manufacture because the customer sometimes changes her mind. Joan is happy to do this because she wants the customer to be really pleased with the dress which is a 'one-off' and individually produced for her.

Joan's work is an example of job manufacturing.

▲ One of Joan's designs

Batch manufacturing

Case study 🔍

Cupid's is a shop in Ballynahinch which sells wedding dresses. The sales manager, Margaret, has been looking at the wedding photographs in the local newspapers. She has been very impressed with the dresses which the newspaper reports of the weddings say were made by Joan.

Margaret approached Joan and asked her to make ten dresses – all the same design, but in different sizes – for sale in Cupid's. She promised that another order would follow for ten dresses of a different style.

Joan agreed with this arrangement and had to employ two temporary dressmakers, Siobhan and Joy, to help with the additional work.

Joan has now moved into **batch manufacturing**. Batch manufacturing is used where several of the same product are made at one time. When the first batch is completed, manufacturing continues with a number of a second product and so on. All the items made in a batch are the same so manufacturing is speeded up. This reduces the cost of labour and results in the final product being less expensive for the customer.

Batch manufacturing is suitable for businesses such as bakeries which bake a number of the same loaves and cakes every day, and where the products do not have to be individual. Newspapers are also produced by this method. The papers are printed every day and each batch must meet a deadline.

Examples of goods made by the batch manufacturing method are:

▶ newspapers
▶ bread
▶ clothing
▶ furniture
▶ motor cars
▶ books
▶ building of housing estates where all the houses are the same.

▲ These houses are all identical – an example of batch manufacturing

Advantages of batch manufacturing

▶ Workers may specialise to some degree.
▶ Labour costs are reduced so the final price of the product is lower.
▶ Machinery may be used.
▶ Manufacturing is faster.

Disadvantages of batch manufacturing

▶ The work is less interesting than in job manufacturing and is repetitive.

▶ More space is required for working and storage.

▶ Larger inventories of raw materials must be kept.

▶ Machines may have to be re-set between batches which loses time.

Flow manufacturing

Case study 🔍

Other shop managers in Cookstown, Ballyclare, Newcastle and Maghera have been contacting Joan to ask if she would supply wedding dresses for their shops.

Joan is certainly interested in this extra work but realises that her manufacturing method would have to change. She rents larger premises, buys additional sewing machines, makes Siobhan and Joy permanent, and employs three additional people – Evelyn, Robert and Pedro. Joan names the business 'Wedding Belles'.

Joan organises the operation on an assembly line basis and each of the six people working in the business is responsible for his/her own separate part of the manufacturing of the wedding dresses.

Although her profits are higher, Joan regrets the fact that the larger number of dresses she now produces are all the same. She also misses the personal contact with her customers which she once enjoyed. Joan has now moved into flow manufacturing.

Flow manufacturing is also sometimes known as mass manufacturing or assembly line manufacturing. It is the method used in factories and most modern manufacturing employs this method.

In flow manufacturing, one product is made continuously and in large numbers. A conveyor belt or assembly line is organised and, as the product moves along the line, parts are added to it. In this way, the item starts at the beginning of the line as raw materials and is packaged and ready for sale when it reaches the end of the line.

Operation of an assembly line requires numbers of employees to sit at their particular places and perform their allocated tasks as the product moves along the line. Each employee's task is very repetitive and simple so those engaged in flow manufacturing tend to be unskilled or semi-skilled. **Motivation** of workers is often a problem, and strategies such as **job rotation** are often used in order to relieve the monotony.

Flow manufacturing is suitable for use where large numbers of identical products are being made. This method is very dependent on machinery, therefore a large amount of capital is needed to establish the factory.

However, since large quantities are being produced in the shortest possible time, wages and other costs are kept to a minimum and the finished product is usually not expensive for the customer.

Examples of goods made by the flow manufacturing method are:

▶ motor vehicles

▶ machinery

▶ televisions

▶ inexpensive clothing

▶ toys.

▲ Goods made by the flow manufacturing method

Advantages of flow manufacturing	Disadvantages of flow manufacturing
Final product is less expensive.	The work is repetitive and boring.
Large quantities can be manufactured.	There is an increased risk of accidents.
The quality of the product is standardised.	Employee motivation is low.
Machinery can be used so labour costs are reduced.	The products are all identical.
Unskilled wages further reduce costs.	Large capital investment is required.
Assembly lines can run continuously.	Large buildings are usually needed.
Manufacturing is fast.	Large amounts of raw materials must be kept.
Takes full advantage of economies of scale.	Machinery breakdown can halt manufacturing.
	There is a loss of traditional skills.

Process manufacturing

Process manufacturing refers to the manufacturing of process goods which cannot be disassembled. For example, when a soft drink is produced, it cannot be broken down into its ingredients. Process manufacturing therefore is the opposite of the previous types of manufacturing, such as cars, clothes and toys which can be manufactured in their parts.

Process manufacturing involves the combination of ingredients according to formula or recipes rather than the assembly of parts. Examples of process goods are chemicals, food and beverages, petrol, paint, pharmaceuticals and cosmetics.

Process manufacturing is the manufacturing of goods which are typically produced in bulk quantities and the manufacturing is continuous. For example, a food processing factory making sauce would make the sauce in a continuous flow.

Process manufacturing has the advantage that it ensures manufacturing consistency with its clear and detailed formula. This increases efficiency and quality.

▲ The manufacturing of HP sauce is an example of process manufacturing

Activity

You are asked to name the most suitable type of manufacturing in each of the following situations.

Situation	Manufacture method
A dressmaker makes designer clothes	
Ford makes thousands of cars for sale throughout Europe	
A bakery makes several varieties of loaves which are sold in retail shops	
A factory produces chemicals	
A kitchen designer makes kitchens to suit individual homes	

Examination question ↻

Capital Magazine Printers Ltd print large numbers of several magazines which are published on a weekly basis. Which method of manufacturing is most suitable for use in the Printers? Justify your choice of method by giving two reasons.　(5 marks)

How to answer this question

You should decide on a method which is suitable for a printer, bearing in mind that they must produce large numbers of each magazine each week. (1 mark) Next give two reasons why this method is most suitable, relating your reasons to printing. (Up to 2 marks for each fully explained reason)

Specialisation

Case study

Joan has had to allocate separate responsibilities to each of her employees in Wedding Belles.

She has retained responsibility for all design work herself. Pedro is the cutter, and passes on the prepared parts of the dresses to Siobhan and Joy who make them up into dresses on the sewing machines. The dresses are then passed to Evelyn who is responsible for the finishing work of sewing on buttons and decorations and pressing the finished garments. Robert is responsible for packing, labelling and transporting the finished products to the shops. Robert also does all the clerical work.

Joan has now started to use specialisation.

Specialisation occurs when an employee concentrates on one particular operation, and does it all the time. It is where each worker, or group of workers, undertakes only a small section of the total work and specialises in that particular part of making the product.

It also occurs when a country concentrates on producing one particular type of goods. For example, areas of France specialise in making wine because the climate there is suitable for vineyards and wine making.

There are four types of specialisation.

Product: for example, the Wedding Belles business specialises in the product of wedding dresses.

Process: for example, in Wedding Belles, Siobhan and Joy have specialised in the process of machining the dresses.

Function: for example, in the Wedding Belles business, Robert has specialised in distribution and clerical work.

Country: for example, France specialises in the manufacturing of wine.

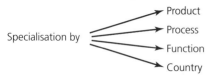

Specialisation by → Product, Process, Function, Country

Advantages of specialisation

▶ People can work constantly at jobs which suit their special skills or training. In this way, each person becomes an expert at that particular function.

▶ The finished product should be of higher quality because of this expertise.

▶ Resources can be effectively used and concentrated in one place.

▶ Goods are made faster, therefore the output from the business is increased resulting in higher profits.

Disadvantages of specialisation

▶ Specialised workers are trained in only one skill, so it may be difficult for them to find other work if they become redundant.

▶ The work may become boring and repetitive, leading to careless mistakes.

▶ Any business concentrating on a small range of work becomes very dependent on other businesses.

▶ An area concentrating on a single industry is very badly affected if that industry should fail. For example, parts of France would suffer greatly if poor weather caused the vines not to grow.

▶ Delays or strikes in one section can cause stoppages throughout the manufacturing.

Activity

If you are a student at a large school you will already be used to specialisation. Your teachers have all specialised in certain subjects which they concentrate on and teach all the time.

1 What is the main advantage for you as a student of having specialised teachers?

2 Which disadvantages, from the teachers' point of view, can you see in specialisation?

Division of labour

Flow manufacturing usually leads to division of labour which is a particular type of specialisation. In division of labour, the manufacture of the product is divided into a number of small stages and each employee is given a single task which may be very narrow.

I once visited a toy factory which used the practice of division of labour. I stood behind a girl whose job was to attach the heads to the bodies of dolls as they moved along the conveyor belt. That was the task which she was given, and she spent the entire day lifting a doll's head from a box with her right hand, lifting the doll's body from the conveyor belt with her left hand and attaching the two in the time the belt had halted in front of her.

Advantages of division of labour

▶ Each worker becomes very practised at one particular task.

▶ Workers have to be trained for only one small task so lengthy training is avoided.

▶ The work is faster so the costs per unit of manufacturing are reduced.

▶ Reduced costs can be reflected in lower prices to the consumer.

▶ Lower prices will raise sales revenue and profits.

- Time is saved because workers do not have to move between jobs.
- Tools and machinery are used economically because each worker will need only one tool which is required for one particular function.

Disadvantages of division of labour

- The work can be very monotonous and boring.
- Bored workers can cause accidents.
- It is difficult for workers to have pride in their work since they do not see the finished product.
- Delays or strikes in one section can cause stoppages throughout the manufacturing.
- There is a loss of traditional skills.
- Goods produced by this method lack variety.
- Workers can feel isolated from each other.
- Redundant employees would have difficulty in finding other work because they are very narrowly trained.

Examination question

Bell & Sons Ltd is a large factory which manufactures televisions. Division of labour is used in the factory. Explain what is meant by division of labour and explain one advantage and one disadvantage of division of labour in Bell & Sons Ltd. (6 marks)

How to answer this question

The first requirement in this question is to define division of labour (2 marks). Next, explain one advantage of division of labour (2 marks) and one disadvantage of division of labour (2 marks) relating both to a factory.

Inventory control

Inventory control is very important in any business – whether it is a manufacturing or a retail organisation. A factory will have to control the levels of two types of inventory – raw materials for use in making its products and finished products ready for sale. A retail shop just has to control the level of inventory of goods it has for sale.

In modern businesses, inventory control is done by computer. Details of items contained in the business are held in the computer system. As goods are sold their barcodes are recorded at the cash desk and those items are electronically deducted from the number in the store. When the computer records that the levels of particular items are low, those goods are automatically re-ordered. A fully computerised system means that the business can get an inventory valuation at any time or see how particular items are selling.

Efficient inventory control ensures that the business is not holding large amounts of goods for long periods, as this would tie up finance which ought to be available for use in the business. At the same time, efficient inventory control also ensures that the business is holding enough inventory to keep its manufacture flowing and to meet the needs of customers. Balancing these two is the art of good inventory control.

Good inventory control will:

- improve efficiency because manufacturing will be constant
- enable the business always to meet demand
- give the business a competitive edge over other businesses
- ensure that capital is not lying idle.

Poor inventory control may:

- mean that consumer demands cannot be met
- lose business and goodwill

- require extra warehouse space
- risk some perishable goods going out-of-date
- use finance inefficiently.

Methods of inventory control

The method of inventory control used varies from business to business and will depend on the type and size of business. The most usual methods are minimum inventory control, batch control, First in First Out, and Just in time.

Minimum inventory level method

This is a simple method where the business works out the minimum amount of inventory with which it can function. Inventory is re-ordered when that minimum level is reached. A major difficulty with this method is that there may be a delay between ordering the goods and having them delivered. If that happens, a factory may have to cease production until the inventory arrives or a retail shop may not have goods to sell.

Batch inventory control method

This method is used in industries that make products in vats and tanks and would be associated with process manufacturing rather than with industries which make products in a continuous flow. It simply calculates the value of the inventory held and available for manufacturing.

First In First Out inventory control (FIFO)

As its name suggests, the First In First Out method of inventory control is based on selling the oldest inventory first and selling or using inventory in rotation. This method accurately assigns costs to inventory as the oldest goods bought may be less expensive. For example, if 1000 units were purchased for £10 each in January and 1000 units were purchased in June for £15 each, the sales price of the first units would be calculated on £10

each and would rise once the first 1000 units were sold.

Just-in-time method of inventory control

The **Just-in-time** system originated in Japan and is widely used in that country and in Japanese factories in other parts of the world.

Using the Just-in-time method:

- products are manufactured just in time for them to be sold. This prevents large amounts of finished goods having to wait to go to market.
- the raw materials or parts which are needed for making the final product, are ordered and arrive just in time for use in its manufacture. Large amounts of goods are not held in warehouses waiting to be used.

In this way the Just-in-time method saves money being tied up for long periods in unused raw materials and unsold finished products. It is therefore effective in reducing costs for the manufacturer.

On the other hand, mistakes in deliveries could hold up manufacturing because there is no reserve inventory to go on using.

Advantages of Just-in-time inventory control

- Capital is used very effectively.
- Warehousing is not needed for storage.
- If faults occur in supplies, the business does not have a large number of the faulty items.
- There is no waste by having excess inventory.
- The finished product should be cheaper for the consumer to buy.

Disadvantages of Just-in-time inventory control

- The business is very dependent on having a very efficient ordering system.
- Manufacturing could be halted if the wrong goods are delivered at the last minute.

▶ It puts severe pressure on suppliers.

▶ The company and its suppliers must work together closely.

Activity

Imagine that you are a Japanese manager of a new car factory being set up in Northern Ireland. You have experience of the Just-in-time method of inventory control and you wish to introduce the system into the new factory.

You plan to give a talk to the employees tomorrow to explain the system to them. Prepare the talk which you will give at the meeting.

The impact of technology on manufacturing

Modern technology has been the cause of the greatest changes in modern manufacturing and businesses invest large amounts of capital in technology in order to be up-to-date and ahead of the competition.

▲ Automotive robots puts the car manufacturing industry in the fast lane

The major impacts of technology on manufacturing are:

1 **An improvement in the quality of the finished product** – As a result of the use of technology, the quality of the products is standardised and the possibility of human error is minimised.

2 **The development of new products** – Improved methods of research and development would lead to new products being added to the business's range.

3 **An increase in the business's manufacturing level** – A fully mechanised business can work around the clock with no interruptions. This would have the effect of increasing the level of output.

4 **A decrease in the manufacturing costs per unit** – Increases in manufacturing lead to benefits of economies of scale which reduces overall costs per unit of manufacturing.

5 **Higher profit levels** – Increased manufacturing and sales, as well as reduced costs, lead to improved profits for the business and improved efficiency overall.

6 **Greater customer satisfaction** – An improvement in the quality of the business's product and the speed of its service would lead to a larger number of satisfied customers. Computers can also monitor inventory levels which would result in better customer satisfaction.

7 **Improved motivation of workers** – Workers enjoy being part of an organisation which is progressive and are also motivated by the opportunities provided in the business. They also benefit from constant training.

8 **Improved information and communication systems** – Internal and external communications are improved by the installation of modern communication systems. Access to information is improved by the provision of computer-based systems.

9 **Possible redundancies of employees** – The increase of automated jobs can cause staff redundancies. Previous skills are no longer required and new ones are needed.

10 **Re-training programmes** – A programme of continuous training is required to keep employees abreast with the latest developments in technology. This is expensive for the business to sustain.

11 **Capital costs** – The installation, up-dating and maintenance of technology requires a substantial capital investment. This costly investment is often impossible for small businesses to fund.

Examination question

Bell & Sons Ltd is a large factory which manufactures televisions. Evaluate the impact of technology on manufacturing for Bell & Sons Ltd. (5 marks)

How to answer this question

In an evaluation type question, you must consider both a positive impact (2 marks) and a negative impact (2 marks). You should then decide whether technology is useful for Bell & Sons Ltd (1 mark).

Checklist ✓

At this stage you should be able to:
○ describe and evaluate the main methods of manufacturing
○ discuss the advantages and disadvantages of specialisation and division of labour
○ identify the most appropriate methods of manufacturing in particular situations
○ describe and evaluate the main methods of inventory control
○ evaluate the impact of technology on manufacturing.

3.3 Quality Assurance

Quality Assurance is the monitoring and evaluation of a product or service to ensure that standards of high quality are being met.

Businesses see **Quality Assurance** as being very important, in fact some companies have a special Quality Assurance Department, but Quality Assurance is the responsibility of every employee.

It is important because it:

▶ prevents mistakes or defects in the company's products

▶ provides confidence in consumers that the products are reliable and safe

▶ gives the company an advantage over competitors

▶ enhances the reputation of the company

▶ increases sales and profits.

For these reasons, most businesses undertake the process to obtain recognised quality standards. Being awarded a recognised standard, such as those described in this section, is an assurance to members of the public that the business organisation has met the high standards required and this gives consumers confidence in dealing with that business.

Customer Service Excellence Standard

The government has developed the Customer Service Excellence Standard for public service organisations to improve their effectiveness and efficiency. This Standard places importance on members of the public and ensures that they are top-priority in public service provision.

To achieve this aim, emphasis is placed on:

▶ delivery of the service

▶ whether the service is delivered on time

▶ level of information available to the customer

▶ professionalism of the service

▶ staff attitude

▶ understanding the customer's experience of the service

▶ constant measurement of the service.

The aims of the Customer Service Excellence Standard are to:

▶ encourage continuous improvement in the delivery of public service

▶ encourage individuals and teams to learn new skills when dealing with customers

▶ reward organisations which deliver good services based on customers' needs.

Activity

Answer the following questions.

1 Why did the government introduce the Customer Service Excellence Standard?

2 As a member of the public, what would you expect of the service in an organisation which had been awarded the Customer Service Excellence Standard?

3 What would your reaction be if you were an employee in an organisation which had been awarded the Customer Service Excellence Standard?

ISO 9001

ISO 9001 is a Business Management Standard award designed to help organisations to manage their processes and is subject to regular validation by external assessors. It concentrates on process management, checks that systems are in place and that everyone is sure of his/her role in the organisation. This Standard looks at how the business has implemented Quality Assurance in the areas of facilities, people, training, services and equipment.

Achieving the award is only the first step as the business must undergo continual assessment to ensure that standards are being maintained.

ISO 9001 looks at how the business:

- trains its staff
- checks that its products or services are of high quality
- handles mistakes and responds to consumers
- conducts sales, design and development, purchases, manufacturing and services
- has systems to improve its products or services
- uses its resources.

The advantages for the business of having the ISO 9001 award are:

- greater efficiency and less waste
- successful working practices
- risk management
- increased customer satisfaction
- greater consistency in its products or services
- advantage over its competitors
- increased profits.

The disadvantages for the business of applying for the ISO 9001 award are:

- the cost involved in getting and keeping the standard
- the time involved in the process
- difficulty of getting some staff to accept change.

European Foundation for Quality Management (EFQM)

The European Foundation for Quality Management (EFQM) was created in order to encourage European business organisations to improve their standards so that European businesses would be world leaders and achieve total advantage over their competitors.

The EFQM model has nine criteria which look at what the business does and what it achieves:

- leadership
- policy and strategy
- people
- people results
- partnership and resources
- processes
- customer results
- society results
- key performance results.

Investors in People (IIP)

At the very centre of the award '**Investors in People** (IIP)' is the importance of the people who work in the business and the need to invest in their training and development.

IIP establishes a level of good training practice so that the people in the business can help the business to achieve its goals. Employees feel motivated by the process, resulting in all-round and continuous improvement.

The idea behind the Investors in People award is that if the people who work in a business are improved, they will improve the business's systems which, in turn, will improve the performance of the entire business.

⌃ The IIP's chain of thought

The Investors in People scheme is externally assessed and is about:

▸ resolving all the people issues in the business

▸ improving the skill levels of all staff

▸ supporting the development of everyone working in the business

▸ getting people to take responsibility for their own development

▸ encouraging people to improve their own performance

▸ getting everyone to understand the business's aims.

Why do businesses apply for quality awards?

By having quality awards, businesses experience the following advantages:

▸ Having an award is good for the image of the business.

▸ Having an award assures the public that the business's product or service is good.

▸ Having an award gives the business an advantage over its competitors.

▸ Having an award should improve the profitability of the business.

▸ Having an award motivates the employees as they feel they are part of a good business.

▸ Working for an award encourages team spirit in the business.

Activity

Answer the following questions:

1 What effect might an Investors in People award have on the careers of employees in the business?

2 Getting employees to understand the business's aims is an important part of the Investors in People award. What benefit would this be to the business?

Activity

Now do some research in two businesses in your area.

Find out if they have been awarded any recognised quality standard or are working for one at the present time.

1 Find out the details of their award(s).

2 Analyse the reasons why those businesses have applied for the awards.

Examination question

Explain the reasons why a business may wish to obtain a quality standard.   (6 marks)

How to answer this question

You are not told how many points to explain. There are 6 marks in total, so you should explain three reasons which would be awarded up to 2 marks each.

Examination question

Define the term 'quality assurance' and name the quality standard which is most concerned with people in the business.   (3 marks)

How to answer this question

This is a straightforward question which deals simply with recall of knowledge. First, say what is meant by quality assurance (2 marks) and then name the appropriate quality standard (1 mark).

Checklist ✓

At this stage you should be able to:

○ explain the term 'quality assurance' and its importance to a business

○ understand the quality awards – Customer Service Excellence Award, ISO 9001, EFQM and Investors in People

○ analyse the reasons why businesses apply for quality standards.

Employers have a general duty to ensure, so far as is reasonably practicable, the health, safety and welfare of their employees at work. They also have a duty towards people who are not their employees but use their premises.

There is legislation covering occupational health and safety in the United Kingdom and in Northern Ireland. This legislation makes employers responsible for the health and safety of employees by ensuring that:

- they provide safe equipment
- employees know how to handle dangerous substances such as chemicals
- employees are trained in health and safety matters.

The law applies to all places of work and sets out the responsibilities of both employers and employees to ensure that the work environment is safe.

Rights and responsibilities of employers in the area of health and safety

Employers are expected to:

- ensure the safe use of articles and substances
- provide health and safety training for employees
- appoint a Health and Safety Officer
- carry out regular fire drills
- provide protective clothing, such as goggles, where necessary

- maintain all machinery and systems in efficient working order
- provide clear signs and enough space for people to move around with ease
- ensure safe practices in the workplace
- have the premises adequately ventilated and well lit
- provide suitable workstations with supportive seating for office-type work
- maintain an indoor temperature of at least 16 degrees Celsius (or 13 degrees Celsius if the work involves physical activity)
- carry out cleaning and the removal of waste regularly
- equip the premises with drinking water, clean washing facilities and toilets
- provide storage space for employees' clothing
- provide facilities for rest periods and to eat meals.

Rights and responsibilities of employees in the area of health and safety

Employees have a duty to support the health and safety procedures in their workplace and to take reasonable care of their own health and safety as well as the health and safety of other people.

Employees are expected to:

▶ take all reasonable care for their own health and safety and the safety of others

▶ co-operate in meeting the business's health and safety requirements

▶ use all equipment carefully to keep it in good working order

▶ wear the protective clothing and equipment provided

▶ undergo health and safety training

▶ report all faults and dangers.

The Health and Safety Executive (HSE)

The Health and Safety Executive is the body which has responsibility for enforcing health and safety legislation. It also produces advice on health and safety matters and guidance on the law. The Executive shares this responsibility with the local councils, depending on the health and safety issue. It also conducts research into the working and effectiveness of regulations, advising Government after consultation with both employers and employees.

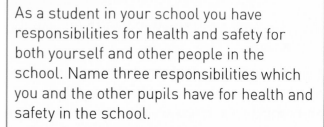

Activity

As a student in your school you have responsibilities for health and safety for both yourself and other people in the school. Name three responsibilities which you and the other pupils have for health and safety in the school.

Examination question ↻

Discuss two responsibilities of an employer and two responsibilities of an employee in relation to Health and Safety. (8 marks)

How to answer this question

There are two distinct parts in this question. First name and discuss two responsibilities which an employer has to keep employees safe (2 marks for each responsibility). Secondly, name and discuss two responsibilities which an employee has for safety in the workplace (2 marks for each responsibility).

Activity

In the following word search, find the words shown in the list. The words can be read in straight lines, horizontally, vertically or diagonally, either backwards or forwards. There is no overlap of words in the grid.

primary	secondary	tertiary	batch	flow	process	job	inventory
quality	health	safety	specialisation		division		labour

p	a	w	s	h	h	r	u	o	b	a	l	z	i	v	w
r	v	n	b	e	g	h	k	j	l	u	p	k	n	m	o
i	z	c	b	n	c	m	q	w	y	k	l	g	v	c	l
m	a	s	p	d	f	o	t	y	j	k	l	q	e	v	f
a	z	x	r	v	h	b	n	m	l	t	y	q	n	w	d
r	w	e	o	r	t	b	n	d	n	m	z	x	t	c	v
y	q	w	c	e	l	r	t	y	a	u	i	o	o	p	l
z	x	c	e	c	a	v	b	v	n	r	m	k	r	l	r
b	r	s	s	w	e	q	w	e	y	u	y	t	y	r	e
o	z	x	s	a	h	s	d	d	r	t	h	j	k	l	m
j	q	w	e	d	f	g	s	a	f	e	t	y	a	d	b
m	n	b	v	c	x	z	l	k	j	h	g	f	d	s	a
z	t	e	r	t	i	a	r	y	u	y	t	r	e	w	t
q	a	z	x	c	d	v	f	v	f	b	g	n	h	j	c
m	n	b	v	c	x	z	a	q	u	a	l	i	t	y	h
d	i	v	i	s	i	o	n	p	o	i	u	y	t	r	e
r	e	w	q	u	i	o	p	l	k	j	h	g	f	d	s
s	p	e	c	i	a	l	i	s	a	t	i	o	n	s	a

Checklist ✓

At this stage you should be able to:
○ understand the implications of health and safety legislation for a business
○ discuss the rights and responsibilities of employers for health and safety
○ discuss the rights and responsibilities of employees for health and safety
○ explain the role of the Health and Safety Executive (HSE).

DEVELOPING A BUSINESS

To develop knowledge and critical understanding of:

▶ recruitment and selection practices

▶ the importance of a business having motivated and well-trained employees

▶ signs of business success and failure

▶ ways in which a business may grow

▶ sources of finance

▶ basic cash flow forecasts

▶ interpretation of simple financial statements

▶ ratio analysis and breakeven.

4 Human resources
4.1 Recruitment

Recruitment is the employment of new workers.

Good employers realise that the most important resource in any business is the people who work there. It is possible for a business to have very modern technology and state-of-the-art premises but unless it employs the best possible work force it will never achieve its best results. For this reason, employers put great emphasis on their recruitment procedures and on getting the best employees to suit their requirements.

Businesses need to recruit new employees for several reasons. They may need to:

- employ extra workers because the business has grown
- bring in people who have skills they need in the business, but do not have
- replace employees who have left because of **retirement**, **resignation**, **promotion** or **dismissal**.

Activity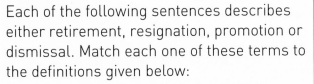

Each of the following sentences describes either retirement, resignation, promotion or dismissal. Match each one of these terms to the definitions given below:

1 This is when a person leaves because he/she has reached the end of his/her working life.
2 This is when a person has lost his/her job because of poor work or behaviour.
3 This is when a person leaves the post to move to a more senior post.
4 This is when a person leaves to go to another job.

Before this recruitment procedure starts, the employer must decide exactly what the organisation needs. For example, the employer will have to carry out a **needs analysis** in order to be clear about the following:

- Which skills and qualifications are required in the organisation?
- How many new employees are needed?
- Are the new employees required full time or part time?
- Should they be **permanent** or **temporary**?
- How soon would the new employee(s) need to start work?

Recruitment procedure

The stages in the procedure may vary from business to business but the following is typical.

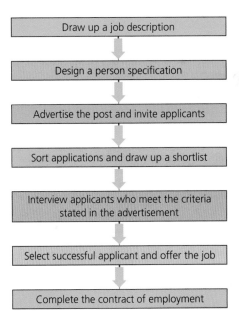

Draw up a job description

Design a person specification

Advertise the post and invite applicants

Sort applications and draw up a shortlist

Interview applicants who meet the criteria stated in the advertisement

Select successful applicant and offer the job

Complete the contract of employment

Case study

In this section we will work through the recruitment procedure to be used in Highwater College, River Road, Strabane for the recruitment of four classroom assistants.

The College Principal has decided on the following needs for the positions:

Duties: Each classroom assistant to assist one special needs pupil at all school activities.

Qualifications Required: Minimum 5 GCSEs at A*–C (must include English and Mathematics)

Number of Employees: Four

Terms of Employment: 30 hours per week   Permanent

Date of Employment: 10 November 2...

The next stage is to design an advertisement. The advertisement for the classroom assistants is shown here:

Highwater College
River Road
Strabane

We invite applications for the following posts:

4 × Classroom Assistant Positions (Special Needs)
30 hours per week £15,882–£16,998 per annum
(£8.4607–£9.0553 per hour).

Applicants must have a minimum of 5 GCSEs Grade A*–C or equivalent qualifications to include English and Mathematics.

It is desirable that applicants have experience of working with children with special needs in a post-primary school setting.

For application forms and further details, please send an A4 S.A.E. to the School Office.
Closing date is Noon, Friday 23rd September 2......

Highwater College is an Equal Opportunity Employer. Posts involving work in educational institutions are subject to the provisions of the Safeguarding Vulnerable Groups(NI)Order 2007

Three other documents are required in the recruitment procedure:

1 Job description

The main purpose of a **job description** is to define the main duties and responsibilities of the post. It also acts as a reference document in the event of later disputes. This document is essential so that both the employee and the employer are clear about what the employee might be expected to do.

A copy of the job description is sent to each applicant for the job so that he/she is clear what is required in the job.

The job description should show:

▶ the title of the job

▶ the place where the job will be done

▶ conditions and hours of work

▶ a list of the main duties required in the job

▶ the person to whom the job holder reports (the line manager)

▶ names of any people who report to the job holder

▶ details of any equipment or parts of premises for which the job holder is responsible

▶ date of first issue of the job description and any updates

Here is the Job Description for the Classroom Assistant post in Highwater College.

Case study

HIGHWATER COLLEGE

Job Description

POST TITLE: Classroom Assistant – Special Educational Needs

PLACE OF WORK: Highwater College, River Road, Strabane

RESPONSIBLE TO: The Principal

Name:

Appointed with effect from: 7 November 2.....

MAIN DUTIES AND RESPONSIBILITIES:
Assist the teacher with support and care of student(s) with special educational needs.
Assist student(s) in moving around school and on and off transport.
Ensure the students are able to use equipment and materials provided.
Assist in motivating and encouraging the students(s) as required.
Meet student's physical/medical needs as required.
Supervise groups of students, or individual students on specified activities.
Assist with classroom administration.
Attend relevant in-service training.

Annual Leave Entitlement: 21/28 days in a full holiday year in addition to 12 public and extra statutory holidays.

Terms and Conditions of Service
The main terms and conditions of employment are those for Classroom Assistants (Special Needs)

Hours of work
30 hours per week

General Conditions of Appointment
Appointments are subject to production of satisfactory evidence of health probationary period of six months sickness and maternity benefit regulations.

Post Holder _____   Date _____

Principal _____   Date _____

2 Person specification

A **person specification** is drawn up after the job description has been prepared. Its purpose is to identify what an ideal applicant for the post should have in terms of personal qualities, knowledge, qualifications, skills and previous work experience. A person specification is

for the use of the employer and would not be seen by the applicant for the post.

Usually the characteristics, achievements, qualifications, skills and previous work experience are listed, under two sub-headings, as essential or desirable.

The person specification for the Classroom Assistants in Highwater College would look like this:

HIGHWATER COLLEGE
PERSON SPECIFICATION
POST: CLASSROOM ASST (SPECIAL NEEDS)

ESSENTIAL CRITERIA
Qualifications (Educational) • 5 GCSEs at grades A*–C or equivalent qualifications to include English and Mathematics • Other relevant courses/training
Experience • Experience of working with children with special needs in a post primary setting • Experience of supporting the work of the teacher
Knowledge • Role of a classroom assistant • Needs of students including physical, educational, emotional and social needs of children • Discipline and safety in school
Skills • Interpersonal skills • Ability to supervise groups of children • Ability to get the best from students • Ability to listen and respond effectively
Personal Qualities • Caring and patient • Self-reliant and showing initiative • Flexible • Tactful and discreet • Common sense
DESIRABLE CRITERIA
Qualification status in childcare
Knowledge of approaches to encouraging children to learn

At this stage, all applicants who meet the criteria will be invited for interview and four successful applicants will be offered the posts of classroom assistants. A Contract will be drawn up and given to each successful applicant within eight weeks of starting work.

3 Contract of employment
Purpose of a contract of employment

The main purpose of a **contract of employment** is to set out the rights and duties of both the employee and the employer. It is an agreement between the two parties and can be enforced by law. Therefore, it gives protection and security to both the employee and the employer. It begins when the employer makes an offer of work with payment of money and the employee accepts the offer at that rate and agrees to work. By law, a **full-time employee** must be given a contract of employment within eight weeks of starting to work for that employer.

Content of a contract of employment

The following details must appear on the contract:

▶ Names of the employer and the employee
▶ Name of line-manager
▶ Date of commencement of the job
▶ Title and description of the job
▶ Hours of work
▶ Agreed rates and method of payment or overtime payment
▶ Details of any pension schemes, **bonuses**
▶ Arrangements for the payment of any **commission**, bonuses or overtime
▶ Length of paid holiday entitlement
▶ Level and duration of sickness, injury and maternity pay entitlement
▶ Length of period of notice to be given
▶ Details of grievance and disciplinary procedures
▶ Name, job title and location of the firm's grievance officer.

A typical contract of employment would look like this:

CONTRACT OF EMPLOYMENT

Between

Employer

Employee

Title of Position held

Date of Commencement

Hours of work

Payment rate (including commission, bonuses and overtime)

Method of payment

Pension schemes which apply

Holiday entitlement

Sickness, injury and maternity pay entitlement

Period of notice of employment termination

Details of grievance and disciplinary procedures

This Contract may be altered only after consultation between the two parties named.

Signed on behalf of the Employer   Employee's Signature

....

Date   Date

Activity

Look in the Job Finder section of either your local newspaper or one of the national newspapers (*Belfast Telegraph*, *Irish News* or *Newsletter*) – there may be more variety in the nationals. Choose any job advertisement which interests you and cut it out.

Design a job description for the post you have selected, using the details in the advertisement to help you.

Next you should design a person specification for the post you have selected. Again, you may get some help from the details in the advertisement.

Make a copy of the details required in a Contract of Employment.

Assume that you have got the post you selected earlier from the newspaper. Call up your copy of the Contract and complete it as a Contract of Employment between yourself and the business named in the advertisement.

Examination question

John is applying for an accountant's post in the accountancy firm of 'Best Accounting'. The firm has sent John a Job Description and also has drawn up a Person Specification.

Explain one advantage for John of having a Job Description and name two details which a Job Description should contain.

Explain two purposes of a Person Specification from the firm's point of view. (8 marks)

How to answer this question

Give details of one advantage of having a Job Description and make sure it is an advantage for the applicant (up to 2 marks). Name two details on a Job Description (2 marks). Simply name the details – no explanation needed. Next, give two reasons why the firm draws up a Person Specification (2 reasons for up to 2 marks each).

Main methods of recruitment

Recruitment may be done either by advertising the post inside the business – known as **internal recruitment** – or outside the business, which is known as **external recruitment**.

Internal recruitment

The usual methods of internal recruitment are to advertise the post:

▶ on notice boards
▶ in internal news sheets

▶ by sending memos or e-mails to all employees.

Advantages of internal recruitment

▶ The applicants are familiar with the business.
▶ Existing employees are given the opportunity to gain promotion within the business.
▶ This improves morale of existing staff and provides motivation.
▶ It is less expensive than advertising externally.
▶ The process should take shorter time to complete.
▶ **Induction** training would not be required.

Disadvantages of internal recruitment

▶ The range of applicants is limited.
▶ It does not bring new skills and ideas into the business.
▶ No existing staff may be suitable.
▶ It could lead to staff discontent if one colleague is promoted over the other employees.
▶ Newly promoted employee may have to be trained for the new post.
▶ The existing job of the newly promoted employee will have to be filled.

Activity

There is a vacancy for a sales assistant in your school tuck shop. The person appointed will be required to work in the shop Monday to Friday before classes in the morning, at break-time and at lunch-time, during term time. Anyone interested in the post should apply to the School Secretary for further details regarding duties and pay.

Using a computer, design an advertisement for the post. The advertisement should be eye-catching and suitable for display on the school's notice board.

External recruitment

There are several reasons for the use of external recruitment:

▶ There may not be a suitable candidate within the business.

▶ None of the present employees may be interested in the post.

▶ Sometimes a business may wish to introduce 'new blood' who will bring in fresh ideas and up-to-date training.

Advantages of external recruitment

▶ The range of applicants is wider.

▶ It brings new skills and ideas into the business.

▶ It avoids jealousies among existing employees.

▶ Fully trained staff may be appointed so expense may be saved on training programmes.

▶ No other internal staff vacancies are created.

Disadvantages of external recruitment

▶ The applicants are not familiar with the business.

▶ Induction training is required for the new employee.

▶ Job opportunities are not created within the business for existing employees.

▶ Existing staff may feel undervalued and demotivated.

▶ Some external recruitment methods are very expensive.

▶ It is a slower process than internal recruitment.

Methods of external recruitment

The main methods are shown below.

The media

The term 'media' includes a range of methods.

Advertising in local newspapers is less expensive but does not reach a wide audience.

It would be suitable for jobs which are not very highly paid and for which people would not travel long distances.

Advertising in national newspapers is more expensive but is read by a greater number of people. Newspapers such as the *Belfast Telegraph*, *The Irish News* and the *Newsletter* have special Job Finder sections. This method of advertising would be suitable for jobs which are more highly paid and for which people would be more willing to travel.

Specialist magazines are read by certain groups of workers and are used to recruit highly skilled or specialist workers. For example, *The Lancet* is a magazine for doctors, the *Nursing Times* is of interest to nurses and the *Times Educational* Supplement is read by teachers and other people working in the field of education.

From time to time some television and radio stations broadcast details of job vacancies. This is usually done on a local basis and would have similar features to advertising in local newspapers.

The internet

There are several websites on the internet which advertise a range of jobs and which businesses may use. Many businesses also have their own websites on which they advertise their vacancies. The main advantages of using the internet are that it:

▶ is not expensive

▶ has a wide audience

▶ attracts candidates who are up to date with the latest technology.

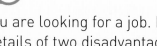

Activity

Imagine you are looking for a job. Name and give details of two disadvantages which using the internet would have for you when job hunting.

Job Centres

Job Centres are run by the government and are found in towns throughout the country. They display notices about available work on behalf of employers on notice boards in the centres, via the internet, on local radio and in newspapers. Job vacancies may also be viewed on www. jobcentreonline.com.

People who are unemployed, or are interested in a change of job, visit the Job Centres to find information and obtain advice about job vacancies and training courses. The Job Centres will help people to apply for suitable jobs and the big advantage is that the service is free. This method of recruitment is often used for finding workers who are skilled or semi-skilled such as factory workers, shop assistants and cleaners.

Activity

If you have access to the internet, search the Job Centre website and make a list of any vacancies in your home area which would be of interest to you.

Private recruitment agencies

There are several private recruitment agencies in Northern Ireland which offer the service of finding suitable candidates for available positions. An example is Diamond Recruitment Group.

People looking for work register with the agency and employers contact the agency with details of available work. The agency matches the candidate with the most suitable work available. When a person is appointed, the firm pays the agency for the service.

The advantage is that time is saved by the employer which is very useful when a temporary worker is required quickly, for example to fill an absence due to illness in an office. However, the service is expensive.

Factors which influence the choice of recruitment method

How a business recruits its employees will depend on several factors:

▶ the size of the business
▶ the amount of money available for advertising
▶ the type of work being offered
▶ where the firm is situated
▶ how many employees are required
▶ how quickly the new employee is needed.

Activity

Name the most suitable method of recruitment for each of the following positions:

1 A part-time office cleaner in Limavady.
2 The Principal of a College in Belfast.
3 A forklift operator in a hardware business in Garvagh.
4 A qualified physiotherapist in Daisy Hill Hospital, Newry.
5 A sales assistant for a supermarket in Coleraine.
6 A clerical officer, needed for two weeks, in an office in Portadown.

Examination question ↻

Explain one advantage and one disadvantage for a business of using external recruitment.   (4 marks)

How to answer this question

This is a straightforward question where you should give details of one advantage (up to 2 marks) and one disadvantage (up to 2 marks) of external recruitment. Make sure you explain an advantage and disadvantage from the point of view of the business.

The role of social media in recruitment

Social media is playing an increasingly important role in recruitment. Newspapers are no longer bought by everyone on a daily basis as was once the case, so not everyone would see an advertisement in the newspaper. Instead people depend on social media such as Twitter, Instagram, Facebook, Snatchat, and Linkedin, so businesses use these as additional channels through which

to recruit employees. Social media reaches people instantly and presents businesses with a great opportunity to get enquiries from people interested in finding work. Social media is a method of advertising posts but it is not possible to make application for work through social media. It is estimated that 39% of companies now use social media services as their primary digital tool.

The advantages of social media are:

▶ it allows for two-way communication with potential employees whereas traditional media such as television and newspapers are static and only allow for one-way communication

▶ it makes customers aware of the vacancies

▶ it has global reach and a blog or tweet or YouTube video can be viewed by millions almost for free.

Legal controls on recruitment and related ethical issues

The overall aim of legal controls on recruitment is to prevent discrimination at work.

Legal controls have been created in order to protect minority groups such as women, the disabled, people from differing religions and cultures, people of various sexual orientations and marital status.

Controls on recruitment fall into six categories – race, religion, disability, gender, marital status and sexual orientation.

Legal controls on race state that:

▶ people of all races, colours, nationalities or ethnic origin must be treated equally during the recruitment and selection process

▶ people of all races, colours, nationalities or ethnic origin must be treated equally in all aspects of employment and in training

▶ in Northern Ireland such conditions also apply to Irish Travellers

▶ the employer would be liable if he/she allowed any of his/her employees to discriminate against other employees on racial grounds.

There are exceptions to these provisions. The law would not have been broken where:

▶ a person of a particular racial group is required for a job – for example, in a dramatic performance or as a photographic model

▶ welfare services are being provided to a particular racial group and those services can best be provided by a person of the same racial group – social workers, for example.

▶ the employment is in a private household

▶ the employment is in a small business where there are fewer than six partners.

Legal controls on religion state that:

▶ people of all religious beliefs and political opinion should have equal opportunities in recruitment and employment

▶ employers must create a 'neutral area' in the workplace. This means that they must prohibit the display of flags, emblems, posters and graffiti or the circulation of materials or the singing of songs which would give offence or cause fear

▶ employers must register with the Equality Commission if they employ more than ten people

▶ employers must annually submit information about the religious composition of their workforces – including **part-time employees**, in order to keep a balance in the workplace.

There are exceptions to these legal provisions on religion. Excluded are:

▶ any occupation where the nature of the job requires it to be done by a person

holding a particular religious belief or political opinion – a minister of religion, for example.

Legal controls on disability state that:

▶ disabled people must have the same opportunities as other people in recruitment, training and selection for employment

▶ disabled people must not be treated less favourably than other people in their conditions of employment

▶ reasonable adjustments should be made to buildings to enable disabled people to work there, such as disabled toilets, ramps and lifts should be installed as well as car parking space provided.

Legal controls on gender state that:

▶ men and women should have equal treatment and opportunity in recruitment and selection and training

▶ men and women should have equal opportunities in promotion

▶ working conditions such as opportunities for retirement and pension provision must not discriminate on grounds of gender

▶ advertisements for jobs should not exclude either men or women

▶ men and women should have equal pay for equal value work. For this to apply, their work must be equally demanding or equally skilful and require equal levels of knowledge, decision making and responsibility

▶ women should not be discriminated against because of pregnancy or maternity leave

▶ the employer would be liable if he/she allowed any of his/her employees to discriminate against other employees on gender grounds.

Legal controls on marital status state that:

▶ it is unlawful to discriminate against someone because he/she is single, married, divorced, widowed, separated or is in a same sex partnership or marriage

▶ people in the above groups must be given equal opportunities in recruitment, selection and promotion in the workplace

▶ everyone must be given equal pay and conditions.

Legal controls on sexual orientation state that:

▶ it is unlawful to discriminate against someone because he/she is in a same sex marriage or relationship or in a heterosexual relationship or marriage

▶ people in the above groups must be given equal opportunities in recruitment, selection and promotion in the workplace

▶ everyone must be given equal pay and conditions.

Activity

Fill in the spaces in the sentences below:

1 Legal controls aim to prevent .... at work. They are designed to protect groups such as ..... and ....

2 Gender law forbids discrimination on the basis of a person's .... Or because he/ she is ....

3 Employers are obliged to make adjustments to the work premises for .... employees.

4 Two exceptions to the Race laws are when .... services are being provided or the work is in a ....

5 The law states that women performing the same, or broadly similar, work as ... must be given the same ....

Activity

You have to decide which legal provision has been broken in each of the following situations:

1 No car parking spaces were reserved for disabled employees.

2 A woman was not given a job because she was married.

3 Irish Travellers were refused part-time jobs.

4 The pay structure in a company stated that male secretaries would be paid £1 per hour above the rate paid to female secretaries.

5 The firm's main building had no wheelchair access.

6 The firm refused to employ any Chinese workers.

7 Political slogans were allowed on factory walls.

8 A job advertisement stated that only women need apply.

Ethical issues underlying anti-discrimination legislation

Legislation has been introduced so that proper rules of conduct are applied to recruitment, selection, training and employment and that discrimination, in all its forms, is prevented.

The ethical foundation of the legislation is that the most vulnerable groups in society – women, the disabled, people belonging to differing religions, other races, and everyone regardless of marital status or sexual orientation – are protected and given their rights.

The government, in passing such laws, is making sure that employers behave in an ethical way. They are obliged to treat all their employees equally and with respect. The underlying principle here is that everyone is equal in the eyes of the law, and therefore each one is entitled to equal treatment. In recruitment terms, the result should be that the best person is employed or given promotion regardless of that person's gender, religion, political opinion or physical ability.

The law makes sure that men and women are given equal opportunities in employment. A woman who has good qualifications and experience must be given the same chance to gain promotion as the men in the business. She cannot be refused a job, for example, because she may have to take maternity leave.

Legislation makes sure that a woman is treated in an equal way, and is given pay equal to that of her male colleagues where the work she does is of equal value.

Legislation also was passed to make sure that people of all religions or political beliefs are given equal opportunities to get employment.

Legally and ethically the disabled must be given equal opportunities to work. Where their qualifications are adequate, disabled people must be treated equally with able-bodied people in the recruitment process. Employers are obliged to overcome any physical difficulties in their premises by installing ramps, lifts and special toilets. In this way, the legislation recognises the contribution which the disabled make to the business world and ensures that their disability does not prevent them from making that contribution.

Laws are also designed to make sure that it would be possible for people from other cultures and races and everyone regardless of marital status or sexual orientation can get employment in Northern Ireland.

Role of the Equality Commission for Northern Ireland

Equality Commission
FOR NORTHERN IRELAND

▲ The Equality Commission

The Equality Commission for Northern Ireland was established under the Northern Ireland Act, 1998. Its aim is to help build a more equal society in Northern Ireland. It is an independent public body which oversees equality and discrimination law in Northern Ireland.

The Commission's mission statement illustrates this aim:

> To value and promote respect for diversity, eliminate unlawful discrimination and achieve equality of opportunity for all.

How does the Equality Commission do this?

Its duties include:

▶ working to eliminate unlawful discrimination
▶ promoting equality of opportunity and encouraging good practice
▶ promoting good relations between people of different racial groups
▶ keeping the relevant laws under review.

The Commission's main work is to give advice and assistance to people who believe that they have been treated unfairly or discriminated against on grounds of their colour, race, nationality, ethnic or national origin (including being an Irish traveller), religious belief, political opinion, gender, sexual orientation, marital status or disability.

In cases where legal action is needed, the Commission will arrange legal representation. It can take legal action against individuals and organisations in some circumstances – for example, if they have published an advertisement which discriminates against someone from one of the groups shown in the previous list.

The Commission also sees that the law on equality is enforced in order to bring about greater equality in the world of work and in society in general. The Commission has powers to ensure that employers monitor and review their employment practices as well as the composition of their workforce. For example, employers must show that they are willing to employ both men and women, both single and married workers, people with different religious or political opinions, people of any race or ethnic origin and people with disabilities.

In addition, the Commission will:

▶ provide information, advisory and training services

▶ publish Codes of Practice which set standards for fairness and equality in employment, pay, housing and the provision of goods and services

▶ make sure that public sector organisations take equality into account

▶ undertake research into equality issues

▶ award grants for promotional and educational work

▶ carry out public education campaigns to raise awareness of equality issues.

Responsibility for implementing the fair employment legislation now rests with the Equality Commission. It is the duty of the Commission to:

▶ work to eliminate religious discrimination

▶ give advice to employers on their practices

▶ help anyone who has a complaint and requests advice.

The Equality Commission has powers to investigate any employer any time and, if necessary, to bring an employer before a Fair Employment Tribunal. The Commission may also issue directions on measures which must be taken by employers.

Activity

Study the following case and answer the questions at the end.

A woman was absent from her company on maternity leave. During her absence, two promotion posts were advertised internally and filled without her being told about the positions.

She said that the company was guilty of discrimination against her because of her sex and pregnancy. She argued that because she was not told about the posts, she had not been able to apply for promotion.

1 In your opinion, is the woman's allegation of discrimination reasonable?

2 What action would you have advised the company to take when advertising the post?

Checklist ✓

At this stage you should be able to:

○ describe and explain the purposes and content of a job description, person specification and contract of employment

○ discuss and evaluate the advantages and disadvantages of internal and external recruitment

○ discuss the role of social media in recruitment

○ understand the legal controls on recruitment in relation to race, religion, disability, gender, marital status and sexual orientation

○ understand the ethical issues underlining the legislation

○ understand the role of the Equality Commission for Northern Ireland.

4.2 Selection

When you become involved in the selection process, remember that this is the first impression the employer will have of you, and first impressions do count. You never get a second chance to make a first impression!

Methods of selection

After the recruitment stage, the next step is for the employer to choose the new employee from the list of applicants who have applied for the position. That is known as the selection process.

In order to choose the most suitable applicant, it is important for the employer to find as much information as possible about all the applicants.

To do this, the following six methods of selection are most commonly used:

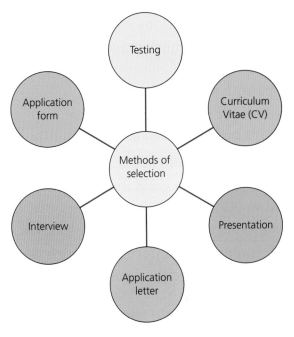

Application form

Sometimes an employer asks the applicants to complete a form on which they must answer all questions.

The advantages of an application form are:
▶ form contains the exact information which the employer needs
▶ this makes it easy for the employer to compare applicants
▶ it helps with short-listing
▶ the employer can see how well the applicant has organised the information.

The disadvantages of an application form are:
▶ does not prove how good the applicant would be at the job
▶ takes time to sift through the information
▶ it may be written by another person
▶ it may contain false information, such as qualifications.

When completing an application form it is important to:
▶ work neatly and accurately
▶ complete all sections
▶ work in black or blue ink – NEVER in pencil
▶ sign and date the form
▶ that all details are correct – untrue information would rule out your application.

Application letter

Sometimes the advertisement states that the applicant should reply by writing a letter of application. An applicant for a job has to show in the application letter that he/she is suitable for the post. The letter should make the employer want to meet the applicant.

The advantages of an application letter are:

▶ shows the level of the applicant's written communication skills

▶ shows the applicant's presentation of work and level of preparation

▶ it helps with short-listing.

The disadvantages of an application letter are:

▶ does not prove how good the applicant would be at the job

▶ takes time to read all the letters

▶ it may be written by another person

▶ it may contain false information, such as qualifications

▶ information is not standardised as on a form.

An application letter should include the applicant's:

▶ personal details

▶ educational background

▶ qualifications and work experience

▶ names of previous employers

▶ names and addresses of two referees

▶ details of personal hobbies, interests and achievements.

All the rules for completing an application form also apply when writing a letter of application – work neatly and accurately, complete all sections, use black or blue ink and check all details.

Activity

HIGHWATER COLLEGE, RIVER ROAD, STRABANE

Classroom Assistant

Required to work in the college.

30 hours per week
Salary Scale £15,882–£16,998 per annum

Applicants for the above post should have a minimum of:
5 GCSEs (Grades A*–C) including English and Mathematics

Application by letter to be received by the Principal by 23 September......

You should now write a letter of application, on your own behalf, for the above position.

Curriculum Vitae

Sometimes the advertisement asks the applicant to include a **Curriculum Vitae** (CV).

A Curriculum Vitae is simply a list of all the applicant's qualifications, work and achievements to that date.

The advantages of a Curriculum Vitae are:

▶ it contains all details of the applicant's education, qualifications and experience

▶ it shows the applicant's presentation and preparation

▶ it helps with short-listing

▶ the employer can see how well the applicant has organised the information.

The disadvantages of an application form are:

▶ does not prove how good the applicant would be at the job

▶ takes time to sift through the information

▶ it may contain false information, such as qualifications.

There is a standard format for a curriculum vitae and it includes the applicant's:

- personal details – name, address, telephone number, nationality, marital status and date of birth
- educational background
- qualifications
- work experience
- positions of responsibility
- previous employers
- details of two referees
- personal hobbies and interests
- other achievements.

When the employers receive all the application forms, letters and CVs they will sort them into two groups – suitable and unsuitable applicants. The 'suitable' group will include those who meet all the criteria in the advertisement, and the 'unsuitable' group will include those who do not meet the criteria.

Unsuitable applicants are then informed by letter that they have been unsuccessful and suitable applicants are invited to undertake a test or an interview or give a presentation.

Activity

You are now ready to design your own Curriculum Vitae. Begin by listing all the results of examinations you have sat, sports awards you have achieved, trips you have gone on, details of your work experience and any school positions you hold or have held such as prefect, sports captain or librarian etc.

Use a computer to arrange all that information, plus your personal details, under the headings given above. Later you can add to the CV as you pass more examinations etc.

Examination question

A candidate for a position of a doctor's receptionist has been asked to include a Curriculum Vitae (CV). Explain what a Curriculum Vitae (CV) is, and why the employer has used it as a method of selection. (4 marks)

How to answer this question

You should provide a short explanation of a CV for which up to 2 marks will be awarded. Explain one advantage of a CV as a reason why the employer has used this method of selection for the remaining 2 marks. Make sure you give an advantage which would apply to a receptionist's position.

Testing

Two types of tests are frequently used – practical tests and psychometric tests.

Practical tests are more usual in the selection process for manual, practical jobs. In a practical test the applicant would be asked to undertake a piece of work which would test skills required in the business. For example, an applicant for the job as a computer operator may be asked to key in a letter or construct a database. This shows the employer whether the applicant's computer skills reach the level required in the business.

Psychometric tests are usually used when management level positions are being filled. Psychometric tests provide a description of the personality of the applicant, and the results are compared with the person specification.

The applicants have to answer multiple choice questions about themselves which are designed to show what they like or dislike and how they would react in certain situations.

The advantages of testing are:

▶ shows the level of the applicant's practical skills

▶ shows the applicant's organisation and approach to the work

▶ proves the information on the application form.

The disadvantage of testing is:

▶ the applicant may become nervous under test conditions.

Examination question

The Sea Shells Hotel uses testing as its method of selection of some new employees. Explain one important advantage for the hotel of this method, and name one type of hotel employee for whom it would be suitable.   (3 marks)

How to answer this question

Name and explain one advantage of testing (2 marks) and then name the type of employee (1 mark). Make sure that your answers relate to a hotel.

Interview

Interviews are very frequently used in the selection process. The applicants who have been short-listed are invited to an interview where they meet representatives of the business to answer questions and discuss the post.

At the interview, all interviewees are asked the same questions and given the same time so that the employer can later compare the answers given.

The advantages of an interview are:

▶ it shows the level of the applicant's oral communication skills

▶ it shows the applicant's personality and appearance

▶ it shows the applicant's attitude and confidence

▶ it allows the employer to check information on the application form

▶ it permits two-way communication between applicant and employer.

The disadvantage of an interview is:

▶ it can be intimidating so the interviewee may become nervous.

It is important for the applicant to:

▶ prepare thoroughly for an interview

▶ do research on the company

▶ dress suitably

▶ act naturally in the interview

▶ show a genuine interest in the organisation

▶ arrive in good time.

Activity

Refer back to the position in Highwater College for which you wrote an Application Letter. You have just heard that you are being interviewed for the job.

1 Draft three questions which you think you may be asked.

2 Draft one question which would be appropriate for you to ask at the interview.

3 What else might you do to prepare for the interview?

Presentation

It is common for applicants for management positions to be asked to give a presentation as well as be interviewed. In this situation, the applicant would be given a title in advance and told the length of time the presentation should last.

The applicant would be expected to talk on the prepared subject which would be related to the work of the particular post. For example, applicants for a shop manager's post may be asked to speak on their ideas for motivating staff or increasing turnover.

The advantages of a presentation are:
▶ it shows the level of the applicant's preparation
▶ it shows the applicant's personality and communication skills
▶ it shows ideas the applicant may have about the job.

The disadvantage of a presentation is:
▶ it can be intimidating so the applicant may become nervous.

Activity

You have been asked to make a presentation when you attend the interview for the position of Classroom Assistant in Highwater College. You have been given the topic in advance and the title is 'The importance of the role of the Classroom Assistant'. You have to speak for a maximum of five minutes and may use PowerPoint or an overhead projector if you wish.

Prepare your presentation for use at the interview.

Responsibilities of employers and employees in the selection process

Both employers and employees have the same responsibilities in the selection process. There are four main obligations which are expected from all parties. They are honesty, objectivity, fairness and confidentiality.

Honesty

It is expected that both employer and employee would be totally honest with each other. For example, documents provided by the employer, such as the job description or advertisement, must be accurate and clear. All other information given about the job – for example pay or holidays – would be expected to be totally honest.

The employees must also provide honest information regarding such details as their qualifications and experience. No information should be left out by the employee if it would influence the final decision – a criminal record, for example.

Objectivity

Both parties are expected to be totally without prejudice about each other. For example, the employer could not reject applicants simply on the basis of their disability, religion, political views, social background, ethnic origin or gender. The employer has a responsibility to find the best person for the position, regardless of any other consideration.

Fairness

Total fairness is required by all parties. The employer, for example, must allocate equal time and consideration to each candidate in an interview and must ask the same questions to everyone. The same conditions must be applied to each person.

The employee must also be totally fair by disclosing full and accurate information.

Confidentiality

Both employee and employer must treat all information learned about each other as strictly confidential. The prospective employee must not talk to others about details of the business and the employer must not give personal details of the applicants to third parties.

Checklist ✓

At this stage you should be able to:
- ○ describe the main methods of selection
- ○ evaluate selection methods in different circumstances
- ○ discuss the responsibilities of employers and employees in selection.

4.3 Appraisal

An **appraisal** is the process of assessing an employee's performance in his/her job.

Reasons for appraisal and its importance

Employers are always anxious to know how to use their employees most effectively and to be aware of their strengths and weaknesses. Performance appraisal is used to discover this information.

Appraisal provides feedback to an employee on his/her performance. The system shows how performance could be improved and considers how the employee's career could be developed.

After identifying the employees' strengths and weaknesses through the process of appraisal, the employer may decide to reward employees who are performing well, or possibly to offer training to other employees where appraisal has shown weaknesses.

Appraisal is also frequently used to decide on the level of an employee's salary. In this case, the employee's effectiveness in the business is linked to his/her pay – a system known as 'performance related pay' – which is not appropriate for all types of work.

The reasons for appraisal are shown in the figure below.

To identify:
- Staff strengths and weaknesses
- The most effective use of employees
- Staff promotion possibilities
- Training requirements for staff
- Appropriate level of pay

Activity

Name two occupations where performance-related pay would be unfair and give reasons why it would not suit those occupations.

Advantages of appraisal for employees:

- ▶ gives them opportunities for promotion and sets pay levels
- ▶ makes sure that they receive training if necessary
- ▶ allows them to achieve their full potential
- ▶ lets them communicate with the employer on a one-to-one basis
- ▶ gives them an opportunity to discuss problems
- ▶ provides clear objectives
- ▶ acts as a motivator.

Advantages of appraisal for employers:

- ▶ helps in the planning and development of the business's human resource provision
- ▶ shows up staff strengths and allows the business to use the best employees efficiently
- ▶ identifies staff weaknesses and helps the business to plan an effective training programme
- ▶ increases staff competence and overall productivity
- ▶ improves the profitability of the business as a result.

Methods of appraisal and their evaluation

There are many methods of staff appraisal and the choice of method depends on the individual business and the type of work it does. The most commonly used ones are discussed here.

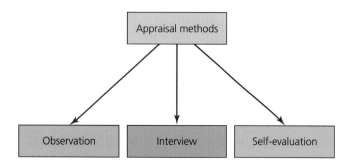

Observation

Observation is where the employee is watched doing his/her work, usually by the person who is that employee's immediate superior. For example, a shop floor worker would be observed by a supervisor and the supervisor may be observed by a manager.

Observation is a useful method of appraisal because:

▶ it allows employees to be observed in their usual surroundings

▶ it gives a true picture of employees' work.

However, some employees may find it off-putting to be observed doing their work. Observation is usually accompanied by an interview.

Examination question

Sportslife is a sports shop which uses observation as the method of appraisal of its sales staff. Describe this method of appraisal and explain two of its advantages. (6 marks)

How to answer this question

Write a description of what is meant by observation (for up to 2 marks). Explain two advantages of observation showing how they could apply to sales persons – up to 2 marks for each advantage fully explained.

Interview

An appraisal interview is a one-to-one discussion between the employee who is being appraised (the **appraisee**) and the supervisor or manager who is carrying out the appraisal (the **appraiser**).

The interview is a very useful method of appraisal because:

▶ it gives both parties a private opportunity to discuss the employee's work and progress

▶ it allows the employee to put forward his/her own ideas

▶ it diagnoses problems in work and tries to find solutions.

At the end of the interview, the appraiser completes a form which shows such qualities as:

▶ employee's level of initiative

▶ employee's ability to cope with pressure

▶ employee's leadership skills.

Self-evaluation

Employees are encouraged to undertake self-evaluation, which is simply looking critically at one's own work and seeking ways to improve its quality or finding easier, more efficient ways of performing it.

Self-evaluation has the advantage of making the employee more responsible for his/her own work. However, one disadvantage is that the worker may not be aware of his/her own faults or know how to improve.

Activity

This is an opportunity for you to carry out self-evaluation of your own performance in school for the school year so far. Take the exercise seriously because it could help you to improve your standard. Include all areas of your school life – examination subjects, sport, extra-curricular activity, etc.

1 Write down what you feel you have done well.

2 List the areas where you have not done so well.

3 Examine why you did not perform so well in those areas.

4 Finally, think of ways in which you could improve your weak points. It may be useful to get the help of your teacher to do this.

Activity

Match the appropriate sections in the following table.

Appraisal is	training requirements for staff
Performance related pay	is watched doing his/her work
Appraisal is used to identify	is known as the appraisee
Employees benefit from appraisal as it	profitability should improve
Employers use appraisal to help them	assessing an employee's performance
As a result of appraisal the firm's	interview
Observation is where the employee	is known as the appraiser
Observation is usually accompanied by	is not suitable for all types of work
The employee who is being appraised	to increase staff competence
The person carrying out the appraisal	allows them to achieve their full potential
An appraisal interview is a one-to-one	at one's own work
Self-appraisal is looking critically	discussion between appraiser and appraisee

Examination question

Appraisal is undertaken each year in Cute Cuts Hairdressing Salon. Explain three benefits which appraisal would have for Cute Cuts as an employer. (6 marks)

How to answer this question

It is important that the benefits (advantages) of appraisal are related to a hairdressing business. There are 2 marks for each benefit which is fully explained.

Checklist ✓

At this stage you should be able to:
- explain the reasons for and the importance of staff appraisal
- analyse the advantages of appraisal for employees
- analyse the advantages of appraisal for employers
- identify and evaluate observation, self-evaluation and interview as methods of appraisal.

Training is defined as 'the acquisition of knowledge and skills which can be applied to a particular job'.

Reasons for staff training

There are three major reasons for staff training.

1 Induction

Induction is the name given to the introduction of new employees to a business. It is not designed to show them how to do their job but it is designed to make new employees feel comfortable in the new workplace and to help them to fit in to their new surroundings. Induction enables new employees to understand the ethos and work of the organisation and to play their part more efficiently.

The content of the induction programme would vary from business to business. It usually includes a guided tour of the buildings, an introduction to work colleagues and line manager, a talk or video on the business's aims and an explanation of the business's health and safety procedures. It may also explain how they are paid and opportunities for promotion within the business. The overall aim of induction training is to make the new employee feel welcome and at home in the business.

2 Change in procedures

Training is not only for new staff. Employees who have been working in the business for years also need to undergo training courses to upgrade their skills and knowledge and to keep up-to-date. This may be necessary because new technology has been introduced into the business and employees need to become familiar with its use.

Sometimes the business's product changes and employees have to learn new information and be trained in the new methods required to make that change.

3 To become more competitive

Businesses also invest in training for employees in order to improve their competitiveness. Their aim is to maximise sales and profits. To do this they are constantly looking for ways to make their product or service better and to produce it in a shorter time, than the product or service offered by other businesses. This requires training programmes designed to improve the efficiency of the employees.

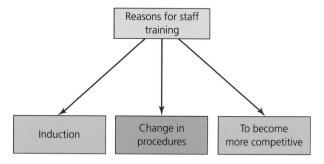

Examination question

Answer the following questions:

1 Name two reasons why induction is helpful for a new employee in a business.

2 Explain one advantage which induction has for the business. (4 marks)

How to answer this question

Simply state two reasons which, if correct from an employee's point of view, will be given 2 marks. No explanation is needed as you are just asked to name the reasons. In the second part, a full explanation is needed of one advantage from the point of view of the business (2 marks).

Advantages of training for the business and employees

Businesses undertake constant training which they consider important and beneficial from the point of view of both the business and the employees for the following reasons:

▶ New employees will be properly inducted into the business.

▶ Employees will be equipped to cope with constant changes in technology.

▶ Employees will have updated skills.

▶ Employees will have the required information for the introduction of new methods.

▶ A highly trained workforce is more efficient and effective.

▶ Having more effective employees improves the quality of the business's products which will lead to increased sales and profits for the business.

▶ This improves customer satisfaction with the products/services.

▶ Training of employees helps the business to keep ahead of its competitors.

▶ Training improves the corporate image of the business.

▶ Training provides motivation for employees.

▶ Training decreases the possibility of accidents in the workplace.

▶ Training decreases the supervision required for employees.

▶ Training reduces the risk of redundancy for employees.

▶ Multi skilled workers are flexible and can undertake different jobs in the business.

▶ Highly trained employees have better opportunities for promotion in the business.

▶ A business which has a highly trained staff and uses up-to-date methods earns a good reputation both as an employer and as a competitor in the marketplace.

Disadvantages of training for the business and employees

▶ Training programmes are expensive for the business.

▶ Employees have to be given time off work to undertake training.

▶ There is a risk that well-trained employees will leave to take work with the competitors.

▶ Highly trained employees may demand higher pay levels.

Types of training

There are two types of training – on-the-job and off-the-job.

On-the-job training

On-the-job training is the most common form of training for unskilled and semi-skilled workers. It is training given at the employee's normal place of work during his/her normal working hours.

Advantages of on-the-job training are:

▶ the content of the training is designed for that business

▶ it uses the equipment/machinery which the worker will be using in his/her work

▶ the employee is supervised by the employer or manager throughout the training

▶ the work of the business is not interrupted and the employee remains at work

▶ everyone knows one another

▶ employees feel at home in their own surroundings

▶ it is less expensive for the company than **off-the-job training**.

Disadvantages of on-the-job training are:

▶ the quality of the training may not be as good
▶ the employee is not able to share experiences with workers from other companies.

On-the-job training may be done in a variety of ways.

Internal courses

Sometimes employers run courses inside their own business and use their own machinery and equipment. This means that the content of the course is designed specifically for that business.

This method is very effective because the employee is shown how to do the work and can practise it under supervision.

Work shadowing

Sometimes the new employee 'shadows' an experienced employee. This means that they work alongside one another and the trainee learns from the experienced worker.

Role play

Sometimes role play is used. In this method, a 'make believe' situation is created and the employees have to work out how they would solve the problem.

Examination question ↻

The hairdressing salon Cute Cuts has employed a new hairdresser who will receive training in the salon. Identify and describe this type of training and explain two reasons why it is suitable for Cute Cuts to use.   (6 marks)

How to answer this question

Name the type of training (1 mark) and describe it (1 mark). State and explain two reasons why that type suits a hairdressing salon (2 marks for each reason). Be careful to relate your answers to a hairdresser business.

Off-the-job training

Off-the-job training is training provided by a specialist and takes place outside the business – perhaps at a training centre, college or university. The training is paid for by the business and may be on a day release basis or for a longer period of attendance at a full-time course for a term or longer.

Off-the-job training has the following advantages:

▶ since the training is done by specialists it usually is of higher quality
▶ employees meet people from other organisations and can exchange ideas
▶ employees visit a new environment and perhaps are introduced to new equipment
▶ employees can attend evening classes which means they do not miss their work and this reduces the cost.

Disadvantages of off-the-job training are:

▶ the equipment/machinery used may not be the same as the employee will be using in his/her work
▶ it is more expensive
▶ the employee is sometimes taken away from work.

Off-the-job training may be done in a variety of ways:

Lectures

Sometimes employees attend lectures where they are given information which they can later apply in their work.

Demonstrations

Demonstrations are effective for showing how tasks should be done. The trainee watches the expert but then must be given an opportunity to practise the skill.

Role play

Role play is used in both on-the-job and off-the-job training and is undertaken to imitate a real-life situation.

Activity

Name the most appropriate method of training for each of the following situations:

1 A business has replaced all its computers. All ten of the office workers need to learn how to use the new computers.

2 An engineering firm has installed one new machine. The business has no experience of this type of machinery. Rory will be working on the new machine but is unfamiliar with it.

3 A school is introducing a new subject to its curriculum and two teachers – Miss Todd and Mr Kenny – have been told they will be teaching the subject next year. They need help.

4 Brian is starting work as a hotel waiter next month. He has not done this type of work before.

5 Nadine is working as a hairdresser but would like to extend her hairdressing skills in order to get promotion in the salon.

6 Billy is tired of his work as a civil servant and has decided to open a garden centre. He needs to learn more about growing garden plants.

Checklist ✓

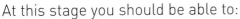

At this stage you should be able to:

- ○ explain the reasons for staff training – induction, change in procedures, and to become more competitive
- ○ describe the advantages of training to employees and to a business
- ○ describe the disadvantages of training to employees and to a business
- ○ describe and evaluate on-the-job training and off-the-job training
- ○ justify the more appropriate method of training for particular circumstances.

4.5 Motivation

Motivation is the way in which a person can be encouraged to make an effort to do something.

Many studies have been carried out on what makes people want to work. Probably the most famous of these studies was by Abraham Maslow, an American psychologist who died in 1970.

Maslow's Hierarchy of Needs

Maslow concluded that people have five levels of need which he illustrated in a 'Hierarchy of Needs' pyramid. He placed the most basic needs at the bottom of the pyramid and the most advanced needs at the top of the pyramid. According to Maslow, when people satisfy one level of need they then move up to the next level.

In his theory, the most basic need is to survive – to have enough money to buy food, shelter and necessary clothes.

When they have satisfied the need for survival, they then need to feel safe and secure – perhaps from unemployment – so the second level of need is for security.

After that, people need to belong to a group and to have friends – these are their social needs. They then move on to needing status. At this stage they need to be respected in the community, to be esteemed and to be given recognition for what they do.

When all these needs have been satisfied, people finally have self-actualisation (or self-fulfilment) needs. This is ambition to achieve as much as they possibly can – perhaps to be promoted to a high level position with more responsibility.

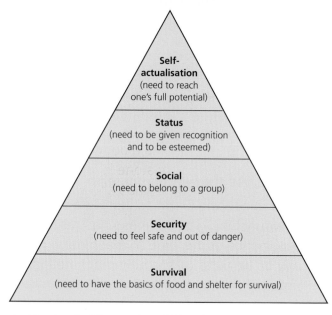

▲ Maslow's Hierarchy of Needs

Importance of motivation

It is very important for a business to have well-motivated employees for the following reasons:

▶ There is likely to be a lower labour turnover. If employees are happy in their work, they are less likely to leave.

▶ Employees would produce higher quality products because they are more interested in their work.

▶ There would be fewer accidents in the workplace since employees are working better as a team and are concentrating on their work.

▶ Employees are less likely to take time off work. Reduced absenteeism improves production rates.

▶ The profitability of the business would be improved.

▶ The reputation and corporate image of the business would be good.

A generous pay system is a good incentive for workers, but money alone is not enough! Maslow's theory has shown that employees need to feel valued in the workplace, they need to feel they belong, and they need to be praised and rewarded for good work.

For these reasons, employers introduce a variety of methods of motivation which offer rewards to employees in addition to their basic pay. These methods of motivation may or may not be for money – in other words, they may be either financial or non-financial. Financial methods involve money for the employee and come at a cost to the employer. There is no finance involved in non-financial methods.

Financial methods of motivation

Bonus

A bonus is an extra payment made to employees who work well and help the business to complete its orders on time or to meet its sales targets. It is paid as a lump sum usually either at Christmas or at the beginning of the summer holidays.

Bonus payments encourage employees to work harder. The advantage for the employees is that they can increase their income while the employer has the advantage of greater production resulting in higher sales and profits.

Commission

Commission is an extra financial reward which is most suitable for a sales person. It is calculated as a percentage of the sales revenue which that person makes. For example, if the commission is 10 per cent and the sales person's sales revenue amounted to £8,000, then the total commission which that person would earn would be £800 on top of his salary.

Commission payments encourage sales staff to increase the amount of their sales. The advantages are that the sales staff increase their income while the business sells more goods and makes more profit.

Profit sharing

Under a profit-sharing scheme, employees receive a share of the total profit made by the business in addition to their basic salary.

Profit sharing acts as a good motivator for employees because it encourages them to increase the business's output and profits of which they can then own a share. It also has the advantage that the employees feel a greater sense of belonging to the business and take a greater interest in its success.

Profit sharing is most usually found in the service sector because, in that type of work, it is not possible to estimate any single employee's contribution to the profits made in the organisation. A slight unfairness of the system is that all employees benefit from the profits made in the organisation – even those who have worked less well and are less deserving.

Fringe benefits

Fringe benefits – sometimes referred to as perks – come with many occupations and are usually related to the seniority of the employee.

For example, directors and senior managers may be entitled to benefits such as company cars, free use of houses, education fees paid for their children, expense accounts, private health care for themselves and their families, pension schemes and trips abroad.

Factory floor workers may be entitled to benefits such as transport to work, free uniforms, discounts on the firm's products, recreational facilities, savings schemes, company shares and luncheon vouchers.

Fringe benefits are classified as a financial method of motivation even though the employee does not actually receive money into his/her hand, unlike the previous methods. This is because they are a financial cost to the business.

Activity ✎

Declan, Jane and Katie all work for the same company. Study the following details and then name the method of financial motivation each one receives.

1   Declan has a management position and has a company car.

2   Jane is a sales person for the company and receives a percentage of the sales she makes.

3   Every Christmas Katie receives a welcome addition to her wages because the employees have worked hard all year.

Non-financial methods of motivation

Job rotation

Job rotation is a method of motivation in which employees move around different jobs in the business in order to avoid the possibility of them getting bored by doing the same work all the time.

The system has the added advantage of giving opportunities for workers to learn more jobs. Job rotation is suitable for unskilled work and is frequently used for factory workers on production lines.

Team working

In a **team working** system, employees are grouped together in teams making sure that the team has the full range of abilities and skills required to make the product or carry out whatever task they have been set. The team may be given responsibility for how they carry out the work and organise it.

This method of motivation has the advantage of making the employees feel more responsible for their own team's decisions. In addition, employees feel committed and will be anxious to make their own team successful so they will work hard to make that happen.

Team working increases job satisfaction for employees and improves morale in the workplace.

Quality circles

Quality circles is a method of motivation which originated in Japan where they are widely and successfully used. They have now become very common in this country, possibly because of the spread of Japanese business in the British Isles. The idea behind quality circles is that quality is the responsibility of not only everyone working on the product, but also those in management, in the offices or working as cleaners. Everyone is expected to ensure that their work is of top quality.

The introduction of quality circles is really another approach to team working. Employees are organised into work teams and meet regularly to examine the quality of what they are doing and to try to find ways of doing the job better and improving the quality of the product or service even further.

Flexible working

A flexible working hours system allows the employee to have some choice about when to start work and when to finish during the working day, as long as the total number of hours are worked per week. Most businesses require their employees to be present during a set period each day (known as the core time). It is especially useful for employees who have responsibilities for children or elderly parents or for those who wish to avoid times of traffic congestion.

This method of motivation has the advantage of giving the employee some flexibility and also means that the business will have workers present for a longer period each day, since some will start early and others will finish later.

The disadvantage of this for the business is the increase in lighting and heating costs. Flexitime works successfully in offices.

Activity

State which method of motivation you think is most appropriate in each of the following cases, giving reasons for your decisions.

1 Catherine is a sales representative for a fashion company and needs encouragement to increase the company's sales.
2 David has been working as a swimming instructor in a leisure centre for several years. He feels that he is being isolated from the other instructors in the centre.
3 Joel is a factory supervisor and is good at his job. However, he often feels de-motivated because he works hard but he thinks his bosses get all the rewards.

4 Patrick is the financial director of the Northern Ireland branch of a multi-national organisation. He agrees that he is very well paid but needs some further encouragement.
5 Elizabeth loves her work as a shop assistant but feels she should have some fringe benefits. Which benefits would you recommend?
6 Jack is bored because for years he has been doing the same work on a production line in a toy factory.

Factors affecting job satisfaction

Job satisfaction is defined as the degree of happiness a person gets from his or her work.

If an employee is to reach his/her full potential and do his/her best work, it is extremely important that he/she enjoys his/her work and gets a high degree of job satisfaction from it.

There are several factors which increase a person's job satisfaction:

Wages/Salaries

Wages/salaries are the monetary payment for work carried out for an employer. Money is obviously a very big factor in any job. The basic reason why people work is in order to earn enough money to buy the goods they need and to be able to have some luxury in their lives. However, money alone is not enough!

Responsibility

Employees need to be given some responsibility in the business – to be in charge of something. This gives an employee a feeling of self-worth, of being trusted and of value. If an employee is given responsibility for a certain process or task, he/she will want to perform that task as well as possible. This may give that employee the opportunity to take on more responsibility or the opportunity to apply for promotion.

Success

People get job satisfaction from succeeding and doing a good piece of work, so a sense of success or achievement is important. Personal success needs to be praised and encouraged by the employer, perhaps by a pay rise or promotion.

Enjoyment

Enjoying the work is also an important factor in an employee's job satisfaction and it is vital to find work which you are happy doing. There is no enjoyment or job satisfaction in work which you dislike, no matter how good the wages are.

Working conditions

The conditions in the workplace can also affect job satisfaction. Such conditions could include a pleasant environment with warm, well-lit buildings, for example. The other people in the workplace can also have a major effect and it is important to have a good working relationship with the employer/manager and the other employees. Liking the people working with you makes the job much more enjoyable and increases job satisfaction to a significant degree.

Praise

Everyone responds to praise and wants to feel that their work is valued. Job satisfaction improves if the employer praises his/her staff and recognises their effort and contribution to the business.

Examination questions

The Sea Shells Hotel is a large, high-quality hotel.

1 Analyse three factors which could affect the job satisfaction of the employees in the Sea Shells Hotel. (6 marks)

2 Explain three advantages for the employers in the Sea Shells Hotel of having employees who are highly motivated. (6 marks)

How to answer these questions

1 To analyse means to thoroughly examine, so in this question you should choose three factors which would apply to an employee working in a hotel and analyse three appropriate factors. Each factor will be given up to 2 marks.

2 Name three advantages of motivation but make sure that you examine these from the employers' point of view and that they are appropriate for a hotel.

Activity

Make a list of the factors which give you job satisfaction in your GCSE work.

Checklist ✓

At this stage you should be able to:
○ explain the importance of motivation for employees
○ identify and evaluate the main methods of financial motivation and their suitability in various circumstances
○ identify and evaluate the main methods of non-financial motivation and their suitability in various circumstances
○ analyse the factors affecting job satisfaction.

5 Business growth
5.1 Business success or failure

Businesses cannot stand still. If they are not being successful, they will be unable to re-pay their loans to banks, to pay their employees or to pay their suppliers for inventory – goods bought. In this case, the bank and other **trade payables** – suppliers to whom they owe money – will force the business to close down in order to recover the money due to them.

Signs of success

▶ **Increasing profit** – A successful business will be increasing its sales, widening its market and making increased profit as a result.

▶ **Attracting new competitors into the industry** – A successful business will be introducing new products onto the market so other competing businesses will want to enter the same market in order to share in the success.

▶ **Expansion** – A successful business will be growing, enlarging its premises, taking over other businesses and opening new branches.

▶ **Favourable customer reviews** – A successful business will be receiving favourable reviews on its website, in reports and on social media from satisfied customers. This will attract more customers to the business and further add to its success.

▶ **Word of mouth recognition** – A successful business will have satisfied customers who will tell other consumers about the good products or service they receive. This will attract those new consumers and further increase sales revenue and profit.

▶ **Increased publicity** – A successful business will have increased good publicity either

through satisfied customers or through sponsorship or community events which it can afford to fund. The business also will feature on social media which will further add to its success.

Signs of failure

▶ **Loss of profit** – An unsuccessful business will lack variety of products and inventory will be low. As a result of decreased sales revenue, profits will fall. If this trend continues the business will close as a result.

▶ **Poor cash flow** – An unsuccessful business will have poor **cash flow** which means that it will not have available cash to pay its trade payables or pay the employees. As a result, suppliers will not continue to supply inventory to the business and the employees will not remain in work there.

▶ **Loss of customers** – An unsuccessful business will lose its customers because of the lack of variety of products, low stocks or poor service.

▶ **Unfavourable customer reviews** – An unsuccessful business will receive unfavourable customer reviews if customers are dissatisfied with the standard in the business, either in goods or service. This will discourage further customers from going to that business.

▶ **High employee turnover** – An unsuccessful business will not be able to attract employees or keep its existing employees. Staff morale will be low and the poor cash flow may mean that employees cannot be paid. They will leave as soon as they find more secure employment.

Activity

Decide whether the following statements are true or false:

1 A **trade receivable** is a person to whom the business owes money.
2 Increasing profit is not a sign of success.
3 Expansion is not a sign of failure.
4 Inventory may be low in an unsuccessful business.
5 Poor cash flow is a sign of business failure.
6 Employees will leave an unsuccessful business.

Examination question

Ashton Ltd is a successful company which manufactures confectionery. Explain two signs of success you would expect to find in this company.   (4 marks)

How to answer this question

This is a straightforward question in which you should name and explain the two most appropriate signs of success for this factory. Each explanation will get up to 2 marks.

Checklist ✓

At this stage you should be able to:
○ identify the signs of business success
○ identify the signs of business failure.

5.2 Business growth

Any form of expansion of the business is an example of business growth.

You will remember from your work on business aims, that growth is one of a business's main aims. This section looks at growth in greater depth.

Different types of growth

Businesses may grow either internally (organically) or externally.

Internal (organic) growth

Internal/**organic growth** takes place inside the business, and without any reference to other sources. **Internal business growth** is slow to achieve and is a gradual process.

To achieve internal/organic growth, a business may:

▶ **Reinvest its profits** – this means that the owner will take little or no profit out of the business but instead will use it to improve the business. The owner will be able to do this for a limited period only as he/she will have little/no personal gain from the business. This is sometimes known as 'ploughing back profit'.

▶ **Expand its product range** – a manufacturing business may extend its range of products or a retail business may introduce new lines of products. For example, large retailers such as Asda, Sainsbury or Tesco have food as their main line but also sell household goods and electrical goods.

▶ **Increase sales activity** – a business may expand by selling its products abroad, it may open new branches to sell its products in a wider area or expand their existing premises in order to create more space for more products.

Activity

There are probably examples of internal growth in your town or area. To complete this activity you should do some local research to discover the information required.

1 Name any shops in your area which have increased their floor space or opened new branches recently.

2 Find out if any of your local hotels have plans to open, or have opened recently, new facilities such as a leisure centre or conference complex.

3 Find examples where any of the local factories are recruiting extra employees, introducing the latest technology, developing new products or expanding their markets abroad.

All of these would be examples of internal growth in your local area.

External growth

External business growth is a much faster type of growth and involves the bringing together of a number of organisations to form a single business. The main implication of external growth is the loss of control of the business and the introduction of shared management and decision making. External growth may be achieved through **takeovers**, mergers, franchising, or integrations.

Takeover

A takeover takes place when one business buys over the control of another business. To achieve a takeover, a business would have to buy a large number of shares so that it could control the voting in the other business. The business wishing to gain control would offer very high prices to the existing shareholders for their shares in order to secure them.

Takeovers frequently are hostile and not welcomed by the business which is being taken over. Where a takeover has been hostile, the main implications for the new business are strained relationships at managerial level and enforced control by an outside company. In other cases, takeovers are agreed and the business being taken over would advise its shareholders to accept the high offers for their shares. In an agreed takeover, the business being taken over welcomes the opportunity to be part of a larger organisation to enjoy greater prosperity and gain from its resources.

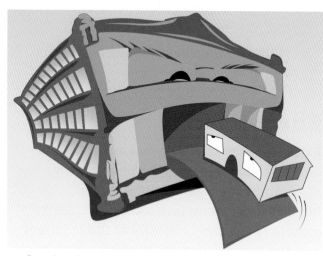

▲ One business swallowing another

Merger

A merger (or **amalgamation**) is a voluntary and agreed joining of two businesses in order to form one larger business. It could be seen as a marriage between two businesses.

In the case of a merger, all the capital as well as all resources and **assets** such as premises, machinery and personnel are joined together in one organisation. The implications for a newly merged business are the increase in business which comes from a larger operation, resulting in economies of scale and greater profits. As with all joined organisations, methods have to be worked out whereby two workforces and two sets of managers can work as one. A merger has the added implication of shared resources without costly duplication. Another implication is the possibility of staff redundancies.

A merger has several advantages:

▶ Savings are made because one merged organisation is able to operate with less equipment and other resources than two.

▶ There would be no duplication in running costs.

▶ Fewer administrative staff and directors are required to run a single business.

▶ The business would be operating on a larger scale so would benefit from economies of scale.

▶ The market share would be increased and sales would be improved.

▶ The businesses would be working together rather than as competitors to one another.

Mergers have some disadvantages:

▶ There is a possibility of staff redundancies as two full sets of staff may not be required.

▶ Consumers have less choice as one business has gone.

▶ Competition is reduced.

▲ One business merging with another

Franchising

Franchising is a popular method by which companies expand their operations and open shops in various parts of the country. McDonald's is the world's largest chain of fast food restaurants and is probably the best example of franchising. There are 31,000 McDonald's restaurants, operating in 119 countries, all over the world. They claim to serve 47 million customers per day. This number grew, through franchising, from the first United Kingdom restaurant which opened in 1974.

A franchised business has to accept that policy is dictated by the franchising company and that there is no opportunity for individuality. The main implication for the business is that it is seen as a branch of a large chain rather than a business in its own right. The owner is seen as a manager rather than as an owner. On the positive side, the implications are that the franchised business enjoys the reputation and ready-made market which come with being part of a **large enterprise**.

(For further details on franchising, you should refer back to Unit 1.3.)

Integration

To integrate means to 'combine parts into a whole'. In business, integration is achieved through mergers and takeovers. There are three main types of integration:

1 Horizontal integration
2 Vertical integration
3 Lateral integration

Horizontal integration

Horizontal integration takes place between businesses on the same level within the same type of business. For example, if two confectionery shops, 'Sweet Temptations' and 'Sweet Things' decided to merge, it would be horizontal integration because they both had previously been selling sweets and chocolate to consumers.

Vertical integration

Vertical integration takes place between businesses on different levels within the same type of business. For example, if a chocolate factory decided to merge with a confectionery shop it would be vertical integration. This is because, although both businesses were involved in the confectionery business, they were working at different stages of the chain of production – one was manufacturing the chocolate while the other was selling it.

Lateral integration

Lateral integration takes place when a business expands by merging with another business which is in a related but different area. They were not in direct competition before integration took place. Their products may be similar but not identical and the types of skills required to make or handle the products are very alike. For example, if the chocolate factory were to merge with an ice-cream factory, the type of integration would be lateral.

Conglomerate

This is the most usual type of merger and brings together businesses whose products are totally unrelated and dissimilar. The businesses may or may not be working at the same level of production.

This type of merger is also known as diversification, and it takes place mainly because the business is expecting a decline in one of its markets and it is branching out into other lines as a safeguard. An example of a conglomerate would be the merger between the chocolate factory, a jewellery shop and a restaurant.

Activity

All of the businesses named here are based in one country. A number of them are considering some type of integration. Study each possibility and write down, in the spaces provided, which type of integration each would be.

Businesses	Type of integration
A filling station links with another filling station	
A bakery takes over a bread shop	
A filling station joins with a chip shop and the bakery	
A supermarket opens another branch in a different area of town	
A large public house and restaurant takes control of a smaller public house and restaurant	
Two hairdressers agree to join their businesses and work together	
A retailer of furniture links with a furniture factory	
The furniture retailer joins his business with a retailer of bathroom fittings	

Factors which may limit the growth of businesses

While the majority of businesses wish to grow and expand for the reasons stated at the beginning of this unit, others may not have the same ambition.

The very nature of specialised businesses such as dress designers or cabinet makers depends on those businesses being small-scale. Their work is done through expensive orders for hand-made articles for which **mass production** would not be appropriate. To grow into large organisations would take away from their high quality and individuality.

Other businesses may, however, wish to expand but may be limited in their efforts to do so. The factors which limit growth are:

▶ **Lack of finance** – Expansion and growth require capital. Capital would be needed to obtain the necessary premises, machinery and other resources for the enlarged operation. If the business cannot raise the required capital it would be impossible for it to expand.

▶ **Competition** – A business may also be curtailed by very strong competition who are much bigger and can sell products to consumers at lower prices. This is the case with small shopkeepers who are unable to expand because of the strength of large chain stores which take away their trade.

▶ **Lack of demand** – Consumer taste changes with the result that some items may no longer be in demand. A business will not be able to grow and keep up with the market unless it either makes alterations to its product or changes to a different product. For example, fax machines were in common use some years ago as a method of communication. They now have been overtaken by more modern technology.

▶ **Difficult economic climate** – In times of recession or when sterling is weaker, it is difficult for a business to grow. Consumers will have less money to spend so the sales of the business go down and profits are reduced.

Economies of scale

Economies of scale are gained when a business increases its production and this causes a decrease in average production costs.

Economies of scale can be illustrated by an example from the newspaper industry. It would be very expensive to produce a single copy of a newspaper because all the major costs in newspaper production – costs of research, writing, designing and laying out the newspaper – would have to be met even for one copy.

However, when production is increased and several thousand copies of the newspaper are printed, the costs do not multiply in proportion to the number of copies. The costs of researching, writing, designing and laying out the newspaper are the same regardless of the number printed, and the only additional costs are extra paper, ink and electricity.

There are four main types of economies of scale:

1 Technical economies of scale

Technical economies of scale are gained in situations where the business can cut its production costs by introducing upgraded technology or by altering its production methods. Increased mechanisation will speed up production and allow the business to use the **flow manufacturing** method. In this way, costs of labour and power are lowered per

unit and overhead expenses such as rates are more effectively used.

Large businesses usually can afford more advanced technology than small businesses, so technical economies of scale are often of more benefit to larger businesses.

2 Financial economies of scale

Financial economies of scale are gained in situations where the business can borrow money or otherwise gain finance by cheaper methods.

Large businesses, in general, provide better security and fewer risks for banks, therefore banks are willing to allow them to borrow larger sums for longer periods of time and at better rates of interest.

3 Marketing economies of scale

Marketing economies of scale are gained in situations where the business can save on expenses associated with marketing such as advertising and distribution.

For example, it costs the same sum to deliver ten boxes of goods in one lorry load as it does to deliver a single box of goods. For this reason, businesses try to combine goods in one consignment and pick up other goods on the return journey to use the vehicle economically.

A large business is charged the same rate for advertising as a small business. However, in a large business advertising expenditure is less per unit of production than it is in a small business which is producing on a smaller scale. For this reason, a large business can afford to undertake more advertising than a small business can. The larger business is also likely to increase its sales, as a result of the advertising, by more than the smaller business.

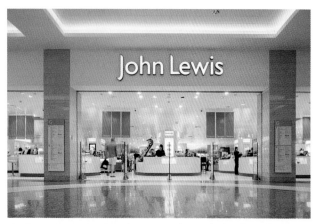

▲ Large organisations such as John Lewis can take advantage of economies of scale

4 Purchasing economies of scale

Purchasing economies of scale are gained when large companies are able to purchase goods in bulk. They will be given discount for buying in bulk which reduces the price per unit they pay. A small business will not be able to purchase in bulk and therefore does not get the same level of discount. These higher costs are then passed on to the consumer, giving the large business an advantage.

Activity ✎

Which type of economy of scale is described in each of the following?

1 Fleet Delivery Ltd uses vans instead of lorries when small loads are being delivered.

2 The Premier Furniture Company has installed computerised machinery in its production plant.

3 A large group of supermarkets, Finest Foods, has been offered a lower rate of interest on a bank loan than Gillian who runs a small grocery shop.

4 Paul, the manager of Finest Foods, uses the same advertisements to promote all shops in the chain.

5 The Fresh Bakery merged with The Daily Bread Company and increased its product range by using the flow production method.

6 The City Book Store is able to purchase books at a discounted price from its main supplier because of the large size of its orders.

Advantages of growth

▶ **Increased profit** – Because the business is larger it will have a larger volume of sales which will result in increased profit for the company.

▶ **Economies of scale** – As a larger business the company will benefit from purchasing economies of scale because it can buy stocks in larger quantities at discounted prices. It will also benefit from technical economies of scale because a larger business can afford to have more modern

technology which speeds up production. Marketing economies of scale will reduce costs such as advertising which are spread over a greater number of units of production or sales. Financial economies of scale will be gained because it is easier for a large business to be given loans or to purchase on credit.

▶ **Greater market influence** – A large business will be more powerful and influential in the market as it is in a position to negotiate better prices with suppliers and buy its stock more cheaply. This means that larger businesses can sell their goods more cheaply and other smaller businesses often have to follow their lead in price setting.

Disadvantages of growth

▶ **Poor communication** – As a business grows it can be difficult for departments to communicate with each other or for management to communicate with all employees. Employees may not know their bosses and this can be de-motivating.

▶ **Lack of motivation** – In a very large organisation, employees may not know one another and they may feel that they are 'small cogs in a large wheel' and that they don't matter as individual workers.

▶ **Difficulties of co-ordination** – A large organisation may be split over a variety of sites and this would lead to difficulties of co-ordination between the different branches or departments.

Ethical implications of growth

Ethical growth is about growing in a way that is morally correct. It ensures that everything is done in a fair, legal, responsible and honest way and that dealings are not simply carried out for the business's competitive advantage. Business is more than just a way to make money – it affects many people such as employees, suppliers and consumers, and it also affects the environment.

The modern tendency in retailing, especially in grocery and light hardware items, is for very large supermarkets to be situated in shopping centres in larger towns or on their outskirts. These large stores are very attractive to shoppers because they offer a wide variety of goods under one roof and at low prices. All of these factors lead to the further success and growth of the large supermarkets. The growth of the large business parks has taken place at the expense of the traditional small retailers in town centres and villages throughout the country.

When growing, businesses are expected to respect the local environment and the people in the nearby community. The business should spend money making the landscape attractive and controlling noise pollution caused by night-time deliveries.

Consumers should be charged fair prices and in-store offers should really be to the advantage of the consumer. An ethical business will pay its employees a fair living wage and give them good conditions.

Suppliers should also be paid at good rates which gives them a fair return for their produce and their work. An ethical business would not buy goods from countries where the goods have been made by exploited workers who earn low wages and are made to work long hours.

As an example of good ethical practice, Levi now makes jeans in Africa. By doing this, they have improved the living conditions there by paying fair wages and creating safe working conditions in their factories. This has cost Levi more than if they had imported cheap jeans from abroad but that would be unethical.

The Competition and Markets Authority (CMA)

The **Competition and Markets Authority** was set up in 2014 to replace the Competition Commission. It is an independent body which has been established for the purpose of investigating mergers and to make sure that mergers between businesses are fair to consumers.

It conducts in-depth inquiries into mergers and the regulation of major industries because a merger between businesses could make one very large business and could eliminate competition. Without competition, it would be possible for a business to charge customers very high prices. The aim of the Competition and Markets Authority is to make markets work well for consumers by increasing the level of competition.

The Authority has three main functions:

▶ It carries out inquiries into monopolies and mergers.

▶ It enforces consumer protection legislation.

▶ It hears appeals against decisions made on monopolies and mergers and on the abuse of market power.

The Competition and Markets Authority publishes the results of its investigations and its decisions on mergers and monopolies are made on the basis of the public interest.

Examination question

Bling is a shop selling costume jewellery. Identify three methods by which Bling could achieve internal/organic growth. Analyse the implications for Bling of each of those methods, stating both positive and negative implications.   (9 marks)

How to answer this question

Identify one method of internal/organic growth which would be appropriate for a jewellery shop (1 mark). Show one good point (1 mark) and one disadvantage of that method (1 mark). Repeat this twice more showing a total of three methods.

Checklist

At this stage you should be able to:

○ describe and evaluate different types of internal/organic growth

○ describe and evaluate different types of external growth

○ discuss the factors which limit growth

○ explain the meaning of the term 'economies of scale'

○ explain different types of economies of scale

○ analyse the advantages and disadvantages of growth

○ analyse the ethical implications of growth

○ explain the role of the Competition and Markets Authority.

6 Finance
6.1 Sources of finance

A business may need finance not only when starting up but also at times during its life. For example, new expensive machinery may be needed. Sometimes large sums may be required for a long period while, at other times, small amounts for a short time may do.

The time for which finance is needed may be:

Short-term	Medium-term	Long-term
May be used to:	May be used to:	May be used to:
Buy extra inventories Avail of special offers Help when trade is poor	Buy short-life assets such as vehicles	Buy long-life assets such as premises

There are several methods by which businesses may raise necessary finance. The method which they choose depends on how much they wish to borrow and the period of time for which it is needed.

Money can be raised internally – inside the business – or externally – from sources outside the business.

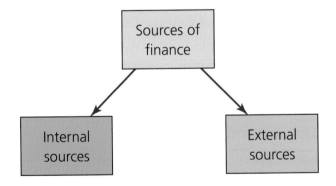

Internal sources of finance

The advantages of internal sources of finance are:

▶ no interest has to be paid
▶ the affairs of the business are kept private
▶ does not have to be repaid.

The disadvantages of internal sources of finance are:

▶ there may not be enough money available.

There are five internal sources of finance:

Owner's investment

In this case, the owners draw on their own private financial resources and invest their private money into the business.

Using the owner's own capital has the advantages of remaining private and does not have to be repaid. The major disadvantage is that not all owners have **additional capital** to call on. This method would be used if the money were required long-term and if the amount was not large.

Retained profits

Sometimes the owners may decide to re-invest or 'plough back' profits from previous years instead of taking them out of the business for their own use. This method also has the advantages of remaining private and does not have to be repaid. The disadvantage is that not all businesses make enough profit to be able to do this. **Retained profits** would be used if the money were required in the medium or long term and the amount required was not very large.

Sale of inventory

Every manufacturing business and every retail shop has inventory which has not been sold. The business can raise finance quickly by holding a sale and offering the goods to the public at a discount. In this way, the business gets its money quickly and can use this money to manufacture or buy new inventory. We are all familiar with the January sales in shops which clear the winter goods, and also raise money and create space for the new spring goods. Selling inventory would be done if the money were required in the short term.

Sale of fixed assets

Businesses have large sums of money invested in their fixed assets such as premises and equipment and sometimes choose to sell some surplus assets – perhaps a machine or a building – in order to raise finance. However, new or small businesses are unlikely to have any surplus fixed assets to sell and even a business which has surplus assets would find the method slow. There is also a limit to the number of assets which a business can sell before it starts to affect its production. Selling fixed assets would be done if the money were required in the medium term.

Debt collection

Most businesses have trade receivables – people who have bought goods and have not paid for them. It is common practice for businesses to allow thirty days' credit, although all the large supermarkets sell only for cash. The money which is owing by trade receivables is not working for the business, so the business has to have a system of debt collection to get the money it is owed. Debt collection is useful if the money is required immediately.

Activity

Name one advantage and one disadvantage of each of the following sources of finance.

Source of finance	Advantage	Disadvantage
Owner's investment		
Retained profits		
Sale of inventory		
Sale of fixed assets		
Debt collection		

External sources of finance

The advantages of external sources of finance are:

▶ larger sums of money are available
▶ the money is usually available more quickly
▶ the borrower has the use of the asset while paying for it.

The disadvantages of external sources of finance are:

▶ it is more expensive as interest has to be paid
▶ the lender requires security in case of non-payment.

There are nine external sources of finance:

Bank loan

This is suitable as a medium- or long-term source of finance. The bank agrees to lend a set sum of money to the business for an agreed period of time. In return, the bank charges interest at a rate which is fixed for the entire period of the loan. For this reason a bank loan can be an expensive way to raise finance.

The bank requires security for its loans. This means that the bank has the right to sell an asset belonging to the business if the loan is not repaid within the agreed time.

Bank overdraft

A bank overdraft is a short-term means of finance. This is an arrangement with the bank whereby the business is allowed to pay out amounts from its bank account to an agreed limit beyond the amount which has been lodged in the account. Interest is paid on the amount actually overdrawn each day and therefore getting a bank overdraft is usually cheaper than a bank loan which has a fixed rate of interest.

Additional partners

If a partnership needs extra finance the partners can agree to invite an additional partner to join the business. The new partner will contribute capital which can be used to finance the purchase of assets or whatever the extra finance is required for in the business. However, the new partner is entitled to a share of the profits of the business.

Activity

Apart from the additional finance which the new partner would contribute to the firm, there are other advantages and disadvantages which taking on a new partner would have for the business.

1 Write down one other advantage which introducing an additional partner would have for the business.

2 State one possible disadvantage for the business of introducing an additional partner.

Share issue

In the case of a limited company, extra finance may be raised by issuing new additional shares in the company. In a private limited company these shares will be issued to family and friends. In a public limited company, additional members of the public may become shareholders by buying the shares on the Stock Exchange. In either type of company, this is a long-term source of finance for the company and no interest is payable although all shareholders are entitled to dividends (share of the profits).

Leasing

Leasing is a method of acquiring assets and is a medium-term method of finance. Leasing is similar to renting and the business does not have to pay a lump sum as it would have to do if it were buying the asset.

The lease is arranged by a finance company and the business makes regular payments to it for the use of the asset. These payments can be very high because they include profits for the finance company. The asset remains the property of the finance company which is another disadvantage of leasing.

Despite these disadvantages, leasing is commonly used in business because it enables firms to have the use of up-to-date equipment (the asset will be updated regularly) and the business is able to get the asset immediately. In addition, maintenance and repair costs are usually paid by the finance company. A common example is a fleet of company cars, which are frequently leased.

Hire purchase

Hire purchase is another method of medium-term finance which is used for the purchase of assets. In the case of hire purchase, the business pays a deposit on the asset

and agrees to pay off the balance in equal instalments over an agreed period of time. The business has the use of the asset while it is paying it off – or hiring it.

The major difference between hire purchase and leasing is that in the hire purchase system, the business eventually becomes the owner of the asset once it has paid off all the instalments.

Hire purchase is a popular method of buying assets because the business can have very modern equipment without having to part with a large sum of money at the outset, and it will eventually own the assets. The major disadvantage is that the total cost of the asset is much higher than if it were bought for cash.

Mortgage

A **mortgage** is a very long-term method of raising finance and is most often used to help in the purchase of premises. The mortgage is arranged with a building society or a bank over a long period of years (usually twenty

Activity

Andrew owns an earth-moving business and is hoping to obtain a new digger soon. He is unsure whether to use hire purchase or leasing and has come to you for advice.

Complete the following table to show Andrew the advantages and disadvantages of both hire purchase and leasing to help him to decide which of these two sources of finance would be better for him to use.

Advantages of hire purchase	Disadvantages of hire purchase	Advantages of leasing	Disadvantages of leasing

to twenty-five) and the sum borrowed, plus interest charges, has to be repaid in instalments over that period. This makes the purchase more expensive than if it were bought for cash. The premises act as collateral which means that the premises can be taken and sold by the building society or bank should the business fail to make repayments.

The big advantage of a mortgage is that the business has the use of the premises from the beginning and can carry on its work there while making repayments. Another advantage is that the premises eventually become the property of the business when all the payments have been made.

Trade credit

Trade credit is a short-term means of finance, and is where suppliers allow their customers to have a period of time (usually thirty days) in which to pay for the goods they have received.

Trade credit gives an advantage to buyers because they have the immediate use of the goods. This would help the **working capital** of a small shop, for example, because the shop could buy the goods on credit, and then sell them and raise money from them before having to pay the supplier.

Trade credit has the added advantage of being free. However, suppliers usually give discount for cash payment which would be lost by using the trade credit facility.

Government grants

Several systems of government grants apply in Northern Ireland to assist businesses financially. These are paid either through the Northern Ireland Assembly, the national government in Westminster, **Invest NI** or the European Union. Details change regularly so you are advised to keep up-to-date.

Government grants are given for a number of reasons but the most usual is to create employment in a depressed area in order to regenerate that area. They are also given in order to attract foreign companies to invest in Northern Ireland. Such government assistance may take the form of tax allowances, rates reduction or help with re-location costs.

Such grants usually do not have to be repaid, although they usually do have conditions. It is common, for example, that the government would specify the location of the business so that some of the unemployment problems in a certain area might be solved.

Activity

In each of the circumstances described here, you are asked to identify the most appropriate source of finance.

1 A company wishes to obtain five new cars for its sales representatives.

2 A small shopkeeper needs to increase his working capital temporarily.

3 A business needs short-term help to buy extra inventory.

4 Elaine and Martin cannot raise enough money for their hardware business to be able to compete with other businesses in their area.

5 A limited company wishes to expand its market and needs more long-term capital.

6 A large company needs to up-date its machinery but does not have enough money available immediately.

7 A business has plans to buy modern premises which would allow it to expand production.

8 A French company is planning to set up a new business in Northern Ireland in an area where there is high unemployment.

Examination question ↻

L&L Flowers is a flower shop which wishes to expand by opening another flower shop. Identify one internal and one external source of finance which might be available to L&L Flowers and explain one advantage and one disadvantage of each source.   (6 marks)

How to answer this question

Name an appropriate internal source.	(1 mark)
Explain one advantage of that internal source.	(1 mark)
Explain one disadvantage of that internal source.	(1 mark)
Name an appropriate external source.	(1 mark)
Explain one advantage of that external source.	(1 mark)
Explain one disadvantage of that external source.	(1 mark)

Checklist

At this stage you should be able to:

○ explain the advantages and disadvantages of internal sources of finance

○ explain the advantages and disadvantages of external sources of finance

○ identify the most appropriate source of finance for particular circumstances.

6.2 Cash flow forecasts

Purpose of a cash flow forecast

You are used to hearing the weather forecast on the radio or television. It predicts what the weather will be like for the following few days and is very useful to people such as farmers and gardeners who can then plan their outdoor work around those conditions. A **cash flow forecast** acts in the same way for a business. It forecasts business activity during the coming period.

A cash flow forecast has the following important purposes:

▶ **Forward planning** – It predicts – or forecasts – the level of spending and level of income which the business will have during the following period of time – usually one year. Perhaps a machine has to be replaced during the year while other expenses such as electricity always have to be paid at regular intervals. Recording all forecasted expenditure enables the business to see if these payments would result in cash shortages at certain times.

▶ **Review performance** – It enables a business to compare the forecasted income and spending against the actual amounts spent and received.

▶ **It shows when finance is required** – Any business wishing to borrow money will see from the cash flow forecast exactly how much needs to be borrowed and exactly when the extra cash is required. This prevents the payment of interest for longer than necessary.

▶ **It shows when loans could be repaid** – Presentation of a cash flow forecast would show the bank or other lender if, and when, the business would be able to repay the loan. This would encourage lenders to give a loan.

▶ **It inspires confidence and acts as a check on spending** – A cash flow forecast gives the owner confidence and shows if the business's financial plans are being maintained.

▶ **It supports the firm's business plan** – A cash flow forecast is required as part of the firm's business plan and can be used to support it. (See Unit 3).

▶ **It sets targets for the business** – A cash flow forecast sets targets for the business to work towards.

Importance of cash flow to a business

Cash flow is the term used to describe the flow of money into and out of a business.

Cash flow is important in a business because:

▶ An even cash flow ensures that the business would never suffer from a shortage of ready money. This shortage could arise if the bills had to be paid at regular intervals but the income was coming in irregularly.

▶ The business must ensure that there is a steady supply of money coming in so that it is able to pay its essential debts such as trade payables (people to whom it owes money) and wages.

▶ Without adequate cash flow the business could be forced to close because suppliers would no longer trade with a business which could not pay for its purchases.

▶ Employees would not continue to work for the business if their wages were not being paid.

▶ It would save the business from having to borrow money which would incur interest charges.

▶ If the business has a good cash flow, it could take advantage of cheaper inventory offers. Taking advantage of offers enables the business to re-sell the goods more cheaply and thus attract customers.

The following diagram illustrates the constancy of the flow of cash in and out of the business.

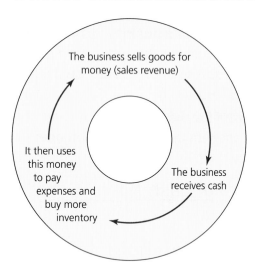

The business sells goods for money (sales revenue)

It then uses this money to pay expenses and buy more inventory

The business receives cash

You can see that a cash flow problem would be created if the goods were not sold quickly and cash was not received in order to pay the expenses or pay the suppliers for the goods. That situation is known as a **liquidity** problem and many businesses have had to close for this reason.

Activity ✎

You are the Financial Director of The Plastic Products Company, a business which manufactures all forms of plastic containers. The factory is very well equipped with state-of-the-art machinery and has a highly trained workforce. Business has been very good for many years and The Plastic Products Company is well established in the market. One new company has come into the plastics market recently and is keen to get new orders.

The Plastic Products Company has experienced some minor cash flow difficulties in the past, and a board meeting has been called to consider ways in which the firm might reduce the risk of future, larger cash flow problems.

As the Financial Director, you have been asked to explain at least four suggestions of how the risk might be reduced.

Consequences of incorrect forecasting

1 It would cause a shortage of working capital. If a business failed to forecast its income and spending accurately it would experience a shortage of working capital. Working capital is used to pay for the essential expenses of the business such as wages. It follows therefore that if incorrect forecasting resulted in a shortage of working capital, the essential expenses could not be paid.

2 Some of the business's assets may have to be sold. If a business forecasts incorrectly and runs short of cash, it may be forced to sell some of its assets. This could affect its production if, for example, machinery were sold.

3 Inventory levels may be inaccurate. If sales revenues were under estimated, sufficient inventory may not have been purchased.

4 Purchases may be made at an incorrect time. This would cause money to be tied up in inventory which could be used elsewhere in the business.

5 Bank loans may be required. These would incur high interest charges.

6 Trading opportunities may be lost. If the forecast is wrong, there may not be enough cash in the business to purchase goods which could have been sold at a profit.

7 The business may have to close. In extreme cases the business may not survive.

➡

Display of a cash flow forecast

A cash flow forecast records:

- **Receipts** – This is the total money the business hopes to receive from sales revenues or other means over the period. These are recorded as separate items and the totals are also shown.
- **Payments** – All payments to be made over the period of the forecast are recorded separately.
- **Balances** – The opening and anticipated closing balances of cash each month.

The following cash flow forecast is displayed for six months for Mary who owns and runs Kutz, a hairdressing salon in Bangor. Mary set up her business on 1 January with her own capital of £18,000. She forecasts that for each of the first three months she will make £3,000 in sales revenue which should rise to £5,000 for the month of April and £6,000 for the months of May and June when she has become established.

She will have to buy shampoo and other supplies of £300 per month during the first three months rising to £900 in April and £1,000 per month in May and June. She will pay herself £600 per month and pay £400 per month to one assistant. During January she plans to buy extra equipment costing £3,000. Mary's rent has been agreed at £600 per month. Electricity costing £250 is due to be paid in March and June and telephone bills of £150 also have to be paid in March and June. £300 for insurance will be paid in January.

Cash flow forecast for Kutz from 1 January to 30 June:

RECEIPTS	Jan	Feb	March	April	May	June	Total
	£	£	£	£	£	£	£
Sales	3,000	3,000	3,000	5,000	6,000	6,000	26,000
Capital	18,000						18,000
Total Receipts	21,000	3,000	3,000	5,000	6,000	6,000	44,000
PAYMENTS							
Purchases	300	300	300	900	1,000	1,000	3,800
Salary	600	600	600	600	600	600	3,600
Wages	400	400	400	400	400	400	2,400
Equipment	3,000						3,000
Rent	600	600	600	600	600	600	3,600
Electricity			250			250	500
Telephone			150			150	300
Insurance	300						300
Total Payments	5,200	1,900	2,300	2,500	2,600	3,000	17,500
Opening Balance	0	15,800	16,900	17,600	20,100	23,500	
+ Receipts	21,000	3,000	3,000	5,000	6,000	6,000	
	21,000	18,800	19,900	22,600	26,100	29,500	
– Payments	5,200	1,900	2,300	2,500	2,600	3,000	
Closing Balance	15,800	16,900	17,600	20,100	23,500	26,500	

Activity

RECEIPTS	Jan	Feb	Mar	April	May	June	Total
	£	£	£	£	£	£	
Sales Revenue	2,000	2,000	2,000	3,000	5,000	5,000	19,000
Total Receipts	2,000	2,000	2,000	3,000	5,000	5,000	19,000
Rent	300	300	300	300	300	300	1,800
Wages	500	500	500	500	1,000	1,000	4,000
Electricity			150				150
Advertising			500	500			1,000
Equipment	4,000						4,000
Total Payments	4,800	800	1,450	1,300	1,300	1,300	10,950
Opening Balance	0	−2,800	−1,600	−1,050	650	4,350	
+ Receipts	2,000	2,000	2,000	3,000	5,000	5,000	
	2,000	−800	400	1,950	5,650	9,350	
− Payments	4,800	800	1,450	1,300	1,300	1,300	
Closing Balance	−2,800	−1,600	−1,050	650	4,350	8,050	

Study the cash flow forecast above and answer the following questions:

1 Choose one business from the following list which the above cash flow forecast might be for – garden centre, toy shop, grocery shop.

2 How could the owner have prevented the low balances during the first three months?

3 Comment on the overall performance of the business.

Activity

Roger put £17,400 into the bank as his own capital on 1 January to open a small café in Portrush. He forecasts that his sales will be £700 for each of the first two months, rising to £1,200 in March. Easter is in April and the daytrippers start coming then so he anticipates his sales will be £3,000 in April and May and will rise again to £5,000 in June when the town has more visitors.

Roger has calculated that his purchases will be £300 in January and February, £500 in March, £800 in April and May and £1,000 in June. Roger plans to employ one part-time waitress in January, February and March.

For April and May he will employ a second part-time waitress, and will take on a third part-time person for June. Each part-time employee will be paid £250 per month. Small items of new machinery are to be bought in January and April costing £400 each. Roger's rent has been agreed at £600 per month. Electricity costing £150 is due to be paid in March and June and telephone bills of £100 will be paid in March and June.

You should now design a cash flow forecast for six months from January to June for Roger. Comment on the overall performance of Roger's business.

Activity

Complete the boxes marked A, B, C and D in the following cash flow forecast.

Cash flow forecast of The Picture Frame Company – January to March

RECEIPTS	January	February	March
	£	£	£
Opening balance	55,000	22,000	**B**
Sales Revenue	42,000	41,000	46,000
Total	97,000	63,000	**C**
EXPENSES			
Purchases	32,000	20,000	15,000
Heat	3,000	0	0
Wages	40,000	41,000	38,000
Machinery	0	0	2,000
Total	**A**	61,000	55,000
Closing balance	22,000	2,000	**D**

Examination question

The Bookworm is a retail shop selling books and magazines in Carrickfergus. It is owned and managed by Carolyn.

a Carolyn sometimes has difficulty in maintaining a good cash flow. Explain the meaning of cash flow. (2 marks)

b Describe one way in which Carolyn might improve the cash flow in the Bookworm. (2 marks)

How to answer this question

In Part A give a short explanation of the meaning of cash flow. Keep it short as it is only given 2 marks.

In Part B just describe one way to improve cash flow and make sure that the method you describe is suitable for a bookshop.

Checklist ✓

At this stage you should be able to:
- ○ explain the purpose of cash flow forecasts
- ○ analyse the importance of cash flow to a business
- ○ complete parts of a cash flow forecast
- ○ calculate and interpret a simple cash flow forecast
- ○ analyse the consequences of incorrect forecasting.

Financial Statements can be described as a story in figures. The story which the Financial Statements tell is about the result of the year's work in the business and the amount of profit or loss made.

There are two Statements – the Income Statement and the Statement of Financial Position. The purpose of the Income Statement is to find the gross and net profits (or gross and net losses) at the end of the year's trading, while the purpose of the Statement of Financial Position is to show the accurate value of the business on any given date.

The Income Statement

▲ Profit or loss? An Income Statement

The Income Statement includes the following sections.

Cost of sales and inventories

In order to sell goods, the business has to purchase them. These new purchases will be added to the opening inventory, which is the amount of goods already in the business. At the end of the year some inventory will be left unsold. This is called the closing inventory and will be kept for the next year.

Cost of Sales = Opening Inventory + Purchases – Closing Inventory

If a business has opening inventory valued at £9,000, purchases of £15,000 and closing inventory of £3,750, then its cost of sales would be £20,250.

Gross Profit/Gross Loss

Gross profit or gross loss is the difference between the money the business makes from the sale of goods (sales revenue) and the cost of sales.

Therefore, if a business has sales revenue of £100,000 and the cost of sales is £75,000, the gross profit would be £25,000. However, if the sales revenue is £100,000 and the cost of sales is £110,000, then the business would make a gross loss of £10,000.

Gross Profit = Sales Revenue – Cost of Sales

Activity

Using the details given, calculate the gross profit or gross loss for five different years for a carrier firm called Speedy Service.

	Year 1	Year 2	Year 3	Year 4	Year 5
Sales	£120,000	£140,000	£155,000	£160,000	£185,000
Cost of sales	£83,000	£97,000	£115,000	£165,000	£165,000
Gross profit					

A loss is shown in brackets.

Expenses

Examples of a business's expenses are rent, rates, electricity, telephone, salaries and heating. These are subtracted from the gross profit to find the net profit.

Net Profit/Net Loss

Net profit is the true profit of the business for that year and takes into consideration all the expenses which have to be paid by the business. Net profit is the amount of money remaining after these expenses have been paid out of the gross profit. A net loss occurs if the expenses are greater than the gross profit.

Net Profit = Gross Profit – Expenses

Therefore, if a business has a gross profit of £15,000 and its total expenses are £9,000, the net profit would be £6,000. However, if the gross profit is £15,000 and its expenses are £19,000, the business would have a net loss of £4,000.

The Income Statement records:
- the total sales revenue for the year
- the cost of sales
- the gross profit
- all expenses
- net profit.

The title of the Income Statement should show the name of the business and the end-of-year date.

Display of the complete Income Statement

The following Income Statement is displayed for Music Makers, a music shop.

▼ Income Statement of Music Makers for the year ended 31 December

	£	£
Sales Revenue		27,500
LESS COST OF SALES:		
Opening Inventory	9,000	
Add Purchases	15,000	
	24,000	
Less Closing Inventory	3,750	
Cost of Sales		20,250
GROSS PROFIT		7,250
LESS EXPENSES:		
Electricity	510	
Stationery	125	
Rates	750	
Interest on Loan	150	
Advertising	845	
Insurance	545	
Telephone	250	3,175
NET PROFIT		4,075

Activity

Using the details given, calculate the net profit for The Bookworm, a bookshop, and The Fish Tank, a fish shop.

	The Bookworm	The Fish Tank
Gross profit	£20,000	£14,000
Expenses	£14,505	£15,210
Net profit/loss		

Activity

Copy the following account and complete the spaces marked A, B, C.

▼ Income Statement of Michael's Mechanics for the year ended 31 December

	£	£
Sales Revenue		35,000
LESS COST OF SALES		
Opening Inventory	7,000	
Add Purchases	**A**	
	25,000	
Less Closing Inventory	3,750	
Cost of Sales		**B**
GROSS PROFIT		13,750
LESS EXPENSES:		
Electricity	630	
Stationery	190	
Rates	750	
Postage	80	
Advertising	**C**	
Insurance	700	
Telephone	240	3,090
NET PROFIT		10,660

Examination question

Study the following Income Statement and answer the question which follows.

▼ Income Statement of Sports Equipment Ltd for the year ended 31 December

	£	£
Sales		120,000
Less Cost of Sales:		
Opening Inventory	13,200	
Add Purchases	66,800	
	80,000	
Less Closing Inventory	11,300	
Cost of Sales		68,700
Gross Profit		51,300
Less Expenses	14,900	
Net Profit		36,400

Suggest two ways in which Sports Equipment Ltd might increase its net profit. [2 marks]

How to answer this question

There are only 2 marks for this question so you should just name two ways – 1 mark for each way. You will not be rewarded for a longer explanation.

The Statement of Financial Position

The Statement of Financial Position lists assets (items owned by the business) and liabilities (items owed by the business). The purpose of the Statement of Financial Position is to show the accurate value of the business on any given date.

Assets are divided into non-current and current assets:

▶ Non-current assets are those assets which are more permanent in the business. An example is machinery.

▶ Current assets are those assets which can quickly be exchanged for cash. An example is inventory or Trade Receivables (money owed to the business by its customers).

Liabilities are divided into non-current and current liabilities:

▶ Non-current liabilities are those liabilities which are borrowed for a longer time. An example is a bank loan.

▶ Current liabilities are those liabilities which must be paid immediately. An example is Trade Payables (people to whom the business owes money).

Activity

Decide whether each of the following items is an asset or a liability.

Money in the bank ....

Money owed to suppliers ....

Machinery ....

Money owed by customers ....

Office equipment ....

Bank overdraft ....

Mortgage ....

Premises ....

The Statement of Financial Position records:

▶ the business's assets – divided into non-current and current assets

▶ the business's liabilities – divided into non-current and current liabilities

▶ the owner's capital (amount of their original investment)

▶ the owner's drawings (cash or goods withdrawn from the business by the owner for their personal use)

▶ the net profit (transferred from the Income Statement).

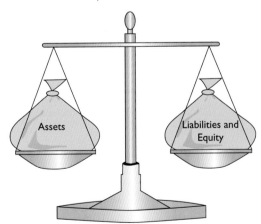

▲ It's all about balance: assets versus equity and liabilities

The title of the Statement of Financial Position should show the name of the business and the date it is being worked on.

The following complete Statement of Financial Position is for Music Makers.

▼ Statement of Financial Position of Music Makers as at 31 December

	£	£
NON-CURRENT ASSETS		
Premises	60,000	
Recording Equipment	13,200	
Motor Van	8,700	
TOTAL NON-CURRENT ASSETS		81,900
CURRENT ASSETS		
Cash in Hand	970	
Bank Balance	10,050	
Closing Inventory	3,750	
Trade Receivables	1,750	
TOTAL CURRENT ASSETS		16,520
TOTAL ASSETS		98,420
EQUITY		
Capital	77,000	
Add Net Profit	4,075	
	81,075	
Less Drawings	3,415	
TOTAL EQUITY		77,660
NON-CURRENT LIABILITIES		
Bank Loan	20,000	
TOTAL NON-CURRENT LIABILITIES		20,000
CURRENT LIABILITIES		
Trade Payables	760	
TOTAL CURRENT LIABILITIES		760
TOTAL EQUITY AND LIABILITIES		98,420

You should note that the total of the assets must equal the total of the equity and liabilities.

Activity

Complete the spaces marked A, B and C in the following Statement of Financial Position.

▼ Statement of Financial Position of Michael's Mechanics as at 31 December

	£	£
NON-CURRENT ASSETS		
Premises	A	
Machinery	4,300	
TOTAL NON-CURRENT ASSETS		45,300
CURRENT ASSETS		
Cash in Hand	B	
Closing Inventory	3,750	
Trade Receivables	750	
TOTAL CURRENT ASSETS		6,020
TOTAL ASSETS		51,320
EQUITY		
Capital	37,150	
Add Net Profit	C	
	47,810	
Less Drawings	2,490	
TOTAL EQUITY		45,320
NON-CURRENT LIABILITIES		
Bank Loan	5,200	
TOTAL NON-CURRENT LIABILITIES		5,200
CURRENT LIABILITIES		
Trade Payables	800	
TOTAL CURRENT LIABILITIES		800
TOTAL EQUITY AND LIABILITIES		51,320

Activity

The following list shows the balances at 31 December for Petals, a flower shop. Use this information to work out an Income Statement and a Statement of Financial Position for Petals.

		£
Sales Revenue		34,500
Opening Inventory		2,000
Capital		30,950
Bank Loan		7,000
Drawings		1,625
Cash Balance		100
Trade Receivables		10,000
Salary		4,900
Bank Overdraft		1,100
Advertising		850
General Expenses		350
Electricity		800
Insurance		175
Rent		750
Trade Payables		12,000
Premises		19,000
Purchases		25,000
Motor Vehicles		20,000
Closing Inventory		3,000

Checklist ✓

At this stage you should be able to:
○ complete simple Financial Statements for a sole trader
○ complete an Income Statement
○ complete a Statement of Financial Position
○ explain and interpret an Income Statement and a Statement of Financial Position and explain their importance.

Examination question

Some amounts are missing in the following Statement of Financial Position.
Complete the spaces marked A, B, C and D.   [4 marks]

▾ Statement of Financial Position of the Teabag Cafe as at 31 December

	£	£
Non-Current Assets		
Buildings	A	
Shop Equipment	15,000	
Total Non-Current Assets		47,000
Current Assets		
Closing Inventory	1,500	
Cash Balance	1,000	
Bank Balance	B	
Total Current Assets		7,500
Total Assets		C
Equity		
Capital	20,000	
Add Net Profit	D	
	22,000	
Less Drawings	1,000	
Total Equity		21,000
Non-Current Liabilities		
Loan	25,000	
Total Non-Current Liabilities		25,000
Current Liabilities		
Trade Payables	8,500	
Total Current Liabilities		8,500
Total Liabilities		33,500
Total Equity and Liabilities		54,500

How to answer this question

Start at the beginning of the Statement and work downwards. Work carefully and make
sure you check your work. Remember that the total assets should equal the total equity and
liabilities.

6.4 Ratios

Now that you understand the **Income Statement** and **Statement of Financial Position**, you can start to interpret them to extract information from them. By reading the Income Statement and Statement of Financial Position it is easy to see the level of profit or loss which the business has made. However, this does not tell us enough to enable us to assess the true performance of the business.

There are a number of ratios and percentages which help us to get an accurate calculation of the performance of the business and also enable us to compare its performance from year to year. All these calculations use figures which are shown in the Income Statement and Statement of Financial Position.

Gross profit percentage

This calculation shows the level of **gross profit** which a business has made on the sales revenue. It is a measure of the business's trading profitability and efficiency – the higher the percentage figure is, the better the trading performance.

The formula for finding **Gross profit percentage** is:

$$\frac{\text{Gross Profit}}{\text{Percentage}} = \frac{\text{Gross Profit}}{\text{Sales Revenue}} \times 100$$

For example, if a business has sales revenue of £68,740 and its gross profit is £29,500:

$$\frac{\text{Gross Profit}}{\text{Percentage}} = \frac{29,500}{68,740} \times 100$$

Gross Profit Percentage = 42.9%

This result means that for every £1 of sales revenue, this business makes almost 43p gross profit – an excellent result!

Net profit percentage

This calculation shows the amount of **net profit** which is made on sales revenue. It measures the business's profitability and efficiency not only in trading but also in keeping its expenses down – the higher the percentage figure is, the better the overall performance.

The formula for finding **Net profit percentage** is:

$$\frac{\text{Net Profit}}{\text{Percentage}} = \frac{\text{Net Profit}}{\text{Sales Revenue}} \times 100$$

For example, if a business has sales revenue of £68,740 and its net profit is £13,500:

$$\frac{\text{Net Profit}}{\text{Percentage}} = \frac{13,500}{68,740} \times 100$$

Net Profit Percentage = 19.6%

This result means that for every £1 of sales revenue, this business makes 19.6p net profit – an average result!

Activity

Calculate the gross and net profit percentages for each year using the figures in the following table.

	Year 1	Year 2	Year 3
Sales	£54,706	£63,750	£70,322
Gross profit	£41,030	£45,900	£49,225
Net profit	£9,300	£10,200	£10,900
Gross Profit Percentage			
Net profit percentage			

Inventory turnover rate

This calculation shows the number of times in a year that the business is able to sell the value of its average inventory. It is, therefore, another measure of the business's trading efficiency – the higher the rate is, the better the business activity.

A business's **inventory turnover rate** depends on the type of goods it sells. If its goods are high value goods – jewellery, for example – it will make fewer sales but each sale is likely to be for a large amount of money. A jeweller may only replace inventory once or twice a year. On the other hand, if the business deals in goods which are low value – fruit and vegetables, for example – it will make a large number of sales but each sale would be for a small sum. Perishable vegetables would be replaced every working day.

The formula for finding the inventory turnover rate is:

$$\frac{\text{Inventory}}{\text{Turnover Rate}} = \frac{\text{cost of sales}}{\text{average inventory}}$$

(Average inventory is opening inventory plus closing inventory divided by 2.)

For example if a business's **cost of sales** is £13,800 and its average inventory is £2,010:

$$\text{Inventory Turnover Rate} = \frac{13,800}{2,010}$$

Inventory Turnover Rate = 6.9 times

This result means that the business sells its stock almost seven times each year.

Return on capital employed (ROCE)

This calculation shows the profitability of the business by comparing the net profit with the capital invested by the owners. It shows the net profit which the owner has received on the capital invested. The owner should compare this result with the profit which would have been received if the money had been invested in shares in other businesses or deposited in the bank, for example. The higher the return, the better the performance of the business.

The formula for finding **return on capital employed** is:

$$\frac{\text{Return on Capital}}{\text{Employed}} = \frac{\text{Net Profit}}{\text{Capital Employed}} \times 100$$

For example if the capital invested in the business is £80,000 and the Net Profit is £13,500:

$$\text{Return on Capital Employed} = \frac{13500}{80000} \times 100$$

Return on Capital Employed = 16.9%

This result means that the owner is making almost 17% profit on his/her investment.

Activity

Statement of Financial Position of Sweet Dreams as at 31 December...

	£	£
NON-CURRENT ASSETS		
Premises	90,000	
Furniture and Fittings	3,200	
Delivery Van	8,700	
TOTAL NON-CURRENT ASSETS		101,900
CURRENT ASSETS		
Cash	1,970	
Bank	9,050	
Closing Inventory	3,750	
Trade Receivables	1,750	
TOTAL CURRENT ASSETS		16,520
TOTAL ASSETS		118,420
EQUITY		
Capital	75,920	
Add Net Profit	11,500	
	87,420	
Less Drawings	8,000	
TOTAL EQUITY		79,420
NON-CURRENT LIABILITIES		
Mortgage	30,000	
TOTAL NON-CURRENT LIABILITIES		30,000
CURRENT LIABILITIES		
Trade Payables	9,000	
TOTAL CURRENT LIABILITIES		9,000
TOTAL EQUITY AND LIABILITIES		118,420

Using the details in the above account, calculate the Return on Capital Employed for Sweet Dreams.

Working capital ratio

This ratio shows the relationship between a business's **current assets** and **current liabilities**. The **working capital ratio** measures the business's ability to pay its debts such as trade payables.

The formula for finding working capital ratio is:

$$\text{Working Capital Ratio} = \frac{\text{Current Assets}}{\text{Current Liabilities}}$$

For example if the current assets in the business are valued at £80,000 and the current liabilities amount to £40,000:

$$\text{Working Capital Ratio} = \frac{80,000}{40,000}$$

Working Capital Ratio = 2:1

This result means that for every £1 which the business owes, it has £2 of assets. Therefore it is very able to pay the debts. The ideal ratio is between 1:5 and 2:1.

Examination question

Easy Connections is a retail shop which is owned by Lisa and sells computers and mobile phones. Lisa's capital employed is £200,000 and she received a total Net Profit of £15,000 in one year.

1 Complete the spaces in the following formula to calculate Lisa's Return on Capital Employed.

$$\frac{\text{Return on Capital}}{\text{Employed}} = \frac{\text{Net Profit}}{\text{Capital Employed}} \times 100$$

Return on Capital Employed = _____ × 100

Return on Capital Employed = _____   (2 marks)

2 Explain the meaning of 'Return on Capital Employed'.   (2 marks)

3 The Return on Capital Employed in Easy Connections for the previous year was 8.2%. Analyse the business performance of Easy Connections and advise Lisa on what action she should take.   (8 marks)

How to answer this question

In Part 1 you should complete the formula with the figures given and work out the Return on Capital Employed for 2 marks. You will lose 1 mark if you do not show the % sign in the answer.

In Part 2 you should write an explanation of ROCE and the information which it gives the business.

In Part 3 you should compare your answer from Part 1 with 8.2% and comment on whether the result is improving or not. You should then comment on how Lisa should respond to the situation.

Checklist

At this stage you should be able to:

○ interpret and analyse an Income Statement and Statement of Financial Position using the following ratios:
   – gross profit percentage
   – net profit percentage
   – inventory turnover rate
   – return on capital employed (ROCE)
   – working capital ratio.

6.5 Breakeven

Before learning about breakeven, it is necessary to understand costs. There are two types of costs – fixed and variable.

Fixed costs

Fixed costs are those costs which are not affected by the quantity of goods produced or sold or by the scale of services rendered. They are called 'fixed' because they do not alter regardless of the volume of work done in the business. For example, factory rent is a fixed cost because it will have to be paid in full whether the factory is manufacturing goods at full capacity or at a reduced level.

On a graph, fixed costs would be shown as a straight horizontal line as is shown here. You can see that the fixed costs stay on one level regardless of the number of units produced. You should also notice that the fixed costs are at that level even if there are no units being produced.

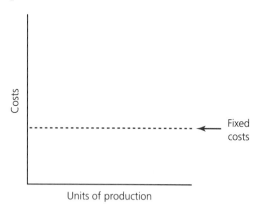

▲ Graph of fixed costs

Variable costs

Variable costs are those costs which vary – or change – according to the level of work being done in the business. For example in a factory, wages will increase if the factory is working at full production level but will decrease if production is reduced and some employees

have to be made redundant. Electricity usage will vary for the same reasons as will the purchase of raw materials.

On a graph, variable costs would be shown as a straight diagonal line because they rise in direct proportion to the rise in production. Notice that there are no variable costs at the point of no production.

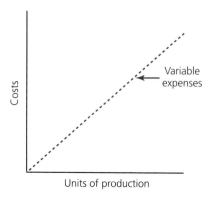

▲ Graph of variable costs

Total costs

The total cost of the business is found by adding together the variable and fixed costs.

Total Costs = Fixed Costs + Variable Costs

On a graph, total costs are shown as a diagonal line but notice that the total costs line starts at the level of fixed costs. This is because, even at the point of no production, the business has incurred total costs equal to the fixed costs.

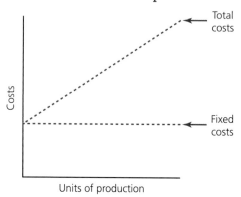

▲ Graph of total costs

Activity

Tick the appropriate spaces in the table to show whether each cost is fixed or variable.

COST	FIXED	VARIABLE
Mortgage repayments		
Rates		
Transport		
Postage		
Machinery repairs		
Advertising		
Telephone		
Rent		

Activity

Complete the table to show the missing amounts of costs for four years in The Paper Mill – a newspaper shop and answer the questions which follow.

YEAR	FIXED COSTS	VARIABLE COSTS	TOTAL COSTS
1	£8,000.00		£13,500.00
2		£6,000.00	£14,500.00
3	£9,000.00		£15,350.00
4	£9,500.00	£9,000.00	

1 Name two fixed costs which The Paper Mill might have.

2 Explain the steady increase in fixed costs over four years.

3 Name two variable costs which The Paper Mill might have.

Breakeven

A business's **breakeven point** is where its total costs equal the total of its sales revenue. It is the minimum point at which the business can survive. At this point the business is making neither a profit nor a loss – it is simply covering its costs.

If it can sell more goods than the level of breakeven it will make a profit. However, if its sales fall below the breakeven level, then the business would be in a loss-making situation.

Significance of the breakeven point

The concept of 'breakeven' is extremely important in business because it can show:

▶ the amount of goods which must be sold in order to make a profit
▶ the level of costs which the business can bear
▶ the price which needs to be charged for goods
▶ how changes in the price would affect the business's profits.

How is the breakeven point worked out?

The most usual method of finding the breakeven point is to work a graph. It is also possible to calculate the breakeven point using a formula. Both methods need to have information on both the business's total costs and its sales revenue.

Calculating breakeven by formula

The formula for calculating breakeven is:

$$\frac{\text{Total Fixed Costs}}{\text{Selling Price Per Unit} - \text{Variable Cost Per Unit}}$$

Study the following example:

Patrick owns a bookshop in Omagh. Calculate his breakeven point if his total fixed costs are £4,000 per month, each book sells on average at £7 and his variable costs are £2 per book.

$$\text{Breakeven} = \frac{4,000}{7 - 2}$$
$$= \frac{4,000}{5}$$

Breakeven = 800 books

This means that Patrick must sell 800 books every month in order to break even. He says that he would find this difficult, so he decides to increase the price of his books from £7 to £9. The new calculation would be:

$$\text{Breakeven} = \frac{4,000}{9-2}$$

$$= \frac{4,000}{7}$$

Breakeven = 571.4 (572)

After the price increase, Patrick must sell 572 books every month in order to break even. He feels he can manage this level of sales but knows that he cannot increase his prices again or else his customers will begin to go to other bookshops.

Activity

Eithne owns a bakery in Toomebridge. Her total fixed costs are £2,100 per month and her variable costs are £1 per unit on average. She sells each cake for £4 on average.

1 Calculate Eithne's breakeven point by formula.

2 Eithne gets the bad news that her rent is being increased by £100 per month. What is her new breakeven point?

3 Calculate Eithne's breakeven point if:
   a she increased the average price of her cakes from £4 to £5 and her rates increased by £50 per month.

Activity

Complete the following table for Tom who is the manager of a toy factory in Magherafelt. The fixed costs of the factory amount to £500 per week and the variable costs are £2 per toy. Each toy is sold for £4. The table is started for you.

Number of toys sold	Total income from sales	Fixed costs	Variable costs	Total costs	Profit/Loss
	£	£	£	£	£
0	0	500	0	500	−500
25	100	500	50	550	−450
50					
75					
100					
125					
150					
175					
200					
225					
250					
275					
300					

Calculating breakeven graphically

A breakeven graph is used to illustrate the:

▶ profit or loss of a business

▶ relationship between total costs and sales

▶ relationship between fixed and variable costs.

Breakeven graphs do have some limitations which you should be aware of:

▶ Perhaps not all the goods will be sold.

▶ Fixed costs are assumed to never change. This is not always the case. Some circumstances such as greatly increased production might mean taking on new premises which would increase the rates for example.

▶ Sales are not always made at a constant level. Businesses sometimes have to offer discounts to clear their inventory.

Before beginning to draw a breakeven chart, it is essential to have details of the business's sales, as well as details of its fixed and variable costs.

Worked example of a breakeven graph

Here is a breakeven graph for David, the owner of a factory in Larne which manufactures small items of office equipment. He needs your help in finding the breakeven point for a new stapler which is just ready to be put on the market.

His fixed costs in the factory amount to £500 per week and his variable costs are £6 per stapler. Each stapler is going to be sold for £11.

It is easier to draw a graph if you first construct a table showing the following details.

Number of staplers sold	Total income from sales	Fixed costs	Variable costs	Total costs	Profit/ Loss
	£	£	£	£	£
0	0	500	0	500	−500
20	220	500	120	620	−400
40	440	500	240	740	−300
60	660	500	360	860	−200
80	880	500	480	980	−100
100	1,100	500	600	1,100	0
120	1,320	500	720	1,220	+100
140	1,540	500	840	1,340	+200
160	1,760	500	960	1,460	+300

We can then use the table to construct the graph and read off the breakeven point.

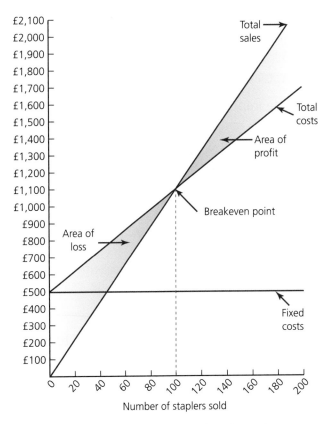

▲ Breakeven chart to show sale of staplers

Note the following:

▶ The total income from sales and total costs may be read off the vertical axis.

▶ The graph should show the total units of sales – staplers, in this case – on the horizontal axis.

▶ The fixed costs should be plotted first.

▶ Next plot the total costs.

▶ Finally plot the income from sales.

▶ Always remember to put on all labels.

▶ The breakeven point should be shown with a broken line drawn to the horizontal axis.

The breakeven point is 100, therefore David must sell 100 staplers per week in order to cover his costs of £1,100.

Activity ✏️

You should now return to the table which you completed for Tom, the manager of the toy factory in Magherafelt.

Use the information in the table to draw a breakeven graph for Tom's toy factory in Magherafelt and indicate the breakeven point on the graph. It is important to label the graph fully.

The margin of safety

The **margin of safety** is the amount which a business sells in excess of its breakeven point.

One of the main aims of a business is to make a profit and expand its market. No business

therefore would be content to operate at the breakeven point for long, so once the business has found its breakeven level it then attempts to exceed it and plan for a higher level of sales. This higher level then becomes its 'selected operating point'.

Let us return to the graph for the sale of staplers where the breakeven point was 100. David now tells us that he is able to sell 140 staplers per week.

Study the following graph to see how the margin of safety is illustrated.

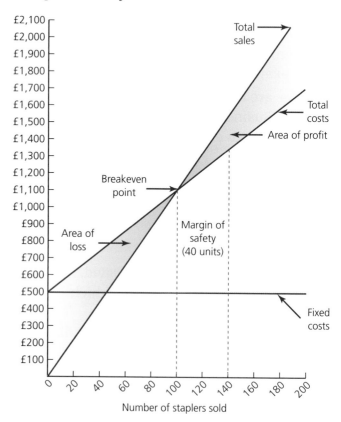

Number of staplers sold

The margin of safety is 40 because David plans to sell 140 staplers per week which is 40 more than the breakeven point.

Activity

The following information was provided by RK Ltd. Study it and answer the questions which follow:

Monthly costs of production of a new toy

Fixed costs	.. ..	£2,000
Labour	.. ..	£6 per unit
Materials	.. ..	£4 per unit
Expected sales	.. ..	450 units
Selling price	.. ..	£15

1 Explain why it is important for a business to calculate the breakeven point.

2 Calculate how many units RK Ltd needs to sell in order to breakeven.

3 What do you understand by the term 'margin of safety'?

4 What margin of safety would RK Ltd have for this product?

5 What difference would it make to RK Ltd if labour costs increased to £7 per unit?

Examination question

The breakeven chart for Office Essential's best-selling calculator is shown below:

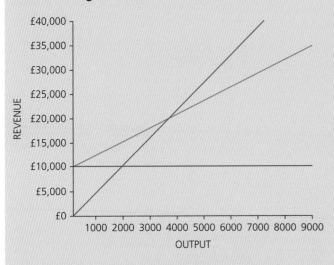

Insert the following labels on the Breakeven Chart:

Breakeven point

Fixed Costs

Total Costs

Total Sales

Area of Profit

Area of Loss   (6 Marks)

Study the Breakeven Chart and state the figures for the following:

Output at breakeven point   ....

Sales revenue at breakeven point   ....

Fixed Costs   ....

The output making a total sales revenue of £30,000   ....

The total costs of manufacturing 7000 calculators   ....   (5 Marks)

How to answer this question

Label the chart very neatly and be careful to read off the amounts accurately.

Checklist ✓

At this stage you should be able to:
- ○ calculate breakeven graphically and by formula
- ○ explain the significance of the breakeven point
- ○ distinguish between fixed and variable costs
- ○ label a breakeven chart
- ○ analyse a breakeven graph
- ○ calculate the margin of safety
- ○ explain the significance of the margin of safety.

PLANNING A BUSINESS

LEARNING OBJECTIVES

▶ To apply knowledge and understanding drawn from the whole specification to a real business context.

▶ To carry out research and apply it, together with their own knowledge, to a range of circumstances.

▶ To examine and evaluate specified areas of a business plan.

▶ To make reasoned recommendations.

When a new business starts up for the first time or when an existing business wishes to expand – perhaps by bringing out new products or by selling in new markets – it is important to write a business plan. Going into business without a business plan is like trying to drive a car without a steering wheel – there is no way of directing it!

A business plan is a detailed description of what a business hopes to do over a period of usually one to five years – after that time it needs to be updated. A business plan acts as a guide for the business and can be referred to frequently to make sure the business is meeting its targets.

The importance of planning in business cannot be over-emphasised. According to a study carried out by the Federation of Small Businesses, 400,000 small businesses were set up one year, 55,000 of which failed. The major factor for failure was given as inadequate planning. Another study found that companies which had planned properly had 50% more income and profit growth than businesses which did not have clear plans.

The business plan shows:

▶ an introduction to the project which is planned
▶ details of what the business plans to do – its objectives
▶ details of resources which are needed
▶ details of how the product will be marketed
▶ details of how the product or service will be produced
▶ costs during that period
▶ expected level of sales revenue and income
▶ timescale for starting to make a profit
▶ expectation of when it would be able to repay loans.

Reasons for developing a business plan

▶ **To show to the bank** – A new business, or one which is hoping to expand, is likely to need to borrow money from the bank or other source. The bank manager would be unwilling to lend money unless he/she was reasonably sure that the business would be able to repay both the loan and the interest on the loan. The purpose of a business plan is to work out accurately the amount of money which is required and then to convince the bank manager that the business idea is viable and that the loan is a safe investment from the bank's point of view.

▶ **To show to shareholders** – The business would probably have shareholders who have invested finance in the business. They will use the business plan to gauge the strength of the business and to decide whether or not they wish to remain as shareholders.

▶ **To show to other possible investors** – The business may hope to encourage other investors to put money into the business. These potential investors would also study the business plan to see if they would receive a worthwhile return on their investment.

▶ **To ensure proper planning of the business** – The actual process of compiling the business plan is a valuable one because it forces the business owners and managers to think about every tiny detail of the business. This makes sure that nothing is left out and that there are no forgotten costs to be discovered later. This fact also adds to the confidence of the bank manager and other investors who can see that the business idea has been carefully thought out.

▶ **To monitor actual performance against the plan** – The business plan is also very useful to the managers in the business who can monitor the actual progress of the business against the plan. The business's managers will be constantly comparing its performance against how it expected to perform, and they will also compare their performance against that of their competitors.

▶ **To keep a check on spending** – The **accounts** produced as part of the business plan will be used to check the monthly figures and any differences can be investigated before they become too great.

▶ **To ensure that aims/objectives are being met** – The business owners and managers would also use the business plan to monitor whether and how the stated aims/objectives are being met in the running of the business.

Style of the business plan

Most businesses go to great trouble to make their business plans very professional. Some are bound, but all are presented in covers with the business name and logo. This is to present a good image to potential financiers and to make them interested in the business.

Components of a business plan

Business plans differ in design and layout but the following information is common to all of them. The sub-headings and their order, may vary according to the type of business being

planned. For example, many business plans have ten to twelve headings, so the following are suggested only as a framework and is all that is required for GCSE.

▶ Introduction to proposed business
▶ Business objectives
▶ Resources plan
▶ Marketing plan
▶ Production plan
▶ Financial plan

Introduction to proposed business

This is where the business makes its first impression and therefore it is very important to get the introduction right. The impact of this page should make people reading the business plan want to invest in the business. The introduction should be short and attention grabbing. It should:

▶ include the business name and address
▶ describe the business idea – what goods or services are to be produced
▶ briefly state why that product is marketable and its benefits.

The business objectives

(Links with Unit 1 – Creating a business)

This section gives details of the business and explains its work. It should include:

▶ the strengths of the business and its past achievements
▶ a brief summary of the value of the business and how it has been funded
▶ the legal status of the business – is it run and owned by a sole trader, partnership or company?
▶ any service awards already awarded
▶ the goals or objectives of the business. These are likely to include levels of profit, sales expectations and future product development

▶ a mission statement would be appropriate in this section

▶ the personal details of the owner.

Resources plan

(Links with Unit 1 – Creating a business)

This section describes the people involved in the business together with details of their special contributions to the business. It also includes:

▶ a description of the premises – its size, location and special features

▶ details of the equipment available

▶ description of raw materials required – if the business is a manufacturing one

▶ required levels of working capital.

Marketing plan

(Links with Unit 1 – Marketing)

This section gives details of the likely types of customers for the new product. It includes:

▶ details of the competition

▶ estimations of the overall demand for the product, projected as far as possible into the future

▶ information received from previous market research about the demand for the new product

▶ a description of where it is proposed to market the product and how it will be distributed

▶ details of any expected future developments to the product

▶ details of the price at which the product is to be sold

▶ details of how the product is to be promoted and advertised.

Production plan (for a manufacturing business)

(Links with Unit 1 – Business operations)

This includes:

▶ a full description of the production process (if the business is involved in manufacturing) *(Links with Unit 1 – Creating a business)*

▶ details of how the premises will be used in the production process

▶ details of the layout of the equipment and the design of the work area

▶ evidence should be provided that features such as health and safety requirements and ergonomics have been catered for.

Financial plan

(Links with Unit 2 – Finance)

It includes:

▶ a breakeven analysis – to show the point at which profit can be expected. This will also show sales revenue estimates

▶ a cash flow statement to explain the likely timing of the business's income and payments

▶ a statement of the capital invested by the owners to show the funding of the business

▶ details of other loans already given to the business together with details of the terms of those loans

▶ details of mortgages on the premises

▶ most recent Income Statements and Statements of Financial Position to show the financial history of the business.

Activity

Match the sentences on the right side to the components named on the left side of the table.

COMPONENTS	
Introduction	States the goals of the business
Objectives	Would include a breakeven analysis
Resources Plan	Shows how the product will be made
Marketing Plan	Describes the people involved in the business
Production Plan	Makes the first impression
Financial Plan	Gives details of the estimated demand

A worked example of a business plan

Case study

Modern Technology is the name of a proposed business in Armagh. The business is being planned by Freddie Carroll and he is preparing his business plan which he hopes to submit to his bank manager.

Freddie has previously carried out market research and he has discovered that there is little competition in the area. He has also found out that there is a demand for high quality PC computers, laptops, tablets and smartphones and for all types of computer software. His research has informed him that his niche market is mainly from the local business community which would like to be able to buy technology locally and quickly. There are large numbers of students in Armagh who would also be an important part of his market.

Introduction

Business Plan for a new retailing outlet selling high-quality technology and associated software products

by Freddie Carroll

The computer products for sale will be sophisticated models offering the best technology at keen prices.

Freddie Carroll's proposed business in Armagh is a completely new one so it has not got any past achievements or awards to show.

Objectives

Modern Technology – the business and its objectives		
Ownership	Freddie Carroll and Anne Carroll	
Rented business premises	32 High Street ARMAGH	
Private address	Deanne House 88 Church Spires ARMAGH	
Legal status	Partnership with two equal partners	
Purpose of the business	Modern Technology is being established for the retail sale of high-quality computers, laptops, tablets, smartphones, other hardware components, high-quality software products and high-quality stationery for computer use.	
Strengths of the business	Freddie Carroll has an established good reputation in this trade and a firm knowledge of this type of business.	
Value of the business	Freddie and Anne Carroll have joint savings of £20,000 for investment in Modern Technology. Additional funding of £20,000 is being applied for from their bank.	
Business objectives	Projected turnover: £75,000 per annum	Projected gross profit: £40,000 per annum
Mission statement	We aim to match the highest quality products with the highest quality service.	

Freddie Carroll's proposed business is a retailing business so it will not have raw materials.

Modern Technology – the Resources Plan	
Management	Freddie Carroll. In year 1 he will withdraw £1,000 per month from the business for living expenses.
Managerial experience	Freddie Carroll has been the manager for ten years with the firm of 'Technology Supplies' in Craigavon. He has established contacts with suppliers in this trade.
Clerical assistant	Anne Carroll, working on a part-time, voluntary basis, will assist in the preparation of accounts while retaining her part-time job in the offices of a local accountancy firm.
Employees	No other people will be employed at the beginning. Later, it is planned to employ one assistant.
Premises	Situated at 32 High Street, Armagh. Premises rented for £300 per month comprising one shop area (40m x 30m), one store (50m x 25m) with street access.
Equipment	Shelving and display stands for small items Six desks for computer display with six chairs New delivery van (on credit until July)
Working capital	£15,000 in Year 1 rising to £20,000 in Year 3

Modern Technology – the Marketing Plan	
Customers	The main customers are the many business organisations in Armagh and the surrounding area which have indicated that they would value a local supplier. A large number of schools and their students as well as university students living in the area would be part of the market.
Competition	There is one other computer retailer in Armagh. The market is too large for one supplier.
Demand	In the first year, the demand is estimated at 50 computers, laptops, tablets or smartphones. Demand for supplies of software is estimated at £15,000 per year and £5,000 for stationery. With increased lines these figures could be doubled within five years.
Suppliers	Main supplier will be 'Ever Ready Technology' who will supply on one month's credit. A second supplier will deliver extra goods in December for cash.
Market place	Sales will be conducted at the premises in Armagh.
Distribution	All products sold will be delivered and installed if necessary. A personal back-up service would be guaranteed.
Future development	Product lines would be extended in later years to include new ranges of popular technology products.
Price	The average prices are: Computers, laptops, tablets and smartphones – £1,100 Ink cartridges – £25 High quality 100g computer paper – £10 per ream
Promotion	Weekly advertising during the first six months in each of the local papers. An opening launch of the business to include viewing and demonstrations of computers. Free mouse mat with every computer sold.

Modern Technology is a retailing business so Freddie Carroll, did not write a production plan.

Freddie Carroll's business is a new one so he has to present a forecasted Income Statement and Statement of Financial Position rather than actual ones. The premises for Modern Technology are rented so Freddie does not have a mortgage. He does not have any loans other than the one he is hoping to get from the bank.

Financial Plan

Statement of Capital Invested on 1 January 20....

	£
Freddie Carroll	10,000
Anne Carroll	10,000

Cash Flow Forecast for Modern Technology for Year 1

	Jan	Feb	Mar	Apr	May	June	July	Aug	Sept	Oct	Nov	Dec	Total
	£	£	£	£	£	£	£	£	£	£	£	£	£
Receipts													
Capital	20,000												20,000
Loan	20,000												20,000
Sales	2,648	2,900	3,885	4,298	5,888	6,915	7,850	5,300	6,250	7,541	11,990	9,535	75,000
Total Receipts	42,648	2,900	3,885	4,298	5,888	6,915	7,850	5,300	6,250	7,541	11,990	9,535	115,000
Payments													
Rent	300	300	300	300	300	300	300	300	300	300	300	300	3,600
Purchases		3,125	4,150	5,000	2,500	3,700	1,000	1,000	1,500	8,500	775	23,125	54,375
Rates	100	100	100	100	100	100	100	100	100	100	100	100	1,200
Electricity			200			200			200			200	800
Shelves	750												750
Desks	720												720
Chairs	300												300
Décor	1,500												1,500
Wages	1,000	1,000	1,000	1,000	1,000	1,000	1,000	1,000	1,000	1,000	1,000	1,000	12,000
Advert	200	200	200	200	200	200							1,200
Van							40,000						40,000
Telephone			120			120			120			120	480
Insurance	500										1,000		1,500
Office Stationery	50												50
Loan Interest	80	80	80	80	80	80	80	80	80	80	80	80	960
Total Payments	5,500	4,805	6,150	6,680	4,180	5,700	42,480	2,480	3,300	9,980	3,255	24,925	119,435
Opening													
Balance	0	37,148	35,243	32,978	30,596	32,304	33,519	−1,111	1,709	4,659	2,220	10,955	
Add Receipts	42,648	2,900	3,885	4,298	5,888	6,915	7,850	5,300	6,250	7,541	11,990	9,535	
	42,648	40,048	39,128	37,276	36,484	39,219	41,369	4,189	7,959	12,200	14,210	20,490	
Less Payments	5,500	4,805	6,150	6,680	4,180	5,700	42,480	2,480	3,300	9,980	3,255	24,925	
Closing Balance	37,148	35,243	32,978	30,596	32,304	33,519	−1,111	1,709	4,659	2,220	10,955	−4,435	

Forecasted Income Statement of Modern Technology for the year ended 31 December:

	£	£
Sales Revenue		75,000
LESS COST OF SALES		
Purchases	54,375	
Less Closing Inventory	20,000	
Cost of Sales		34,375
GROSS PROFIT		40,625
LESS EXPENSES		
Electricity	800	
Stationery	50	
Rates	1,200	
Rent	3,600	
Interest of Loan	960	
Wages	12,000	
Insurance	1,500	
Decoration	1,500	
Advertising	1,200	
Telephone	480	23,290
NET PROFIT		17,335

Forecasted Statement of Financial Position of Modern Technology as at 31 December:

	£	£
NON-CURRENT ASSETS		
Fixtures and Fittings	750	
Furniture	1,020	
Motor Van	40,000	
TOTAL NON-CURRENT ASSETS		41,770
CURRENT ASSETS		
Trade Receivables	3,125	
Closing Inventory	20,000	
TOTAL CURRENT ASSETS		23,125
TOTAL ASSETS		64,895
EQUITY		
Capital	20,000	
Add Net Profit	17,335	
TOTAL EQUITY		37,335
NON-CURRENT LIABILITIES		
Bank Loan	20,000	
TOTAL NON-CURRENT LIABILITIES		20,000
CURRENT LIABILITIES		
Bank Overdraft	4,435	
Trade Payables	3,125	
TOTAL CURRENT LIABILITIES		7,560
TOTAL EQUITY AND LIABILITIES		64,895

Appendices

An appendix is usually added and acts as a place to show any additional background material. This material might include:

► any technical information on the product which has not been included previously

► any additional material from market research

► CVs for the staff (if any)

► photographs and drawings

► copies of legal documents such as partnership agreements or loan agreements.

Freddie Carroll decided to include the following in his business plan:

1 His own CV.

2 A copy of his partnership agreement with his wife and business partner, Anne.

3 A photograph of the premises he was planning to rent.

Evaluation of a business plan

Activity

The GCSE specifications require you to be able to evaluate a business plan. It is extremely unlikely that you would have access to a real business plan, but that doesn't really matter.

You will be working business plans in class. Swap your work with another student and evaluate each other's work constructively – that means that you look for its positive points but also should point out any omissions or details which are unclear.

As you study the business plan you are evaluating, ask yourself:

► Would I lend money to the proposed business?

► Does this business sound profitable?

► Would I want to buy from or sell to the proposed business?

► Do I need any additional information about it?

Examination question

Melanie is a qualified chemist who would like to open her own pharmacy. She knows that she should produce a business plan but is unsure how to write one.

Explain two reasons why it is important for Melanie to write a business plan. (4 marks)

How to answer this question

Give details of two reasons explaining the importance of a business plan. Each reason carries 2 marks.

Checklist ✔

At this stage you should be able to:

○ explain the reasons for developing a business plan

○ understand the components of a business plan

○ complete a simple business plan

○ evaluate a business plan.

Assessment objectives and command words used in the GCSE (CCEA) Business Studies examination

Assessment Objective	Controlled Assessment Weighting	Paper 1 Weighting	Paper 2 Weighting	Overall Weighting
AO1	5.00%	15.00%	15.00%	35.00%
AO2	9.00%	11.00%	15.00%	35.00%
AO3	6.00%	14.00%	10.00%	30.00%
TOTAL	20.00%	40.00%	40.00%	100%

The GCSE examination must examine three assessment objectives and the table above sets out the weightings for each one in the GCSE qualification. A variety of key terms – known as command words – is used to do this. This list is presented to show the exact requirements of each term used.

AO1

The first assessment objective finds out if candidates can recall, select and communicate knowledge and understanding of concepts, issues and terminology.

Define or explain	Give the details of a topic to show understanding. An example makes the explanation clearer.
Name, state or list	Give examples. No explanation is needed.
Identify	Name or list the required information.
Outline	Write a short description or a brief summary.
Show your calculation	Show the steps leading to the final answer.

AO2

The second assessment objective finds out if candidates can apply their knowledge and understanding in a variety of contexts.

Apply	Put into effect in a recognised way.
Comment on	Write an explanation or make remarks on the situation.
Calculate	Work out the answer to a mathematical question.
Demonstrate or show why	Explain understanding of the business concept being discussed.
Describe	Write about the main features of the topic to show knowledge.
Distinguish between	Show the difference between two terms.
Examine	A thorough explanation is necessary but a conclusion is not.
Explain	As for AO1
Suggest	Give views on reasons why something has occurred or perhaps on ways to solve a problem.
Use the data etc.	Select the data and apply it to the question being asked.
Which	Choose the best option.

AO3

The third assessment objective finds out if candidates can analyse and evaluate evidence, make reasoned judgements and present appropriate conclusions.

Advise	Give ways in which a problem might be solved or show the best way to do something.
Analyse or examine	Breakdown information and identify its characteristics. A thorough explanation is necessary but a conclusion is not.
Assess	Make an informed judgement about how effective something is. The candidate must show both the strengths and limitations and must make a definite judgement.
Compare and contrast	Consider the similarities and differences between two options. To do this involves looking at the points for and against each option.
Consider	Weigh up the arguments for and against two courses of action.
Decide	Make a judgment between the alternatives being discussed.
Discuss	Investigate or examine the topic giving reasons for and against it. A conclusion is necessary.
Evaluate	Make an appraisal of a situation to judge its value. Weigh up both strengths and weaknesses of something and reach a conclusion.
Illustrate	Clarify the topic by means of either an example or visual material.
Interpret	Examine and translate the data.
In your opinion or Judge	Make a personal judgement by considering the positive and negative points.
Organise	Select relevant information and put it in.
Recommend	Make a decision which you feel is best in the circumstances.
Select or suggest	Choose from a variety of alternatives and pick the most relevant.

Glossary

Accounts The records of the financial transactions of a business

Additional Capital Extra capital brought into a business, perhaps for expansion

Amalgamation A voluntary and agreed joining of two or more businesses in order to form one large business. Can also be known as a merger

Appraisal The process of assessing an employee's performance in his/her job

Appraisee The person who is being appraised

Appraiser The person who is carrying out the appraisal

Articles of Association A legal document used in the setting up of a limited company

Asset An item owned by a business such as premises or vehicles

Batch Manufacturing A method of production in which several of the same product are made at one time

Bonus An extra payment made to employees who work well and help the business to achieve its objectives

Breakeven Point The point at which a business's total costs equal the total of its sales revenue. It is the minimum point at which the firm can survive

Business Growth Any form of expansion of a business

Business Plan A detailed description of what a business hopes to do over a future period of usually one to five years

Business Resources Four resources of land, labour, capital and enterprise which must be present before production can take place

Capital Is contributed by the owners and is wealth which is invested in order to create further wealth

Cash Flow The flow of money into and out of a business

Cash Flow Forecast A prediction of the level of spending and level of income which a business will have during the following period of time

Channel of Distribution The means by which goods are passed from the producer to the consumer

Commission An extra financial reward for sales staff. It is usually expressed as a percentage of sales

Communication The passing of information from a sender to a receiver

Competition and Markets Authority (CMA) An independent body set up to investigate mergers and monopolies to ensure they are fair to consumers

Competitive Marketing Any market in which there are many firms competing for customers

Competitive Pricing See Market-led Pricing

Competitor - based Pricing When a business accepts the price its competitors are charging for a product and then prices its own product at the same level or slightly lower. Also known as 'market - led pricing'.

Consumer A person who is the final user of the product

Contract of Employment It is an agreement between the employer and the employee and its main purpose is to define the rights and duties of both parties

Cost-based Pricing A pricing policy which is based on the firm's total fixed and variable costs plus a percentage profit

Cost of Sales A firm's opening inventory plus purchases less closing inventory

Current Assets Items owned by the business which can be quickly exchanged for cash, for example inventory

Current Liabilities Amounts owing by the business which must be paid immediately, for example to the bank

Current Working Capital Ratio Shows the relationship between a firm's current assets and its current liabilities

Curriculum Vitae (CV) A list of a person's qualifications, work and achievements which is used as a method of selection

Decline The final stage of the product life cycle when sales have fallen and the product is unprofitable

Deed of Partnership A legal document which may be drawn up for business partners to replace the Partnership Act

De-industrialisation A situation where there is a decline of manufacturing industries in an area

Demand The quantity of goods which will be bought at a given price

Desk Research See Secondary Research

Destruction Pricing A pricing policy which is designed to destroy competitors' sales and drive them out of the market

Director A person who is appointed to a company's board and has responsibility for the running of the company

Discount A sales promotion method in which a percentage is taken off the price of the product

Dismissal Is where an employer discontinues an employee's work because of incompetence or dishonesty

Division of Labour A type of specialisation in which the manufacture of a product is divided into a number of small stages

E-Business (electronic business) Is the on-line transaction of goods and services and the digital transfer of funds

Economies of Scale Economies which are gained when an increase in production causes a decrease in production costs

Entrepreneur A person who has a business idea and is willing to take a risk in order to make it work

Equity The value of the shares issued by a company

External Business Growth Growth which takes place outside the business. This may be by takeovers or amalgamation for example

External Recruitment A system in which advertising for new employees invites applications from people who do not work in the business

Field Research See Primary Research

Financial Economies of Scale Economies which are gained in situations where a business can obtain finance by cheaper methods

Fixed Costs Costs which are not affected by the quantity of goods produced or sold, or by the scale of services rendered

Flow Manufacturing A method of production in which one product is made continuously and in large numbers. Also known as mass production

Franchise A system in which a business idea is hired out to other businesses

Franchisee A person who buys a franchise

Franchiser A person or company who sells a franchise

Fringe Benefit Is a method of motivation and includes such perks as company cars, pension schemes, private health care and free housing

Full-time Employment A system in which an employee is engaged to work the total number of specified hours per week

Generic Advertising A method of advertising which advertises a whole industry or a particular type of goods regardless of where the goods are sold

Global Market Trading on a worldwide scale

Gross Profit The difference between a firm's income from sales and the cost of sales. It is found in the Income Statement

Gross Profit Percentage The amount of gross profit which a business has made on sales. It measures a firm's trading efficiency

Growth The stage of the product life cycle when sales are growing rapidly

Hire Purchase A medium-term method of finance used for the purchase of assets. A deposit is paid at the beginning and the remainder paid in instalments while the business uses the asset

Income Statement Is the account in which the gross and net profits are calculated

Induction Is the training given to new employees and is designed to make them fit into their new workplace easily

Informative Advertising A type of advertising which is intended to give information

Internal Business Growth Growth which takes place inside a business such as ploughing back profits. Also known as organic growth

Internal Recruitment A system in which advertising for new employees is done inside the business

Interview A method of appraisal in which a one-to-one discussion takes place between the appraiser and the appraisee. Can also be when an applicant for a job is called to meet representatives of the business

Inventory Turnover Rate The number of times in a year that a business is able to sell the value of its average stock. It measures a firm's trading efficiency.

Invest NI Northern Ireland's economic development agency which was created in 2002

Investors in People An award given to a business organisation which has invested in the training of the people working there

Job Description A document used in the recruitment process to define the duties and responsibilities of the post being offered

Job Manufacturing A method of production in which one single item is made at a time – often to a customer's individual specification

Job Rotation A system in which employees move between different jobs in order to avoid boredom

Job Satisfaction Is the degree of fulfilment and happiness which an employee gets from his/her work

Just-in-time Production A method of inventory control in which products are manufactured just in time for them to be sold

Large Enterprise A business which has more than 250 employees

Launch The stage of the product life cycle when the product is introduced to the market

Leasing A medium-term method of finance used for acquiring assets. Similar to renting, the business makes regular payments for the use of the asset

Liabilities Amounts owed by a business, for example to the bank

Liquidity The ability of a business to pay its debts

Loss-Leader A sales promotion method in which the price of one or two products is reduced to a very low level in order to attract customers to the shop

Loyalty Cards A sales promotion method in which each purchase in the store earns points which can be exchanged later for cash or air miles

Manager A person on the second layer of authority in a business who has responsibility for its day-to-day running

Manufacturer See Producer

Margin of Safety The amount which a business is able to sell in excess of its breakeven point

Market-led Pricing A pricing policy in which a business accepts the price which competitors are charging and prices its product at the same level. Also known as 'competitive pricing'

Market Research The collection of information from consumers to find out if they like, or will buy, certain products

Market Segmentation The selection of groups of people with similar tastes who would be most interested in a particular product. Segmentation may be by age, gender, background, class or geography

Marketing The process which identifies, anticipates and satisfies customers' requirements profitably

Marketing Economies of Scale Economies which are gained in situations where a business can save on expenses associated with marketing

Marketing Mix All the key activities which are used in marketing a firm's goods – price, promotion, place and product

Mass Production See Flow Manufacturing

Maturity The stage of the product life cycle when sales levels are maintained and the product has become established on the market

M-Business Refers to new business services using mobile technologies

Memorandum of Association A legal document used in the setting up of a limited company

Merger See Amalgamation

Micro Business A business which has fewer than ten employees

Mission Statement A statement of a business's main aims and objectives

Monopoly A situation in which one business controls more than 25% of the market

Mortgage A long-term method of finance often used for the purchase of premises.

Motivation The way in which a person can be encouraged to make an effort to do something

Municipal Undertaking An activity organised by a local authority

Needs Analysis The first stage in the recruitment procedure where the employer decides exactly what the firm needs from new employees

Net Profit The true profit of a business which is found in the profit and loss account by subtracting all expenses from the gross profit

Net Profit Percentage The amount of net profit which a business has made on sales. It measures a firm's trading efficiency and also its ability to keep expenses low

Non-Current Assets Items owned by a business which cannot be turned into cash quickly, such as buildings

Non-Current Liabilities Amounts owed by a business which may be owed over a longer period of time, for example a mortgage

Observation A method of appraisal in which the employee is watched doing his/her work

OFT Stands for the Office of Fair Trading, which is an independent body set up to promote and protect the interests of consumers

Off-the-job Training Training which is provided by a specialist outside the employee's normal place of work

On-the-job Training Training which is given at the employee's normal place of work

Organic Growth See Internal Business Growth

Overdraft A short-term means of finance in which the business is allowed to write cheques beyond the amount of the balance in the account

Owner A person who has invested money in a business

Partnership A business which has at least two owners and is most often found in professional businesses and those giving a service

Part-time Employment This is where an employee works less than a full week – three mornings per week, for example

Penetration Pricing A pricing policy in which a low price is set at the beginning. The price is increased when the product's place in the market has been secured

Permanent Employment Is where an employee is contracted to work for a business until he/she leaves because of retirement, resignation, redundancy or dismissal

Person Specification A document drawn up as part of the recruitment procedure to identify the qualities, skills and experience which an ideal applicant for the post should have

Persuasive Advertising A method of advertising which is intended to create a need and to encourage members of the public to purchase the advertised product

Ploughed Back Profit See Retained Profit

Price War A pricing policy which cuts the price of some products to a very low level in order to attract customers

Primary Production The first stage of production which is extracting raw materials and using the earth's resources to grow crops

Primary Research A method of market research which collects original information and is carried out by making direct contact with consumers and members of the public. Also known as 'field research'

Private Limited Company A company which cannot sell its shares on the Stock Exchange. Its shares are owned by a small group of people

Private Sector Businesses Businesses which are owned by private people

Producer A person who manufactures goods or services

Product The goods or services which a business is offering for sale

Product Life Cycle The lifespan of a product showing the path from the beginning of the product to its withdrawal from the market

Profit Sharing A financial method of motivation whereby employees receive a share of the profit made by the business

Promotion (in Employment) Is where an employee has been given a job at a higher level in the same firm

Promotion (in Marketing) All methods by which businesses inform customers about their products and encourage them to buy those products

Public Corporation A government-controlled market body

Public Limited Company The largest type of private sector organisation. Its shares are traded on the Stock Exchange

Public Relations Any activity where the public's awareness of a business is raised and the business is seen to be generous and public spirited

Public Sector Businesses Businesses which are owned by the country and run by the government

Purchasing Economies of Scale Economies which are gained in situations where a business is able to purchase in bulk

Quality Assurance The need to achieve constant, high standards in all that customers require

Quality Circles A similar system to team working. Employees are organised into groups and meet regularly to examine the quality of what they are doing and try to find ways of improving it

Questionnaire A means of primary research and is a list of written questions which members of the public are to be asked in order to find information

Quota Sampling A method of sampling in which interviews are held with a set number of people who fall into pre-determined categories, for example, male or teenager

Random Sampling A method of sampling in which people are randomly selected and questioned

Recruitment Is the employment of new workers

Resignation Is where an employee leaves a firm voluntarily because he/she has decided to give up work or is leaving to go to a different job

Retailer The shopkeeper who is the final seller of goods to the consumer

Retained Profit Profit which the owner re-invests in the business. Also known as 'ploughed back' profit

Retirement Is where an employee leaves a firm because he/she has reached the end of his/her working life

Return on Capital Employed (ROCE) Shows the net profit which the owner of a business has received on the capital invested

Salary Payment given to an employee in return for work done. Usually paid monthly

Sales Promotion See Marketing

Sampling A method of primary research which questions a sample of people as being representative of the whole population. Sampling may be random, quota or target

Saturation The stage of the product life cycle when sales are at their highest and new customers cannot be found

Secondary Production The second stage of production which works on raw materials to manufacture finished goods

Secondary Research A method of market research which uses published statistics, data and other information all of which have been collected previously. Also known as 'desk research'

Self-Employment An employment system in which a person sets up his/her own business and works for himself/herself

Self-Evaluation The process of assessing one's own work to find ways of improving its quality

Shareholder A person who has invested money in a limited company by buying shares. This makes the shareholder a part owner in the company

Skimming A pricing policy which sets a relatively high price initially in order to skim the market. The price is reduced later when other firms enter the market

Sleeping Partner A partner who contributes capital to a partnership business but does not work in it or take part in its organisation

Small Enterprise One which has between ten and fifty employees

SME Stands for small to medium-size enterprise

Social Enterprise A business which has the interests of the community at heart

Sole Trader A person who owns and runs his/her own business

Specialisation Is when an employee concentrates on one particular operation and does it all the time. Specialisation may be by product, process, function or country

Sponsorship A method of promotion in which a company meets the costs involved in running an event or providing a service.

Stakeholder A person who has an interest in the activity

Statement of Financial Position A list of assets and liabilities which shows the accurate value of a business on any given date

Start-up Capital The capital needed to get a business started

Stock Exchange The place where shares in companies are bought and sold

Supervisor A supervisor is on the lowest level of management in a business and has direct contact with the workforce

Takeover Is when one business buys the control of another business

Team Working A system in which employees are grouped together in teams, making sure that each team has the full range of skills and abilities required to carry out the task required

Technical Economies of Scale Economies which are gained in situations where a business can cut its production costs by introducing upgraded technology or by altering its production methods

Temporary Employment A system in which an employee is engaged to work for a specified period of time – one year, for example

Tertiary production The stage of production which provides services to members of the public and to other industries

Total Costs The sum of a business's fixed and variable costs

Trade Payables Refers to amounts of money owed by the business to other traders perhaps for inventory bought but not paid for

Trade Receivables Refers to amounts of money owed to the business by other traders for goods sold to them but not paid for

Training Is the acquisition of knowledge and skills which can be applied to a particular job

Variable Costs Costs which change according to the level of work being done in the business

Wage Payment given to an employee in return for work done. Usually paid weekly

Wholesaler The wholesaler purchases goods in bulk from the manufacturer, stores them, and sells them to retailers in smaller quantities

Working Capital Capital required to pay the day-to-day running expenses of the business

Working Capital Ratio This measures the business's ability to pay its debts such as trade payables.

Index

A

advertising   73–7

Advertising Standards Authority
        (ASA)   81–2

after-sales service   78

age, market segmentation   55

appraisal   149–50

apps   106

assembly line   115
    see also flow manufacturing

assets
    current   184–6, 191
    non-current   6, 172, 184–6
    sale of   172

B

bank loans   173

batch manufacturing   114–15

Board of Directors   17, 44

breakeven point   193–6

business
    aims   37–43
    growth   39, 161–70
        economies of scale   12, 20, 39,
            92, 167–8
        ethical implications of   169
        factors limiting   166–7
        types of   163–6
    location   31–6
    ownership   9–30, 44
    plan   200–7
    resources   6–8, 32–3
    stakeholders   44–6
    starting   9
    types of   9–10

C

capital   6–7, 17, 20, 22, 26, 122, 171

cash flow   161, 177
    forecast   177–80

channels of distribution   84–6

charity   29, 79

cinema advertising   75

commission   157

community
    social enterprise   29
    social responsibility   40
    stakeholders   46

competition   88–9, 93, 166

competitions   78

Competitions and Markets Authority
        (CMA)   169–70

competitor-based pricing   60

confidentiality   148

conglomerate   166

consumer panels   52

Consumer Protection Act 1987   72

Consumer Rights Act 2015   71–2

consumers
    legal protection   71–2, 80–2
    as stakeholders   45
    see also customer service

contract of employment   134

corporate image   39

cost-based pricing   60

credit rates   64

cultural background, and market
        segmentation   55

cultural differences, and trade   93

customer service   89–91, 106

Customer Service Excellence
        Standard   123

D

debt collection   172

Deed of Partnership   15–16

de-industrialisation   111

demand   7, 67, 85
    lack of   166
    and price   62–4

destruction pricing   60

directors   44

disability legislation   139

discounts   77

discrimination legislation   138–41

distribution   83–6, 93, 94

division of labour   118–19

E

E-Business (electronic business)   95–6,
        101–3

economic climate   167

economies of scale   12, 20, 39, 92, 167–8

employee

motivation   156–60

responsibilities   127–8

self-evaluation   150

as stakeholder   45

turnover   161

working conditions   43, 160

employer responsibilities   127

enterprise   3, 7–8

'enterprise culture'   3

entrepreneurship   2–5, 7–9

environmental issues   39–40, 43

equality   43

Equality Commission   141–2

ethical issues   42–3

ethnic background, and market
        segmentation   55

European Union   98–9

exhibitions   75–6

expert demonstrations   76

F

failure, signs of   161

finance
    analysis and calculations   188–91
    breakeven point   193–6
    capital   6–7, 17, 20, 22, 26, 122, 171
    cash flow   177
    cash flow forecast   177–80
    financial statements   182–91
    fixed costs   192–6
    lenders   45
    margin of safety   196
    sources of   171–5
    variable costs   192–6

fixed costs   192–6

flexible working   159

flow manufacturing   115–116, 118

footfall   33

franchising   10, 21–3, 165

free gifts   78

free samples   78

fringe benefits   157–8

G

gender
    legislation   139

market segmentation   55
global market   96
   see also international trade
government incentives   34, 175
gross loss   182–3
gross profit   182–3, 188
growth   39, 161–70
   economies of scale   12, 20, 39, 92, 167–8
   ethical implications of   169
   factors limiting   166–7
   product   67
   types of   163–6

H
health and safety   127–8
Health and Safety Executive (HSE)   128
hire purchase   174
hoardings   74
horizontal integration   165
human resources
   appraisal   149–50
   confidentiality   148
   contract of employment   134
   discrimination legislation   138–41
   induction   152
   interview   146–7
   job description   132–3
   recruitment   131–42
   selection   143–8
   staff training   152–5
   testing   145

I
Income Statement   182
incorporation   18
independence   5
induction   152
international trade   92–9, 103
internet advertising   75
internet shopping   86
   see also E-Business
interview
   appraisal   150
   job selection   146–7
inventory
   control   119–21
   sale of   172
   turnover rate   189–90
Investors in People (IIP)   124–5
ISO 9001 award   123–4

J
job centres   137
job description   132–3
job manufacturing   113
job-rotation   158
job satisfaction, factors affecting   159–60

L
labour   6
   see also human resources
land
   as business resource   6
   availability and cost   33
   premises   31–3
large businesses   10
lateral integration   165
launch stage, of product   67
   see also product: life cycle
leasing   173–4
legislation   71–2, 80–2, 138–41
lenders   45
liabilities   184–6
liability
   limited   18
   unlimited   11, 14
life span, of goods   85
limited companies   17–21
   see also private limited company (ltd); public limited company (plc)
limited liability   18
Living Wage   43
location   31–6
loss-leaders   77
loyalty cards   78

M
M-Business (mobile business)   105–7
magazine advertising   75
mail shots   76
managers   44
manufacturer   83
manufacturing
   division of labour   118–19
   impact of technology   121–2
   inventory control   119–21
   specialisation   117–18
   types of   113–16
margin of safety   196
market research   9, 49–54
   consumer panels   52
   interviews   51

observation   52
questionnaires   51
sampling   53–4
testing   52
market segmentation   55
marketing, definition   49
marketing mix   58
   place   83–6, 89, 94
   price   59–64, 70, 77–8, 88, 94
      factors affecting   62–4
      pricing policies   59–61
   product   66–72, 88, 94
      legal constraints   71–2
      life cycle   66–70
   promotion   73–82, 88–9, 94
      advertising   73–7
      legal constraints   80–2
      public relations (PR)   79
      sales promotion   77–8
      social media   79–80
      sponsorship   79
Maslow's Hierarchy of Needs   156
medium-sized businesses   10
merger   164, 169
micro businesses   9–10
mission statements   37
mobile
   banking   106
   payments   105
   ticketing   106
money-off coupons   77
mortgage   174–5
motivation   156–60
municipal undertakings   25, 27–8

N
net loss   183
net profit   183, 188
newspaper advertising   75
non-current assets   6, 172, 184–6

O
observation   52, 150
Ofcom (Office of Communication)   82
Office of Fair Trading (OFT)   82
off-the-job training   154–5
on-the-job training   153–4
ordinary shares   17
overdraft   173

P
parking   35
partnerships   10, 14–16, 173

penetration pricing   59
person specification   133
point-of-sale displays   78
posters   74
praise   160
preference shares   17
premises   6
     see also location
pressure groups   45
price   59–64, 70, 77–8, 88, 94
     factors affecting   62–4
     guarantees   78
     pricing policies   59–61
     reductions   77
     wars   60
primary production   109–10
private limited company (ltd)   10, 18–19
private sector   10, 42
process manufacturing   116
producers   44–5, 83
product   88, 94
     decline   68
     definition   66
     growth stage   67
     launch stage   67
     legal constraints   71–2
     life cycle   66–70
     saturation stage   68
production   109–12
     cost of   62
profit   39
     gross   182–3, 188
     net   183, 188
     and pricing   62
     sharing   157
     as source of finance   171–2
     see also income statement
promotion   73–82, 88–9, 94
     advertising   73–7
     definition   73
     legal constraints   80–2
     public relations (PR)   79
     sales promotion   77–8
     social media   79–80
     sponsorship   79

psychological pricing   60
psychometric testing   145–6
public corporations   26–7
public limited company (plc)   10, 20–1
public relations (PR)   79
public sector   25–8, 42

Q
quality assurance   123–5
quality circles   158–9
questionnaires   51
quota sampling   54

R
radio advertising   75
random sampling   53
raw materials   32, 44
     cost of   62
     primary production   109
recruitment   131–42
     see also human resources
recycling   40
region, market segmentation   55
religion, legislation   139
Research and Development   66
retailer   83–4
retained profits   171–2
return on capital employed (ROCE)   189
risk, and entrepreneurship   3–5
role play   155

S
sales promotion   77–8
sampling   53–4
saturation   68
seasonality, and price   63
secondary production   110
shareholders   17–20, 39, 41, 44
shares   17–20, 173
shop window displays   76
Single Market   99
skimming   59
'sleeping partner'   14
small and medium sized businesses
          (SMEs)   10
small businesses   10

SMART targets   37
social enterprise   29–30
social media   79–80, 138
social responsibility   40, 43
socio-economic class   55
sole trader   10, 11–13
special offers   77
specialisation   117
sponsorship   79
staff training   152–5
stakeholders   44–6
starting a business   9
Statement of Financial Position   184–6
Stock Exchange   17, 20, 173
success, signs of   161
survival   38

T
takeover   164
team-working   158
television advertising   75
tertiary production   110–12
trade credit   175
Trade Descriptions Act 1968   81
trade journals   75
trade unions   45
transport   95–6
     advertising   76
     infrastructure   34
turnover   39

U
unemployment   34
unlimited liability   11, 14

V
variable costs   192–6
VAT (Value Added Tax)   11
vehicle advertising   76
vertical integration   165

W
wages   43
wholesaler   83–4, 86
working capital   175
working capital ratio   191
working conditions   43, 160